San

When Hollywood Was Right

How Movie Stars, Studio Moguls, and Big Business Remade American Politics

Hollywood was not always a bastion of liberalism. Following the Second World War, an informal alliance of movie stars, studio moguls, and Southern California business interests formed to revitalize a factionalized Republican Party. Coming together were stars such as John Wayne, Robert Taylor, George Murphy, and many others who joined studio heads Cecil B. DeMille, Louis B. Mayer, Walt Disney, and Jack Warner to rebuild the Republican Party. They found support among a large group of business leaders who poured money and skills into this effort, which paid off with the election of George Murphy to the U.S. Senate and of Richard Nixon and Ronald Reagan to the highest office in the nation. This is an exciting story based on extensive new research that will forever change how we think of Hollywood politics.

Donald T. Critchlow is Professor at the School of Historical, Philosophical, and Religious Studies, Arizona State University. He has authored and edited numerous books, including *The Conservative Ascendancy: How the GOP Made Political History* (2007, revised 2011); *Phyllis Schlafly and Grassroots Conservatism* (2005); and *Intended Consequences: Birth Control, Abortion, and the Federal Government* (1999). He is currently working on a data-driven book, *American Democracy Now and Its Future*. He is editor of the *Journal of Policy History*, an interdisciplinary quarterly published by Cambridge University Press, and is general editor of the Cambridge Essential Histories series.

"Hollywood wasn't always a stronghold of the political Left. Back in the days after World War II, many movie moguls and movie stars – Louis B. Mayer, Cecil B. DeMille, Walt Disney, John Wayne, George Murphy – worked to revitalize the Republican Party. Donald Critchlow tells the exciting story of how they did, and how they helped elect Richard Nixon and Ronald Reagan president."

– Michael Barone, Senior Political Analyst, *Washington Examiner*; Resident Fellow, American Enterprise Institute; co-author, *The Almanac of American Politics*

"Few people have more insightful things to say about modern politics than the historian Donald Critchlow. Now Critchlow has focused his keen political and historical skills on Hollywood. The result is a provocative, smart, original, and entertaining book that should be required reading for all students of American politics and popular culture."

– Steven M. Gillon, Scholar-in-Residence, The History Channel

"Don Critchlow has done it again. *When Hollywood Was Right* is the most comprehensive and detailed account of an epic that is too often told in black and white cartoonish tones. Critchlow captures the paradoxes of how the left-right clashes of the mid-twentieth century affected Hollywood, in many cases for the better. This fine-grained narrative, brimming with new detail Critchlow has unearthed from unused archives, leaves us wondering what is being lost in today's almost monolithically leftist Hollywood."

– Steven Hayward, Thomas Smith Distinguished Fellow, Ashbrook Center, Ashland University

"This incisive, first-rate study is based on extensive archival research. *When Hollywood Was Right* masterfully tells how anticommunism drove film industry executives, directors, and stars, allied with business leaders, to remake the Republican Party in California after World War II. As Professor Donald T. Critchlow astutely argues, the result had national implications. These conservatives backed Richard Nixon and ultimately put one of their own, Ronald Reagan, in the White House."

– William J. Rorabaugh, Professor of History, University of Washington, author of *The Real Making of the President: Kennedy, Nixon, and the 1960 Election*

When Hollywood Was Right

How Movie Stars, Studio Moguls, and Big Business Remade American Politics

DONALD T. CRITCHLOW
Arizona State University

CAMBRIDGE
UNIVERSITY PRESS

CAMBRIDGE
UNIVERSITY PRESS

32 Avenue of the Americas, New York, NY 10013-2473, USA

Cambridge University Press is part of the University of Cambridge.

It furthers the University's mission by disseminating knowledge in the pursuit of
education, learning, and research at the highest international levels of excellence.

www.cambridge.org
Information on this title: www.cambridge.org/9780521199186

First published 2013

Printed in the United States of America

A catalog record for this publication is available from the British Library.

Library of Congress Cataloging in Publication Data
Critchlow, Donald T., 1948–
When Hollywood was right : how movie stars, studio moguls, and big business remade
American politics / Donald T. Critchlow, Arizona State University.
pages   cm
Includes index.
ISBN 978-0-521-19918-6
1. United States – Politics and government – 1945–   2. Motion picture producers and
directors – Political activity – United States – History – 20th century.   3. Motion picture
actors and actresses – Political activity – United States – History – 20th century.
4. Motion picture industry – United States – Influence.   5. Republican Party
(U.S. : 1854–) – History – 20th century.   I. Title.
E743.C75   2013
320.973'0918–dc23   2013015873

ISBN 978-0-521-19918-6 Hardback

Contents

Players

Douglas Fairbanks – American actor, director, screenwriter, and producer; most famous for playing Zorro and Robin Hood

John Ford – Irish-American director famous for westerns; won four Academy Awards for best director

Clark Gable – American film actor, most famous for playing Rhett Butler in *Gone With the Wind*

Bob Hope – English-born American actor and comedian; hosted the Academy Awards fourteen times

Hedda Hopper – Influential syndicated *Los Angeles Times* newspaper columnist

Elia Kazan – Turkish-born American director; testified as a friendly witness before the House Un-American Activities Committee

John Lee Mahin – American screenwriter active in films from the 1930s to the 1970s, including *The Wizard of Oz* and *Scarface*

Albert Maltz – American author and screenwriter, one of the Hollywood Ten who were blacklisted

Raymond Massey – Canadian/American actor, famous for being in the first movie with sound, and many others

Adolphe Menjou – American actor, worked from 1914 to 1960; nominated for an Oscar in 1931 for *The Front Page*

Robert Montgomery – American actor and director famous for his films and for being elected president of the Screen Actors Guild (SAG) in 1935 and 1946

Mary Pickford – Canadian actress known as "America's Sweetheart"

Dick Powell – American director, producer, actor, and singer

Ayn Rand – Russian-American writer known for her two best-selling novels *The Fountainhead* and *Atlas Shrugged*

Ginger Rogers – Actress and dancer who was in more than seventy-three films

Morrie Ryskind – American screenwriter nominated for two Academy Awards

Randolph Scott – American actor most famous for westerns

Barbara Stanwyck – Academy Award–nominated film and television star; during her sixty-year career, she made eighty-five films in thirty-eight years before working in television

Jimmy Stewart – American stage and film actor, known for his distinctive voice and personality

Gloria Swanson – American actress famous for playing Norma Desmond in *Sunset Boulevard*

Robert Taylor – American film and television actor, considered one of the most popular celebrities of his time

W. S. Van Dyke – Famous American actor/director nominated for several Academy Awards and known for his versatility

John Wayne – American actor famous for his westerns; named the all-time top money-making star; seen as an American icon famous for his demeanor

Sam Wood – American film director and producer, known for making hits and winning five Academy Awards

MOGULS

Walt Disney – International icon and owner of Disney

Sam Goldwyn – Helped build Paramount, MGM, and United Artists

Howard Hughes – Maverick film producer of controversial films and owner of Trans-World Airlines

Louis B. Mayer – Head of Metro-Goldwyn-Mayer (MGM)

Benjamin Schulberg – Associate producer at Paramount pictures and producer for Columbia

David O. Selznick – Head of production at Radio-Keith-Orpheum (RKO)

Warner Brothers – One of the largest film studios, founded by Harry, Albert, Sam, and Jack Warner

Darryl Zanuck – Vice president of Twentieth Century Fox; won three Academy Awards

POLITICOS

Edmund "Pat" Brown – Governor of California (1959–1967)

Hiram Johnson – Governor of California (1911–1917), U.S. senator (1917–1945)

William Knowland – California senator (1945–1959); defeated in a run for governor in 1958

George Murphy – Californian actor and politician serving as president of the Screen Actors Guild (SAG) (1944–1946) and as U.S. senator and state senator (1965–1971)

Richard Nixon – Californian Senator (late 1950–1952), also the president of the United States (1969–1974)

Ronald Reagan – Actor and politician, served as president of the SAG; governor of California (1967–1975); president of the United States (1981–1989)

Nelson Rockefeller – Governor of New York who sought the presidential nomination in 1960, 1964, and 1968

Upton Sinclair – Famous author and candidate for governor of California

J. Parnell Thomas – Elected seven times to represent New Jersey's Seventh District (1935–1950) before being convicted of corruption

Earl Warren – Governor of California, 1943–1953

Wendell Willkie – Corporate lawyer and Republican nominee for president in 1940

BUSINESS

Harry Chandler – *Los Angeles Times* publisher-owner

Justin Dart – Son-in-law to Charles Walgreen, known as the "boy wonder" of drugstores

Leonard Firestone – Staunch Republican and son of Harvey Firestone
William Randolph Hearst – American newspaper publisher famous for creating
   the largest newspaper chain and for his effect on journalism
Henry Salvatori – Founded Western Geophysical; a philanthropist and conservative activist

Acknowledgments

Researching and writing a book are arduous and lonely processes are made easier through the support of institutions, professional colleagues, friends, and family.

This book began at Saint Louis University and was finished at Arizona State University. Arizona State University provides a wonderful environment for research and writing. I want to thank five people in particular who supported my coming to Arizona State University in 2010, first as a visiting professor then permanently: Michael Crow, president of the university; Elizabeth Langland, dean of Humanities; and my colleagues in History, Mark Von Hagen, Philip VanderMeer, and Matthew Garcia.

Saint Louis University provided me with two excellent research assistants: Cynthia Stachecki, who helped me find archival, biographical, and bibliographical sources, and Amy Wallhermfechtel, who tracked down and researched myriad other sources, including Federal Bureau of Investigation files, the *Hollywood Reporter*, newspapers, magazines, and congressional hearings. Later, she shared with me her own extensive notes in the Cecile B. DeMille and William Knowland papers for her own study of Cecile B. DeMille and right-to-work legislation. While at Arizona State University, Sam Tufford, an undergraduate student, assisted me in finding articles from California newspapers about state and presidential elections.

Early research support for this project came from a semester fellowship at the Social Philosophy and Policy Center at Bowling Green University. The Earhart Foundation provided a research grant that allowed me to conduct further research in the Cecile B. DeMille papers at Brigham Young University, the Richard Nixon Papers and Ronald Reagan Papers in California, the Herbert Hoover Papers in Iowa, and the Barry M. Goldwater Papers in Arizona.

Lisa Forshaw, with the keen eye of a practicing attorney, read many iterations of this manuscript from early drafts to the final copy. Her willingness to do so went beyond the norms of friendship, nonetheless ensuring my deep gratitude and appreciation that she and her husband, Joe Forshaw, are friends. In preparing the manuscript for publication, Beatriz Kravetz proofread and indexed the book. In addition, I want to thank in particular my two editors at Cambridge University Press, Lew Bateman and Eric Crahan, who supported this project from the outset.

Two of my best friends, both notable historians, William Rorabaugh and Irwin Gellman, read drafts of the manuscript, finding stylistic and factual errors, challenging interpretations, and making useful comments on making a better book. Irv provided relevant chapters on the 1962 California governor's race from his forthcoming book on the Eisenhower-Nixon administration. Greg Schneider, with his great knowledge of the history of conservatism, directed me to sources and alerted me to new books on the subject. Alan Gallay provided encouragement, as well as insight into this project, even though his own interest in history is centuries before modern America. Also, I want to thank Kathryn Cramer Brownell, a young historian who graciously shared her dissertation on Hollywood politics. Her work and personal exchanges provided me with an immense amount of information, especially on the liberal side of Hollywood politics.

Without family support, especially my wife Patricia, this book would not have been written. She put up with my long hours in the office away from home and joined me when she could on research trips under the guise of "family vacations." We were joined on many of these trips by our grandchildren – Andrew, usually visiting from Prague, and his cousin Alex. These summer trips persuaded both of them not to become historians. One day, perhaps, we will be joined by Andrew's brother, our third grandson Joshua. Through an ersatz holiday, I might dissuade him too from becoming a historian, while convincing him that history itself is worth knowing and can sometimes be entertaining.

Introduction

When the Academy of Motion Picture Arts and Sciences announced that film director Elia Kazan would receive an honorary Oscar at the January 1999 ceremony, the Hollywood Left erupted in anger. Hollywood leftists could not believe that the Academy was going to recognize Kazan's achievement. Everyone knew that Kazan was one of the witnesses who appeared before the House Un-American Activities Committee (HUAC) in 1952 to "name names" of communists. Kazan, the squealer, the opportunist, the careerist, and a moral coward was now getting artistic recognition for "his work." What about his other work, his work before HUAC that had destroyed lives and encouraged others to testify? So what if he had won two Academy Awards for Best Director for *Gentleman's Agreement* (1947) and *On the Waterfront* (1954)? He broke, recanting his communist past and gave names to Congress of past communist associates.

Actor Karl Malden, winner of an Oscar for his performance in Kazan's *A Streetcar Named Desire* (1951), pushed for the award. Malden believed that Kazan deserved to be in the company of people like Cary Grant, Alfred Hitchcock, and Howard Hawkes, who had won previous honorary Oscars for their life's work. Malden first proposed Kazan for the award in 1989. In the ensuing decade, Kazan was denied lifetime achievement awards from the San Francisco Film Festival and the Los Angeles Film Critics. Malden's persistence paid off. After much debate, the Motion Picture Academy agreed with Malden that Kazan deserved an honorary Oscar.

The announcement stirred up deep resentment, feelings that had never really died down for those who lived through the Hollywood Red Scare beginning in 1947, as Congress investigated Red infiltration in the entertainment industry. Good men and women with progressive views had been blacklisted from working in Hollywood once they were named in a HUAC hearing. Exactly what had these people done to have their careers ruined? The Hollywood Left believed they had stood up against fascism before it was politically correct. They had stood up on behalf of African Americans at a time when black actors were relegated to playing stereotyped "steppin-fetchit" roles. And, after the Second World War, they came forward as witnesses for continued cooperation with the Soviet Union. For these actions, these progressives did not deserve to be placed in exile, their careers ended, and their lives ruined.

On Oscar night, directors Martin Scorsese and Robert De Niro escorted eighty-four-year-old Kazan to the stage. Many in the audience rose to applaud him. Others refused to stand. They were mostly younger actors such as Ed Harris, Nick Nolte, Ian McKellen, Ann Madigan, and Ed Begley, Jr., joined by some middle-aged actors, such as Richard Dreyfus. They viewed themselves as men and women of principle, standing for freedom of speech, witnesses to the evil done nearly a half century earlier during the Hollywood Red Scare.

Outside the Dorothy Chandler Pavilion, where the Oscar ceremony was being held, hundreds of placard-carrying demonstrators noisily denounced Kazan. Among the protesters was Norma Barzman, widow of a Hollywood blacklist screenwriter. When Norma first heard about the award, she joined forces with other surviving blacklisted artists, including Abe Polonsky, Bernie Gordon, Jean Butler, and Bobbie Lees. They collected money for ads in *Variety* and *Hollywood Reporter* and condemned the Academy for giving the award.

When Kazan received his award, the Left appeared to have won the ferocious political battles in Hollywood. The story of repression, hysteria, betrayal, the Inquisition, those scoundrel days of the late 1940s and early 1950s had become the accepted canon. On November 20, 2012, the leading Hollywood entertainment newspaper, *The Hollywood Reporter*, again picked up the story of the blacklist era in a multiple-page story, "The Most Sinful Period in Hollywood History." Left-wing actor Sean Penn, son of a blacklisted actor, recounted in another story published by the newspaper how his father suffered because of the blacklist. Children of other blacklisted actors and directors described the destructive consequences that the Hollywood Red Scare had on their families. Billy Wilkerson, publisher of *The Hollywood Reporter* and son of the former publisher who had been instrumental in attacking communists in the film industry in the 1940s and 1950s, concluded that this period was nothing short of a "Hollywood holocaust." However excessive these terms – "Hollywood holocaust" and "the most sinful period" – in an industry full of scandal, the story of the blacklist has obsessed reporters, filmmakers, and scholars over the last half century.

This book, *When Hollywood Was Right*, tells an equally dramatic story that has been ignored in the often-told history of the film industry's Red Scare: the rebuilding of the Republican Party in California. The storyline begins in the 1930s and concludes in 1980.

Ronald Reagan's election to the White House marked the culmination of an effort by a small group of Hollywood conservatives to rebuild the Republican Party in their state after the Second World War. What brought these men and women together was a commitment to a vibrant Republican Party at a time when Democrats in the state began to surge ahead in voter registration. Those involved in the effort to reconstruct a party that had dominated California politics prior to the 1930s believed that by appealing both to the patriotic instincts of average Californians and to their desire for economic opportunity, the Republican Party could once again become the party of the people.

In rebuilding the Republican Party, an informal alliance took shape gradually among Hollywood studio moguls, movie stars, and Southern California businessmen. These allies contributed celebrity, money, media expertise, and political involvement to the Republican cause. This project called for each group – moguls, celebrities, businessmen – to become involved in contributing money, organizing rallies, speaking to local Republican clubs, developing party organization, and acting as media consultants. Movie producers involved themselves directly in state party organization and political campaigns.

Hollywood actors, directors, and screenwriters provided celebrities for political rallies, local party clubs, and campaign advertising, even as they were tapped for huge donations by party fundraisers. Big money donors, such as Justin Dart of Rexall Drugs, played an important role in shaping party organization on the precinct level in Southern California. He also coordinated the disbursement of campaign contributions to various Republican candidates. Rebuilding the California Republican Party took money, lots of money. Political advertising was costly in such a sprawling state, but California's media-driven politics would eventually become a national model. The project also called for rebuilding the party on a grassroots level, especially in populous Southern California. Southern California business interests joined with Hollywood to provide this money. Film stars gave money and attracted crowds at fundraisers and rallies. Republican strategists and party leaders used celebrities to foster enthusiasm for the party at the grassroots, and Republican politicos sent stars to speak to local women's groups, Rotary Clubs, the American Legion, and party clubs throughout the state as luncheon and evening speakers. The party relied on a stable of superstars such as John Wayne, Ronald Reagan, Robert Taylor, and Fred Astaire's dance partner and Academy Award–winning actress Ginger Rogers to mobilize the Republican grassroots and the general electorate. Republicans lauded June Allyson, a popular star of the 1950s and wife of actor/producer Dick Powell, for her work for the party. *Los Angeles Times* gossip columnist Hedda Hopper organized Republican women throughout Southern California and spoke frequently at campaign events. Dozens of actors urged citizens to become politically active Republicans.

George Murphy, a longtime actor whose film career waned in the postwar period, served as a liaison between business and Hollywood. He arranged for celebrities to attend rallies, appear at fundraisers, and make radio and television ads for Republican political candidates. Republican movie stars were not simply trotted out during election years. In off-election years, party officials and strategists arranged through Murphy to have film celebrities speak to local Republican groups and community organizations throughout the state. Many involved in these campaign activities remained lesser lights, such as character actor Adolphe Menjou. Spanish-speaking Leo Carrillo, whose acting career had been resuscitated playing sidekick "Pancho" in the popular western television series *The Cisco Kid*, appeared as a frequent speaker. In the 1960 presidential campaigns, he spoke before large Hispanic crowds. Murphy's work for the party laid the foundation for his own career in politics; he won election to the U.S. Senate in 1964, and this victory set the stage for Reagan's election as governor in 1966.

The drama of rebuilding the California Republican Party cast many players: studio heads such as Louis B. Mayer, Darryl Zanuck, Cecil B. DeMille, the Warner brothers, and Walt Disney; Southern California businessmen such as Justin Dart, Leonard Firestone (heir to Firestone Tires), Walter Knott (founder of Knott's Berry Farm), oil man Henry Salvatori, and Patrick Frawley, owner of Schick razor and Technicolor. The endorsement of Norman Chandler, publisher of the *Los Angeles Times*, proved necessary for any Republican candidate running for office in California. Actors such as Gary Cooper and Bob Hope played leading roles in this campaign to resurrect the Republican Party. Beginning in the 1970s, Charlton Heston, a former Democrat, assumed the conservative banner by becoming a Reagan Republican who supported strong national defense and gun rights.

Western stars had particular appeal because of their movie and television roles. Randolph Scott, who at the age of fifty-eight was still playing the leading man after appearing in close to a hundred films, remained a conservative who gave money and time to the party when he could. Ward Bond, who appeared in NBC's hit television series *Wagon Train*, was notorious for his right-wing sentiments, as was Walter Brennan, star of the heartwarming *The Real McCoys* television series. Movie and television actor Richard Boone, who played the suave gunslinger Paladin in *Have Gun Will Travel*, was no less vociferous in his political views. Former major league baseball pitcher Chuck Connor from *The Rifleman* proved to be a favorite in Republican circles, and many saw him as an up-and-coming political candidate.

A few film aficionados and film historians remember these stars, but, for the most part, history has forgotten many of these celebrities of movies and early television. Most of the other stars are unknown to younger movie audiences, and, if remembered for their films, few know of their politics.

Cameo performances by an array of other stars, movie moguls, screenwriters, politicos, and fat-cat Republicans appear in this drama. Even Hollywood's most attractive leading man in the late 1950s and early 1960s, Rock Hudson, was a right-wing Republican. His party affiliation might have surprised his myriad of female fans who projected themselves into the characters played by his co-star, singer Doris Day (another Republican) in their numerous romantic comedies. Movie stars like Hudson kept their personal lives separate from their film personas, but their politics were often on public display in political rallies and in their involvement in political causes. Hudson appeared at anticommunist rallies and campaigned for conservative Republican presidential candidate Barry Goldwater in 1964. If Hudson's fans would have been surprised by his politics, they were even more surprised when it was revealed in 1985 that he was a homosexual dying of AIDS.

Surprisingly many conservative Republicans once populated Hollywood. Given the relatively few in Hollywood today who are declared Republicans, this appears to be a historical anomaly, a brief period in the film industry. The Hollywood Right is important because Hollywood conservatives led the way in taking control of the California Republican Party and eventually changing the political landscape of modern America.

Anticommunism brought many conservatives in Hollywood together in the postwar period. Contrary to the perceived history of the Red Scare in Hollywood, anticommunists in the film industry were not united as to the extent of the problem in 1947, in how to treat the issue of communists in the industry, or in their support of congressional investigations. Hardline anticommunists, such as screenwriter Ayn Rand, were less forgiving. Neither was Hedda Hopper, whose nationally syndicated newspaper column influenced millions of movie fans; she proved unforgiving of former communists. Others proved more generous in their attitudes and behavior toward former party members. Among the anticommunist Right in Hollywood, members were divided over basic issues such as whether the Communist Party should be outlawed. Anticommunism in Hollywood remains only a small part of what was happening behind the scenes. By focusing on the Hollywood Red Scare in the early Cold War years, the larger story of Republican mobilization in postwar California has been neglected.

The ascendancy of the Republican Party in California was by no means a straight advancement. Factionalism characterized the Republican Party in these years, reflected within the Hollywood Right and among Southern California businessmen. Often these divisions revolved around personalities and politicians. Ideology divided some. Schisms and profound differences appeared at every step of the Republican advance – and retreat. There were hardline anticommunists who supported the blacklist. Others believed the communist issue had been taken care of even before HUAC swept into town to investigate alleged communist influence in the film industry. The Hollywood Right and its allies in the Southern California business community were divided over who to support in the 1952 Republican primaries, Dwight D. Eisenhower or Robert Taft, and divisions reemerged between Nelson Rockefeller backers and Barry Goldwater supporters in 1964. These divisions were seen among studio moguls, Hollywood celebrities, and the business community. They stood united in rebuilding the Republican Party. The question was how and which candidates would best serve this goal.

When Hollywood Was Right tells how men and women dedicated to a conservative political cause transformed American politics and the course of American history. The story is one of courage and disappointment, but ultimately about politics and power displayed in the elections of Vice President

Richard Nixon, U.S. senator George Murphy, and Governor Ronald Reagan. Nixon or Reagan were on the national ballot for every election from 1952 to 1984, except in 1964 and 1976. Between them, they won six national elections, including four presidential victories. California's ascendancy was Hollywood's, too. For the Hollywood Right, Nixon and, especially, Reagan marked Hollywood's true Golden Age.

These men and women of the Hollywood Right viewed themselves as patriots and defenders of American values of individualism, patriotism, and free enterprise. They accepted an abiding faith in the American dream and the spirit of American individualism, even though some were motivated by personal advancement, careerism, vindictiveness, financial gain, and political calculation. This book tells of electoral victory, and, more frequently, defeat at the polls and a minority at odds with a liberal political culture that prevailed throughout most of this period in the film industry. Theirs is a drama of striving and ultimate political success – one that began in the mid-1930s as Hollywood became politicized and then continued into the Cold War and the anticommunist fight. There was a steady and eventually successful effort to rebuild the Republican Party in California in the following years that led to significant state and national power.

In the end, Hollywood itself was more about making movies and money than it was about politics, and politics is only a small part of the overall Hollywood story. The history of the Hollywood Right remains worth telling because it reveals how a small group of dedicated men and women, often at odds with one another, changed the course of politics in a democracy and remade both their state and their country.

CHAPTER I

Setting the Stage in the 1930s

Republicans on Defense

The economic depression of the 1930s transformed America into a nation of haves and have-nots. This was especially the case in Hollywood, where movie moguls made huge profits, film stars such as Gary Cooper received salaries that were the highest in the nation, and screenwriters earned incomes of more than $100,000 a year. Beneath the Hollywood elite, as novelist Nathaniel West so graphically captured in his haunting *Day of the Locust* (1939), swarmed actors looking for bit parts, extras hoping to be used in crowd scenes, old vaudeville performers looking to resuscitate their careers, and young writers hoping to break into the business.

In the first years of the Great Depression, Hollywood remained a generally nonpolitical town. A few studio chieftains, such as Louis B. Mayer, head of MGM, actively participated in Republican Party politics, but Mayer stood out in this regard. As the Depression continued, the nation swung to the left in support of Franklin D. Roosevelt's New Deal and in response to the growing threat of fascism in Europe. Hollywood became increasingly politicized by the mid-1930s. The change in Hollywood's political atmosphere accelerated when socialist author Upton Sinclair won the Democratic Party nomination for governor in 1934, and studios and the Republican establishment successfully organized to defeat him in the general election. Other factors contributed to this growing politicization: the unionization of studio technicians, cartoonists, screenwriters, actors, and directors split Hollywood into warring camps, and the anti-Semitic rhetoric of Nazi leader Adolph Hitler, who came to power in Germany in 1933, pushed many in Hollywood further to the left. In this environment, some in Hollywood joined the Communist Party. Embattled Hollywood Republicans fought a rearguard action to thwart what seemed to be the shifting tide of history as the political left gained momentum in Hollywood and California and global capitalism seemed to many to be in its final death throes. The political battles of 1930s Hollywood set the stage for a historic confrontation between the left and the right that followed the Second World War. In 1930s Hollywood, nobody foresaw just how deeply divided Hollywood would become just one decade later. The left in the 1930s seemed ascendant and the right in decline.

The New Deal hit California Republicans like an earthquake. A seismic shift occurred as Democratic registrations soared in the state, leaving Republicans worried about the future of their party. Republicans everywhere fought back as best they could, aided in their efforts by Hollywood Republicans, who were mostly studio executives and a few movie stars. California Republicans kept believing victory was just around the corner, but it never quite came.

In the 1930s, the state Republican Party – reflecting the national party – began suffering from a severe, perhaps unavoidable, identity crisis, not quite sure whether to mimic the Democratic Party or declare itself the last remnant in opposition to the perceived advance of socialism that had occurred under Franklin Roosevelt's New Deal. Although Republican candidates continued to have success in statewide and local elections, California Republicans were divided into an array of nearly indecipherable and shifting factions that cut across ideological lines. The Roosevelt years left California Republicans reeling as party registration in the state fell precipitously and Democratic registration grew.

Within Hollywood, Republicans had become a distinct minority in the movie industry. For the most part, studio executives remained loyal to the party. Louis B. Mayer, head of MGM and the highest paid executive in the country, personified the Republican Old Guard, and producer Cecil B. DeMille, who had voted for Roosevelt in 1932, later shifted his loyalties to the Republican Party, even going so far as trying to promote himself as a senatorial candidate. But even studio executives were no longer unanimously anti–New Deal. The Warner brothers, upstarts who had only made it into the big time with the invention of sound, were considered by most Hollywood insiders pro–New Deal.

The real strength of the Democrats in Hollywood – and progressives in general – rested with the actors, screenwriters, and studio technicians. Furthermore, the Communist Party, although small in numbers, had made considerable advances in Hollywood, especially in unions such as the Screen Writers Guild (SWG) and a number of studio technicians' unions. Even so, communism in the film industry was not much of a concern to many in the early 1930s. Anticommunist voices within the industry remained isolated and did not play much of a role in Hollywood politics, nor, for that matter, within the California Republican Party. Anticommunism was, however, vociferously articulated by conservative Democrat William Randolph Hearst's newspaper chain, whose five California daily papers had circulations that equaled that of all other newspapers in the state combined.[1] Many California Republicans, as well as many Hollywood studio heads, did not like Hearst for personal and political

---

[1] Greg Mitchell, *The Campaign of the Century: Upton Sinclair's Race for Governor of California and the Birth of Media Politics* (New York, 1992), p. 5.

reasons, especially when his papers ignored or panned their films. Hearst endorsed Roosevelt in 1932 and continued to enjoy good relations with the Roosevelt administration until the late 1930s, when Hearst's isolationism crashed head-on with the administration's interventionist policies.

Although the American Legion, the Los Angeles Police Department's Red Squad, a few fundamentalist radio ministers, such as gun-packing Martin Luther Thomas, and isolated eccentrics kept up a steady anticommunist drumbeat, for the most part, the great mass of Californians in the 1920s and early 1930s were not given to anticommunist fervor. This was not surprising, given the small numbers of Communist Party members in California in these years: when twenty-five-year-old Sam Darcy was appointed California state organizer of the Communist Party in 1930, there were only an estimated fifty party members in the Los Angeles area.[2]

CALIFORNIA POLITICS IN THE '30S: REPUBLICAN DISORIENTATION, PROGRESSIVE REVIVAL

In 1928, California was a Republican state, and Hollywood was a Republican town. A decade later, the political fortunes of the Republican Party had reversed. Although Republicans continued to enjoy political success in state races, by the mid-1930s, Hollywood and the Golden State were overwhelmingly Democratic when it came to voting for president and in voter registration. In the 1924 presidential election, Democratic presidential candidate John W. Davis received only 8 percent of the vote in California, but by 1936, 60 percent of the state's voters were registered Democrats. In 1936, Franklin Roosevelt won an overwhelming 67 percent of the California vote, compared to the 32 percent who voted for Alf Landon, the Republican candidate.

For Republicans in the 1930s, the real problem was not communists in the state or in Hollywood. What frightened them was the sheer popularity of Roosevelt in California and growing Democratic registrations. Republicans held on to state offices, but to do so they had to absorb and condone much of the New Deal program.

The disorientation of Republican leadership brought about by the popularity of Roosevelt and the New Deal was evident in *Los Angeles Times* owner Harry Chandler's correspondence with the forlorn former Republican president Herbert Hoover in the 1930s. In 1933, a year after the presidential election that had thrown Hoover out of the White House with a resounding victory to Roosevelt, Chandler wrote that so many experiments and programs had been brought forward by the administration that "millions of average citizens" had "lost their bearings." He feared that "erratic and radical thinkers and actors everywhere feel that they are in the saddle and the millennium is just around the

---

[2] This figure is given in Mitchell, *The Campaign of the Century*, p. 264.

corner. . . . No poison so deadly as mental poison." He adamantly believed that the electorate would quickly reject the New Deal once it was "demonstrated false" and then turn to Republican leadership that had been "proven to be safe, wise, and practical."[3]

Underestimating the extent of the Depression, as did many businessmen in 1933, Chandler was convinced that New Deal spending programs were going to lead to inflation. So certain was he that he prepared a "simply-worded" inflation primer for readers of the *Los Angeles Times*.[4] A year later, Chandler was still predicting a turn around in the electorate and a "very definite swing away from the 'New Deal.'"[5] What Chandler actually meant was that none of his rich friends, including the paper's advertisers and a few of the paper's readers, liked the administration's policies.

Following the trouncing that the GOP received in the 1936 election, the sobered Chandler accepted the fact that the Republican Party had become a minority party. He sent Hoover, who had risen in national politics through California ties, a long memorandum prepared for him by the Southern California Republican Campaign Committee. The memo declared the need to organize a "militant minority to speak for the great mass of voters who would not accept the New Deal." The core of this militant minority, the memo urged, should be a "powerful group of business and professional leaders representing the soundest heads of the minority thought." The Republican Campaign Committee observed that, before 1932, nomination on the Republican ticket was tantamount to election. Personal political machines were effective merely because a Republican could not be beaten. Since 1932, however, "the times have changed."[6] Chandler and Southern California Republicans understood that the party, in the state and nationally, was going to have to be rebuilt from the ground up, beginning with business and professional groups and then moving toward capturing the average voter.

California Republicans enjoyed surprising electoral successes in the '30s, given the surge in Democratic registration and the precipitous decline in Republican registration. Despite Democratic-leaning voters, Republicans still claimed the loyalty of many attorneys, physicians, and successful business-people. The educated elite from which many statewide candidates tended to be drawn were often Republicans.

One of the saving factors for Republicans was a state system of candidates being able to cross-file in both parties during primaries and the general election.

---

[3] Harry Chandler to Herbert Hoover, December 14, 1933; and Chandler to Hoover, April 15, 1933, Herbert Hoover Papers, post-presidential files.
[4] Harry Chandler to Herbert Hoover, April 26, 1933, Herbert Hoover Papers, post-presidential files.
[5] Harry Chandler to Herbert Hoover, November 19, 1934, Herbert Hoover Papers, post-presidential files.
[6] Southern California Republican Committee to Harry Chandler, November 18, 1936, Herbert Hoover Papers, post-presidential files.

Cross-filing had emerged as a reform measure at the turn of the century by a citizenry fed up with Southern Pacific Railroad Company's virtual control of state government that extended down to local-level elections.[7] As one leading state reformer, John R. Haynes, acidly wrote, "From the village constable to the governor of the state ... the final selection lay" with the "railroad machine."[8] Opposition to corrupt government and corrupt control encouraged progressive reformers to win control of the Republican Party, a movement led by Hiram Johnson, a San Francisco district attorney who combined high moralism with pragmatism. Winning election as governor, he went on to the U.S. Senate in 1917, a seat he held until his death in 1945. Among the many reforms instituted by reform-minded progressive Republicans was a measure that permitted candidates to cross party lines in primaries, with one result being that party structures and loyalties tended to become diluted in the process. As one of the most astute observers of California politics, journalist Carey McWilliams, noted, "California is a state that lacks a political gyroscope, a state that swings and sways, spins and turns in accordance with its own peculiar dynamics."[9]

Prior to the 1930s, California Republicans had profited from the state's booming population and growing wealth. Throughout the 1920s, Republicans outnumbered Democrats in the state by as much as five to one. Republicans dominated state politics, but the party was sharply divided between its progressive and conservative wings, North and South, and party leaders who claimed the mantles of reform or economy and efficiency. The line between "progressive" and "conservative" was often blurred. This line was made even murkier by the alcohol prohibition issue, the "dry" versus "wet" debate. After Johnson went to the U.S. Senate, William D. Stephens stepped into the governor's mansion, proclaiming himself a progressive and a "dry." He epitomized the conflicting political views of the day: during his administration, the anti-union Criminal Syndicalism Act was enacted in 1919, a law that was ruled unconstitutional in 1927. Stephens vetoed pro-labor legislation, but, at the same time, he raised corporate taxes by 35 percent and increased the state's biennial budget by 50 percent.[10] Stephens fell prey in the Republican primary of 1922 to the flamboyant conservative Friend W. Richardson, who was encouraged to run for office by Kyle Palmer, political editor of the *Los Angeles Times*.[11]

---

[7] The main authority on this subject remains George E. Mowry, *The California Progressives* (Berkeley, 1951). Also useful is Joseph P. Harris, *California Politics* (Berkeley, 1967, fourth edition). Although California politics needs more scholarly study, useful studies are found in Jackson K. Putman, *Modern California Politics* (San Francisco, 1984); Harris, *California Politics*; Gladwin Hill, *Dancing Bear: An Inside Look at California Politics* (Cleveland, 1968); Eugene P. Vorin and Arthur J. Misner, *California Politics and Policies* (Reading, MA, 1966).

[8] Quoted in Mowry, *The California Progressives*, p. 16.

[9] Carey McWilliams, *California: The Great Exception* (New York, 1949), p. 192.

[10] Putnam, *Modern California Politics*, p. 7.

[11] Hill, *Dancing Bear*, p. 70.

Conservative Republicans under Frank Merriam took control of the legislature. The conservative ascendancy in California proved short-lived. In 1926, progressive C. C. Young defeated Richardson. Young completed the government reorganization begun under Stephens; established aid for the physically disabled, needy, and blind; and created the first comprehensive old age pension law in the nation. He also secured public financing for the Central Valley Project.[12] When the "dry" vote divided in 1930, a conservative and "soaking wet" Republican, Mayor James Rolph of San Francisco, won the governorship. When he died suddenly while campaigning for renomination in June 1934, Lieutenant Governor Frank Merriam captured the Republican nomination.

Throughout these years, the California Democratic Party was in disarray, plagued by poor organization and its own factionalism. From 1920 until 1932, no Democrat was elected to the U.S. Senate from California. Although three Republican governors failed to win renomination, Democrats failed to elect a governor throughout the 1920s. In 1924, at the apogee of Republican control in the state legislature, Democrats only held 7 of 120 seats.[13] Although Franklin Roosevelt won the state during the Depression years, Republicans continued to control state government for the greater part of the 1930s. Although Democrats controlled the majority of the California congressional delegation from 1932 to 1946, they were unable to win control of the California state legislature. Throughout the decade, they elected only one governor, Culbert Olson, in 1938, and this success proved short-lived.[14]

FOUR CHEERS FOR ROOSEVELT

Before the Great Depression, Hollywood was a largely apolitical town. Caught up in the prosperity of the 1920s and the success of silent movies, the film industry was obsessed with profits, social glamour, and lavish lifestyles.[15] Studio owners were Republicans, but politics was not central to their lives. They mostly wanted government to stay out of the film business by not imposing moral codes on the industry.

Louis B. Mayer was the great exception to this phlegmatic political attitude in Hollywood. Mayer's involvement in Republican politics can be traced to his enthusiastic support for Herbert Hoover, which began in the early 1920s when Hoover served as Secretary of Commerce in the Warren Harding and Calvin Coolidge administrations. Hoover had strong California connections. He had graduated from Stanford University, and he often lived in later years in a mansion

[12] Putnam, *Modern California Politics*, p. 11.
[13] Hill, *Dancing Bear*, p. 71.
[14] Harris, *California Politics*, pp. 8–9.
[15] For a synoptic take on Hollywood within the larger cultural context of Southern California, see Mark Shiel, *Hollywood Cinema and the Real Los Angeles* (New York, 1998).

he built on campus, which is today the Stanford president's house.[16] In 1923, Mayer arranged for Herbert Hoover to visit MGM studios. Mayer was so impressed after the visit that he sent Hoover photos of the two of them together with a note, "I wish the responsible citizens of our glorious country could know you intimately as you deserve to be known."[17] This relationship became tighter through their mutual friendship with Ida Koverman, Hoover's longtime secretary and his political ears in the state. She arrived in California in 1924 to help organize Republican women for the Calvin Coolidge presidential campaign. Koverman, who became a major force in California state politics, met the young Hoover while working for the Consolidated Gold Fields of South Africa, Ltd. in New York. Through him, she became interested in politics. In 1923, she became the executive secretary of the Republican County Central Committee. The following year, she was appointed executive secretary for the Coolidge presidential campaign.[18]

When Hoover declared himself a presidential candidate in 1928, Mayer was one of the first aboard his election effort. He offered to take to the stump for Hoover, but was refused by state campaign officials. Still, Mayer arranged for Hoover and his people to meet with producers Joseph Schenck and Cecil B. DeMille, as well as with powerful newspaper publisher William Randolph Hearst. Mayer had convinced Hearst at the Republican National Convention to throw his support to Hoover after it was clear that his preferred candidate, Andrew Mellon, was not going to garner the delegate votes necessary to win the nomination.[19] It turned out that Hoover did not need Mayer's help to win the state: in the fifteen counties surrounding Los Angeles, registered Republicans outnumbered Democrats 600,000 to 217,000, and Hoover beat his Democratic rival Alfred Smith easily.[20]

Mayer, the son of poor Jewish immigrants, took great pride in his association with the president of the United States, even though Hoover, for his part, did not see Mayer as a great political player in the state. Indeed, Koverman took it on herself to urge Hoover to give some recognition to Mayer, suggesting that Mayer might be invited to Florida to visit with Hoover before the inauguration. She understood Mayer and knew what she was asking. "This is another small boy," she wrote about Mayer, "new at the game and used to a great deal of attention.

[16] Mayer's biographer Scott Eyman mistakenly dates the Mayer-Hoover connection to the 1928 presidential campaign, but Mayer's involvement with Hoover began much earlier. See Scott Eyman, *Lion of Hollywood: The Life and Legend of Louis B. Mayer* (New York, 2005), pp. 136–137.

[17] Louis B. Mayer to Herbert Hoover, July 11, 1923, Herbert Hoover papers, Commerce series, Box 20, Herbert Hoover Presidential Library, Iowa City, Iowa.

[18] "Mrs. Ida Koverman, Film Leader, Dies," *Los Angeles Times* (November 25, 1954); Ida Koverman to W. C. Mellendore, June 26, 1923, Hoover papers, Commerce, Box 360.

[19] Steven J. Ross, *Hollywood Left and Right: How Movie Stars Shaped American Politics* (New York, 2011), pp. 64–65.

[20] Insight into the California campaign is found in George B. Bush to Lawrence Richey, November 17, 1928, Hoover papers, Campaign and Transition series, Box 41.

I know he would strut around like a proud pigeon."[21] The first dinner guests to the Hoover White House were Mayer and his wife.

With his activity in the Hoover campaign, Mayer's role in politics was just beginning. He became vice chairman of the California Republican Party in 1930, then served as state chairman in 1932 and 1933 as Republican influence in the state waned with the Depression. The title was grander than the actual job, given the weakness of the state committee in California Republican politics. His most important political role came when he joined in organizing the movie studios against socialist upstart Upton Sinclair, who ran for governor as a Democrat in 1934.

For his part, Mayer was so impressed with Koverman that he appointed her his executive secretary. In this role, she became Mayer's chief political operative, as well as a power in MGM studios. She became, in the words of Mayer's biographer Scott Eyman, "one of the invisible power centers in both MGM and the city of Los Angeles."[22] She served as either director or an officer of the Opera Guild, the Municipal Art Commission, and the Los Angeles and Hollywood Chambers of Commerce. A member of the Los Angeles Federation of Republican Women and a regular at Republican national conventions, she brought politicos, celebrities, and business interests together. She furthered Mayer's relationship with Hoover, a relationship Mayer, the once poor Jewish kid, doted upon. For his part, Mayer sent new talkie films to the White House for the president and his wife to see, and he stuck by Hoover, even in 1932, when most people realized that the Republicans were going to lose the White House.

Mayer also tried to introduce glamour and media savvy to a distressed Republican ticket headed by the embattled incumbent president. He staged the Republican National Convention to project a more festive mood than the dull 1928 convention. Voters, hardly in a cheery mood following the Crash of 1929, heard the convention on their radio sets, along with live music and radio announcers describing a screening of a talking film of Hoover and the exuberant floor demonstrations celebrating Hoover's nomination. Mayer continued to try to bring excitement to the Hoover campaign following the convention. He summoned stars such as Ethel and Lionel Barrymore, Wallace Beery, Al Jolson, and others to appear at political rallies on behalf of Hoover. Six days before the election, Mayer staged a massive campaign rally at the Shrine Auditorium in Los Angeles, which showed how glamour and politics could be combined in this new age of celebrity and mass consumption. The event featured a twenty-five-piece band, a Hoover address to the huge crowd via radio from Washington, D.C., and a stage packed with MGM movie stars.[23]

---

[21] Ida Koverman to Lawrence Richey, January 29, 1929, Hoover papers, Campaign and Transition, Box 41.
[22] Eyman, *Lion of Hollywood*, p. 137.
[23] On stage were featured stars Lionel Barrymore and Wallace Berry, comedians Buster Keaton and Jimmy Durante, as well as Conrad Nagel, Mae Murray, and Colleen Moore. Mayer's role in this campaign is discussed in fascinating detail by Ross, *Hollywood Left and Right*, pp. 69–70.

Mayer was not alone in Hollywood in thinking that Hoover was going to beat Roosevelt in 1932. Shortly before the Democratic National Convention in 1932, producer Cecil B. DeMille hosted a dinner party that drew some of Hollywood's most powerful men. Included were Mayer, MGM attorney Edwin Loeb, MGM executive Irving Thalberg, and head of Paramount production Benjamin Schulberg (Schulberg was a known liberal Democrat). During the dinner, discussion turned to politics. Emotions became heated and tempers flared. This led to bets: Mayer and Edwin Loeb wagered Irving Thalberg that Al Smith, the presumed Democratic nominee, would not be the next president of the United States. Loeb claimed that he bet $300 that Hoover would be the next president.[24] Such bets – absurd as they were to put money on Hoover in 1932 – reveal just how far out of touch many studio heads were with the actual political climate of the country. Roosevelt easily won California in 1932 by a higher margin than his national popular vote, 58.4 percent of the state vote to 57.4 percent nationally. And he won the state three more times before his death in 1945.

Although most studio heads stuck by the Republican Party, the Depression in Hollywood pushed actors, directors, screenwriters, and technicians to the left. Typical of this movement was director John Ford, who, in a public speech to the Directors Guild, blamed the Depression on the banking industry. Why had the banking industry gone on a sit-down strike to bring down the market, he asked? Simple: "So that wages and wage earners can be pushed back to where they were in 1910."[25] He was not alone in this sentiment: the Crash of 1929 caused the entire country to move to the left, although few studio heads followed.

National trends favored the rise of liberalism within the Democratic Party (outside the South) and within the general electorate. The Great Depression and the rise of fascism in Europe during the 1930s drove many Americans, especially artists, writers, and intellectuals, increasingly to the left. Hollywood, home to some of America's best paid people connected with the arts, became a hotbed of antifascist activities and leftist politics. By the 1930s, as John Wayne biographers Randy Roberts and James Olson note, Hollywood had become "a town of causes," from the Scottsboro Boys, to the struggle to organize labor, the fight against fascism, and the Spanish Civil War (which broke out in 1936). As liberal journalist and student of California politics Carey McWilliams observed in 1934, "meetings are now held at which the denizens of Hollywood foregather to discuss the most portentous of problems and to hail the dawn of world communism until about two o'clock in the morning when, their brows weary with the travail of thought, they sojourn to some nearby café and apotheosize the new God of their devotion."[26]

[24] Cecil B. DeMille to Edwin Loeb, Benjamin Schulberg, Louis Mayer, Irving Thalberg, February 10, 1932, Cecil B. DeMille papers, Box 27.

[25] Speech File, 1933–34 Speeches, John Ford papers, Box 1, Lilly Library, Indiana University.

[26] Carey McWilliams, "The Hollywood Gesture," *Panorama*, September 1934, p. 1, quoted in Saverio Giovacchini, *Hollywood Modernism: Film and Politics in the Age of the New Deal* (Philadelphia, 2001), p. 40.

In this politicized environment of the mid-1930s, Hollywood liberals, radicals, and communists joined together in a Popular Front to fight fascism. The Popular Front took organizational form through myriad groups, including the Motion Picture Democratic Committee, the Hollywood Anti-Nazi League, and the Joint Anti-Fascist Refugee Committee. Hollywood activists were kept busy attending benefit dinners and fundraising cocktail parties. Of the 50,000–60,000 workers in film, an estimated 15,000 or 25 percent joined one or another of these political organizations, although the core of this activity was centered on about 2,000 individuals. Many of the most radical within this grouping were screenwriters.[27]

As the 1930s progressed, some actors stepped forward to embrace liberal and radical causes. As high-paid stars anxious to protect their careers and public images, these actors were circumspect, generally not going too far out on the political limb. Given the popularity of Franklin Roosevelt and strong antifascist sentiment in America, endorsing the Democratic Party or joining antifascist organizations did not take great political courage, although correspondence, interviews, and later memoirs and testimony illustrate that these activist actors knighted themselves with heroism. James Cagney, one of Hollywood's top film stars and known for his many roles playing a gangster, was quite visible in progressive circles, as was another star of gangster movies, Humphrey Bogart. Also prominent in left-wing causes was John Garfield, known for his role in *They Made Me a Criminal* (1939) and the postwar hit *The Postman Always Rings Twice* (1946). Orson Welles, director of the dark portrait of Hearst, *Citizen Kane* (1941), was well known in Hollywood progressive circles. The moody and Academy Award–winning Bette Davis, always a thorn in the side of the studios, identified herself publicly with the labor wing of the Democratic Party. Perhaps the most prominent of stars identified with the left was brilliant comic actor Charlie Chaplin, best known for his silent films.[28]

Screenwriting was a hotbed of Hollywood progressivism, and, within this circle, the Communist Party had particular recruiting success. The exact number of party members within the SWG, the union representing screenwriters, remains unclear because party membership was kept secret. Some screenwriters who were party members did not keep secret their allegiance to the Communist Party. For example, playwright John Lawson, who had helped organized the SWG, was considered cultural commissar within the Hollywood party. Dalton Trumbo, the highest paid screenwriter in Hollywood, never hid his sympathies with the party, although he claimed he did not join it until 1943. Other party members within the SWG kept their allegiances quieter, but nine of the Hollywood Ten, those later fired from the studios in 1947 because of their Communist Party affiliations, were screenwriters. Journalist Eugene Lyon called

---

[27] Randy Roberts and James S. Olson, *John Wayne: American* (New York, 1995), p. 177.
[28] Nick Clooney, "Actors of the 1930s, '40s Were Active Politically," *Cincinnati Post*, September 4, 2003.

them the "$2,000-a-week proletarians," "the swimming pool peasantry," and "caviar and champagne communists."[29]

In an industry rebounding from significant losses in the early 1930s, studio owners did not pay much attention to an employee's politics. From 1930 to 1932, weekly movie attendance fell by 50 million, dropping from 110 million to 60 million. It rose to 70 million in 1934, steadily climbing to 90 million by the outbreak of the war in Europe in 1939. Driven by profits, studios were willing to hire writers who could produce engaging scripts, quickly and in abundance, and studio chiefs did not much care about a writer's politics. At the same time, the Hollywood Production Code, a self-imposed industry code written in 1930 to appease Catholic and Protestant moral concerns, was more concerned about sexual morality and pro-family values depicted in films than in political messages.[30] Most political messages, when they were slipped into films, were indirect and often found expression through an outrageous character – the unscrupulous businessman, the enlightened worker, or the comic sidekick commenting on the virtues of "the people."[31] The studios turned a blind eye to political affiliation unless it might cost them money, and Hollywood censors were too busy looking on top of beds for sex and not under beds for Reds. As blacklisted screenwriter Dalton Trumbo recalled, the studio heads at MGM were "never deceived about my political affiliation. ... There were no objections."[32] Unless an actor's or writer's politics adversely affected the studio's image with the movie-going public, executives ignored political ideology.

The result was that political activism flourished in late 1930s Hollywood, even while the studios were turning out Fred Astaire–Ginger Rogers musicals, Marx Brothers comedic romps, and light mystery capers such as *The Thin Man* series starring William Powell and Myrna Loy. Many of the scripts for these movies were written by writers on the left, including communists, but few people cared. Why should they? The purpose of Hollywood was to make money by producing movies that people were willing to reach into their pockets to see. If it took a leftist to make Hollywood capitalism work, so be it. These leftist writers, actors, directors, and technicians could do what they wanted on their own time.

---

[29] Quoted in Gerald Horne, *Class Struggle in Hollywood, 1930–1950* (Austin, TX, 2001).

[30] Gregory D. Black, *Hollywood Censored: Morality Codes, Catholics and the Movies* (New York, 1996), and Black, *The Catholic Crusade Against the Movies, 1940–1975* (New York, 1998); and William D. Romanowski, *Reforming Hollywood: How American Protestants Fought for Freedom at the Movies* (New York, 2012).

[31] For an excellent discussion of propaganda in film, see Giovacchini, *Hollywood Modernism*, p. 58.

[32] Dalton Trumbo to Murray Kempton, March 5, 1957, in Dalton Trumbo, *Additional Dialogue: Letters of Dalton Trumbo, 1942–1962*, edited by Helen Manful (New York, 1970).

A BOLSHEVIK COMES TO TOWN: THE STRANGE CASE
OF SERGEI EISENSTEIN

One thing about Hollywood was certain: profit trumped ideology. No episode better reflects the ambivalent stance of the Hollywood studios toward communists in the early 1930s than the strange case of Sergei Eisenstein, the acclaimed Soviet film director who was invited to Hollywood in 1930 to work for Paramount. Eisenstein publicly proclaimed himself a committed Bolshevik, and Hollywood took him at his word. Hollywood appreciated his skills as a director, which were evident in films that took the world by storm with their cutting edge "montage" editing, as seen in *The Battleship Potemkin* (1925) and *Ten Days That Shook the World* (1927). Eisenstein was deeply admired in European and American intellectual and artistic circles. In 1926, Eisenstein had been visited by film pals Douglas Fairbanks and Mary Pickford, representing their United Artists studio, who promised to try to bring him to Hollywood. The stock market crash and the high costs of transition from silent movies to sound prevented United Artists from fulfilling this promise.[33]

Already under criticism in the Soviet Union for being an intellectual dilettante, Eisenstein received a rare travel visa to leave the Soviet Union in 1928. The Soviet Union at this point had not begun the full crackdown that would occur under Stalin and the purge of hundreds of thousands of "enemies of the state." Soviet officials allowed Eisenstein and his entourage to travel to Europe, but granted them little in the way of funds. Rumor later had it that Eisenstein was given only $40 in hard cash when he left the country. The expectation was that he had to earn his own way, through lectures and the good graces of the many friends of the revolution in Europe. Eisenstein and his Russian entourage were nearly out of money when Jesse L. Lasky at Paramount Pictures offered him a $100,000 contract to come to Hollywood as a director. Eisenstein the Bolshevik welcomed the opportunity to cash in on Hollywood's success. However strange Eisenstein's definition of Bolshevism (which he equated with montage film technique and the dialectic of bisexuality), Hollywood welcomed him.[34] Although Eisenstein floundered in Hollywood, his arrival reveals just how little studio executives cared about an artist's politics unless it became a large public issue, such as James Cagney's support of striking longshoremen a few years later in 1934.

[33] Oksana Bulgakowa, *Sergei Eisenstein: A Biography* (San Francisco, 2001), p. 99.

[34] There is a more than small cottage industry in Eisenstein studies. The following discussion of Eisenstein draws on a small selection of these studies, including Bulgakowa's exceptionally useful *Sergei Eisenstein: A Biography*; David Bordwell, *The Cinema of Eisenstein* (New York, 1998), especially pp. 17–39; James Goodwin, *Eisenstein, Cinema and History* (Urbana, 1993); and Sergei Eisenstein and Upton Sinclair, *The Making and Unmaking of Que Viva Mexico!* edited by Harry M. Geduld and Ronald Gottesman (Bloomington, IN, 1970), pp. 35 and 92. Professor Bulgakowa's assistance in understanding Eisenstein's definition is acknowledged. See Oksana Bulgakowa to author, October 18, 2011, in author's possession.

Eisenstein's projects had been turned down already by the studio heads when he came under attack from Major Frank Pease, leader of a one-man anticommunist crusade. History has generally forgotten Pease, a right-wing, anticommunist nationalist who in the mid-1930s called for the United States to undertake imperialist expansion into South America as a remedy to the Depression.[35] At the same time, he denounced Hitler and Mussolini, warned that the New Deal was headed toward fascism, and declared that "too many capitalists and other patriots" were being misled by "some hate-exploiting, bigotry-mongering, racketeering anti-Semites."[36]

Nevertheless, when Eisenstein arrived in Hollywood, Pease attempted to organize an effort to get the Soviet director "expelled" from town. He produced a vile, anti-Semitic, twenty-four-page pamphlet, *Eisenstein, Messenger of Hell*, an effort that earned him some notoriety, but the question still remains: "What kind of influence did Pease have in Hollywood?" The answer is: not much.

Historical literature describes studios, concerned with a public backlash as disowning Eisenstein[37]. Contrary to this claim there is no evidence that Pease was able to exert this kind of influence on the studios or on the public. The claim that Eisenstein was expelled because of political pressure brought about by an organized right wing served both men,

---

[35] Pease was a disabled veteran who was discharged after losing his leg. In the '20s, he worked as a journalist and tried his hand at motion picture writing. He formed the Hollywood Technical Directors' Institute and in 1929 he organized the American Defenders, a right-wing organization, which appears to have attracted few members. In 1930, he gained some notoriety in Hollywood circles when he produced a telegram he sent to Herbert Hoover demanding the banning of Universal's recently released *All Quiet on the Western Front*, which he characterized as a "subversive film" that would lead American youth to become "a race of yellow streaks, slackers, and disloyalists." Major Frank Pease, "Shall the Movies Go Red Too?" (telegram), April 27, 1930, in author's possession.

    Pease is mentioned in passing by a few scholars. For example, see Andrew Kelly, *Filming All Quiet on the Western Front: "Brutal Cutting, Stupid Censors, Bigoted Politicos"* (London/New York, 1998). Kelly describes Pease as "manager of the Hollywood United Technical Directors Association (UTDA), a right-wing pressure group of uncertain size" (p. 108). Pease is described as a "well-known American Fascist" later revealed as a German agent. His newsletter, *American Defender*, does not appear in the exhaustive *The Conservative Press in Twentieth Century America*, edited by Ronald Lora and William Henry Longton (Westport, CT, 1999). In a similar vein, Marie Seton, a film critic who enjoyed a close friendship with Eisenstein, declares, "Pease was not speaking for himself alone; he was not merely an isolated 'crank' seeking publicity, although self-aggrandizement probably played a part in his activities. In linking 'Communist' with 'Jews,' Pease reflected the anti-Semitism in California and elsewhere in America. ... He was the spokesman of many individuals and groups." Mary Seton, *Sergei M. Eisenstein* (New York/London, 1952), p. 168.

[36] Major Frank Pease, *Pole to Panama: An Appeal for American Imperialism and A Defense of American Capitalism* (New York, 1935), pp. 25–26 for quotation, and for his denunciations of European fascists and the New Deal as a fascist state, see pp. iii, 3, 6, 26, and 39.

[37] For example, see Thomas Patrick Doherty, *Hollywood's Censor: Joseph I. Breen and the Production Code* (Columbia, 2009); Bordwell, *The Cinema of Eisenstein*, p. 17.

Eisenstein and Pease. For Eisenstein, the claim that right-wing political activism ruined his chances in Hollywood created an appealing excuse for his failure in the American film industry.

Similar claims have been made about Pease's role in bringing Hamilton Fish, chairman of the House Special Committee to Investigate Communist Activities and Propaganda, to Los Angeles in 1930. The Fish hearings elicited strong emotions on the left at the time, and this characterization of a Hollywood witch hunt was perpetuated by later commentators. Writing in the November 1930 issue of the *New Republic*, playwright Conrad Seiler warned of a witch hunt having arrived in Los Angeles. Seiler reported in his essay, "Redmongers Go West," that the hearings in Los Angeles had gathered exhaustive testimony from "prominent officers" of the Better America Federation, the American Legion, and the Chamber of Commerce about (as Seiler put it), "the great Red plot against the sacred institutions of this country."[38]

Based on a closer reading of the documentary evidence, there is a different story to be told about the hearings that shows that Fish and his committee were not interested in communist activity in Hollywood. In its final 100-page report, the Fish Committee devoted less than an eighth of a page to the issue of communism and the cinema. What concerned the committee were not communists in the film industry or the threat of a communist revolution in the country, but the introduction of Soviet propaganda films to the United States. The committee warned that "communist and ultra-pacifist propaganda is being introduced and attractively circulated in this country through Russian moving-picture propaganda films" being circulated in the United States and playing in small movie houses. The report mentioned "Serge Eisenstein" in passing, stating that he had arrived in Hollywood, but the nature of any film he might direct "remains to be seen." In short, Hamilton Fish, arguably the most notorious anticommunist crusader in Congress, was more concerned about Soviet films in America, not the Hollywood film industry.[39]

Fish actually did not think that the Communist Party presented much of a threat in the United States.[40] Fish declared, "I do not believe that there is any likelihood of a Communist revolution in the United States this year or next or for many years to come. ... We have nothing to fear in this country from a revolutionary point of view until there is a Communist revolution in Germany." He added that "[o]n the question of a revolution in this country, there is another good, sound reason why we will not have one. There are only, as our Committee

---

[38] Conrad Seiler, "Redmongers Go West," *The New Republic*, November 12, 1930, pp. 346–348, quoted p. 348.

[39] U.S. Congress, "Investigation of Communist Propaganda" (1931), Report 2290, pp. 80–81.

[40] As examples of Fish as a precursor to McCarthyism, see Seton, *Sergei M. Eisenstein*; and Bulgakowa, *Sergei Eisenstein*, p. 112. It should be noted that Bulgakowa's study is an excellent scholarly study that places the director in a larger context of Soviet film history.

found, 500,000 to 600,000 communists out of an entire country of 120 million people."[41]

Eisenstein left Hollywood because he failed to convince the studio heads at Paramount that he could direct a commercially successful film.[42] Eisenstein's post-Hollywood years, however, would have direct implications for the California governor's race in 1934, and this part of the Eisenstein story is bizarre, even by the standards of Hollywood and American politics.

With his visa about to expire, and not wanting to return to the Soviet Union as a perceived failure, Eisenstein turned to America's leading socialist author, Upton Sinclair, to save him. He proposed to Sinclair and his wife Mary Craig that they provide him with $25,000 for three or four months to finance a nonpolitical documentary film about Indian and peasant life in Mexico. Mexico had become fashionable in left-wing circles since John Reed's *Insurgent Mexico* was published in 1914. Mexico appealed to left-wing intellectuals because it combined revolution with what was seen as an exotic peasantry.[43] A formal contract was signed, with Eisenstein stipulating that all negative and positive prints were to be the property of Mrs. Sinclair. A codicil to the contract provided that the Soviet Union be given a finished print for screening inside the Soviet Union.

Eisenstein and his crew traveled to Mexico to begin filming. Months passed. Mary Sinclair continued to send checks. It's estimated that 170,000–250,000 feet of film was shot. Meanwhile, Eisenstein socialized with Mexican artists Frida Kahlo and Diego Rivera, enjoying Mexico's social life. After fourteen months of filming and more than three times the amount of money agreed on, and what Upton Sinclair described as months of "treacheries, falsehoods, and worse," Mary Craig Sinclair shut down the project. Eisenstein returned to the Soviet Union, but difficulties for Upton Sinclair and his wife were just beginning.[44]

After trying to get the film made in the Soviet Union, Sinclair secured the services of film distributor Sol Lesser, who reduced the 200,000 feet of negative film into two short feature films, *Eisenstein in Mexico* and *Death Day*, and a short documentary, *Thunder Over Mexico*. When *Thunder Over Mexico* opened in Los Angeles on May 10, 1933, the communist left went on the attack.

---

[41] Hamilton Fish Jr., "The Menace of Communism," *The Annals of American Academy of Political and Social Science*, July 1931, pp. 54–61, quoted pp. 117–119.

[42] For an excellent discussion of Paramount's rejection of Eisenstein's script, see Bulgakowa, *Sergei Eisenstein*.

[43] Bulgakowa, *Sergei Eisenstein*, p. 122; and Goodwin, *Eisenstein, Cinema, and History*, p. 129.

[44] For Sinclair's take on what he considered Eisenstein's antics in Mexico, see Sinclair letter to editor of the *New Leader*, March 26, 1934; Sinclair, "Eisenstein Comes to Hollywood"; and Sinclair, "The Eisenstein Picture," Upton Sinclair Papers, Box 31. The Eisenstein episode is discussed by Upton Sinclair and Mary Craig Sinclair in their autobiographies, Upton Sinclair, *The Autobiography of Upton Sinclair* (New York, 1962), pp. 262–264; and Mary Craig Sinclair, *Southern Belle* (Phoenix, 1957), p. 331.

The International Defense Committee for Mexican Film sought to have the film banned, and there were protests throughout Latin America. Sinclair was accused of trying to "ruin" Eisenstein and profit from his artistry.[45] Sinclair believed that these attacks were coordinated and encouraged by the Communist Party. Sinclair defended himself in print; privately, he took delight in discovering that Eisenstein had been humiliated in the Soviet Union by Stalinist authorities who forced him to declare publicly that his "unripened revolutionary feelings" were "objectively harmful" to the workers' state. Sinclair smugly noted that this kind of "group control" is more than most Americans can understand and "far more than we think we should enjoy."[46] Sinclair noted that Eisenstein did not protest the infringement of his "artistic freedom" under Stalin's regime – criticism of any kind was forbidden to artists and intellectuals who found themselves in the throes of a brutally repressive regime.[47]

Sinclair's alienation from communist left-wing circles was complete. His reputation as a socialist had been severely damaged, and this came back to haunt him when he won a surprising victory in the Democratic primary for governor in 1934. That year, the public's mood had turned so sour that California voters were willing to give socialist Sinclair a chance to turn the economy around through his radical program, End Poverty in California.

ONE CHEER AND MANY TEARS FOR SINCLAIR

Sinclair's nomination to head the Democratic ticket seemed to have come out of nowhere. Best known for his novel *The Jungle* (1904), which exposed foul practices in the meatpacking industry, Sinclair and his wife Mary moved to Southern California in the 1920s. When the 1930s Depression worsened, Sinclair, now in his fifties, proposed in a series of self-published pamphlets and

---

[45] Sinclair correspondence in 1934 details these attacks; see Upton Sinclair to Hunter Kimbrough, June 11, 1935; Sinclair to New Britain, January 27, 1934; Sinclair to Bernard Ernst, January 25, 1934, and Sinclair to Eric McKnight, Sinclair Papers, Box 25. The campaign against Sinclair is discussed by Bulgakowa, *Sergei Eisenstein*, pp. 150, 157

[46] Sinclair, "Eisenstein Repents" (n.d.), Sinclair Papers, Box 25.

[47] Stalin personally ordered the removal of any depiction of Trotsky in Eisenstein's film *The General Line*, released in 1927. The removal of Trotsky was reported in the German press, which Sinclair later used against Eisenstein. In 1927, Eisenstein fell under further criticism for his film *October*, which was denounced by his film collective as a "historical lie." Returning to the Soviet Union in the spring of 1932, Eisenstein came under attack for his "formalism" and lack of understanding of the working class. He was forced to admit publicly that he lacked true Bolshevik consciousness and was given to idealism. The purge of artists, intellectuals, and writers had begun and would accelerate with party purges in the late 1930s. Although the number of film artists imprisoned and executed did not rival the numbers of other groups persecuted in these purges, it is nonetheless surprising that film historian James Goodwin wrote that "not a single prominent film artist was exiled or executed in this period." Goodwin, *Eisenstein, Cinema, and History*, p. 140. For Eisenstein's travails in the Soviet Union, see Bulgakowa, *Sergei Eisenstein*, p. 76; also pp. 181, 188, 189.

then a book (*I, Governor of California and How I Ended Poverty* [1933]) a socialist scheme to restore the Californian economy. Sinclair's plan called for California state government to take over unproductive factories and turn them over to the workers who would produce goods for consumption and trade with agricultural cooperatives. His End Poverty in California (EPIC) plan attracted wild enthusiasm from Californians stricken by the economic downturn. EPIC clubs began springing up spontaneously throughout the state. At Sinclair's first campaign rally, held at the Hollywood Bowl in June 1934, an estimated 25,000 people showed up. Sinclair switched his party registration from Socialist to Democrat and declared his candidacy for governor in 1934. On August 28, 1934, Sinclair swept the Democratic primary, easily defeating his major rival, George Creel, by 150,000 votes.[48] Sinclair won by carrying Los Angeles and Long Beach by a three-to-one margin. Close to fifty other EPIC candidates, including Jerry Voorhis, a future Congressman later defeated by Richard Nixon, won primary races for the state legislature.

Sinclair's nomination threw Republicans and the Democratic establishment into turmoil. Sinclair had revitalized the Democratic Party in California, and Democratic registration had surged past Republicans' for the first time in state history.[49] Sinclair had polled 436,200 votes, which were almost 90,000 more votes than Republican incumbent Governor Frank Merriam had received in his primary race. Republicans and Democrats alike saw Merriam, who had taken office following the death of Governor "Sunny Jim" Rolph that June, as an exceptionally poor candidate. The sixty-eight-year-old Merriam was seen by his opponents as a reactionary, old-time politico without much to offer in Depression-ridden California. He had angered organized labor and many progressive Republicans when he called out the state National Guard after rioting broke out in connection with a general strike in support of the left-wing longshoremen's union in July, shortly after Sinclair had won the Democratic Party nomination.

Most progressive Republicans distanced themselves from the strike. Longtime progressive Republican U.S. senator Hiram Johnson did not support the general strike. After winning the endorsement of both the Republican and Democratic Parties, incumbent Johnson refused to endorse Merriam or Sinclair. Some old progressives, such as sugar millionaire Adolph Spreckels, supported Sinclair, but others broke either to Merriam or to Commonwealth Progressive Party candidate Raymond Haight, a reform-minded attorney from Los Angeles. Haight drew modest support from Hollywood, including actors Wallace Beery and Robert Montgomery, but most of the Hollywood Left broke for Sinclair. Early endorsers of Sinclair included Charlie Chaplin, actors Victor

---

[48] This discussion of the EPIC campaign relies on Mitchell, *The Campaign of the Century*, which details the anti-Sinclair part of the campaign, as well as Sinclair's extensive collection of papers located at the Lilly Library, Bloomington, Indiana.

[49] Mitchell, *The Campaign of the Century*, p. 11.

Joey and Irving Pichel, and screenwriters Dudley Nichols, Frank Scully, and Morrie Ryskind.[50] Ryskind's support proved especially interesting because he became a leading anticommunist in the SWG just a few years later. Gene Fowler, a well-known playwright and screenwriter, best known for his play-turned-movie, *The Mighty Barnum* (1934), came out in support of Sinclair. Leftist screen writer Dorothy Parker also supported Sinclair.[51]

In one of the most expensive and vicious campaigns up to that point in California history, the 1934 gubernatorial race revealed the power of mass media in shaping an election's outcome. With Democratic registration surging and Republicans stuck with Merriam, most political insiders (including Franklin Roosevelt) believed until the final weeks of the campaign that Sinclair was going to win. The anti-Sinclair forces turned the election into a Republican victory.

Critical to the anti-Sinclair campaign was a massive radio and billboard advertising campaign, as well as short, extremely slanted "newsreels" that appeared in movie houses across the state. One of the ironies of this vicious media campaign was that Sinclair had taken an early interest in the possible use of film as a propaganda tool. He had suggested to his friend, comedian Charlie Chaplin, film plots that promoted bringing socialist values to the masses. Sinclair's interest in film as political propaganda did not translate into a political tool for his own campaign in 1934. Instead, his opponents employed film against him as a crude propaganda tool.

Because polling was still in its infancy, it is impossible to discern exactly how much of a role this media campaign had in changing the average voter's mind. During the campaign, Sinclair found himself under assault by every major newspaper in the state, radio preachers with large audiences, and organized interest groups from fruit growers to California realtors. Sinclair drew unrelenting attack from popular Southern California evangelist Aimee Semple McPherson, *Los Angeles Times* owner Harry Chandler, supporters of Long Beach dentist Francis Townsend (who was advocating old age insurance), and the California Republican Party headed by up-and-coming Earl Warren. Sinclair was attacked for being an atheist, a proponent of free love, a loon, a socialist, and a tool of the Communist Party.

Sinclair was many things – a health faddist, utopian, and socialist – but the one thing he was not was a communist. American communists despised Sinclair. When Sinclair won the Democratic nomination, the Communist Party attacked him as a "social fascist," an opprobrium saved for their most despised opponents. Party boss Earl Browder instructed California party organizer Sam Darcy

---

[50] Ryskind was best known for writing plays that were turned into Marx Brothers hits, *Cocoanuts* and *Animal Crackers*. Ten years later Ryskind was one of the founders of the Motion Picture Alliance that called on Congress to investigate Communist infiltration into Hollywood. After leaving Hollywood, Ryskind helped found *Human Events*, a leading periodical on the right.

[51] See Frank Scully to Upton Sinclair, October 20, 1934; Frank Scully to Sinclair, October 13, 1934; and Jack Preston to Richard S. Otton, October 7, 1934, Sinclair Papers, Box 29.

to attack Sinclair as a fraud misleading the masses. Communist Party cartoonist Robert Minor traveled to California to appear on radio to denounce Sinclair, warning that Hitler had used socialist phrases as well in his rise to political power. Plain people of California, he asked, "Do you not remember Hitler raised the cry 'Deutschlands Armut Vereden' – End Poverty in Germany?" Minor dubbed Sinclair, "Adolf Sinclair of Pasadena."[52] Pasadena was well known for its haughty, conservative business community; a real leftist would not live there, Minor hinted.

The campaign against Sinclair was not concerned with the nuances of Sinclair's vision of democratic socialism versus Soviet communism. At first, the anti-Sinclair forces were disorganized, especially in Southern California. Critical in bringing them together was C. C. Teague, who owned the world's largest lemon ranch and was president of the California Walnut Growers Association, which had created the Diamond brand. Teague also headed the state Chamber of Commerce. In 1932, Teague had chaired Hoover's reelection campaign in Southern California and had helped write the Republican platform. He was fanatically anti-union.[53] In early September, Teague traveled to Los Angeles to meet with Harry Chandler and major financial and business interests in Southern California to organize against Sinclair. Attending the meeting was Mendel Silberberg, the attorney for Louis B. Mayer.[54] Teague warned that if Sinclair won he would "destroy the prosperity and industry of this fair State of ours, and his poor misguided followers will find their standard of living and their ability to make a living greatly lowered."[55] At the end of the meeting, the group pledged $50,000 to launch a campaign that was to be based on mass advertising, radio support, speakers, and other media. To ensure full mobilization of the Republican Party, Earl Warren, a young district attorney in Oakland, was selected to become head of the Republican State Central Committee. Many thought Warren an odd choice because he had opposed Merriam in the Republican primary. Political strategist and *Los Angeles Times* columnist Kyle Palmer, a major player in state GOP politics, believed otherwise. He felt that Warren could win over wavering Democrats and independent voters. Palmer spoke for *Times* owner Harry Chandler, so his voice carried weight.[56] In the campaign, Warren directly appealed to disenchanted Democrats and independent voters. He also encouraged major Republican donors such as Colbert

---

[52] For Darcy's attack on Sinclair, see Mitchell, *The Campaign of the Century*, pp. 263–265 and 464.

[53] Teague's critical role in organizing anti-Sinclair forces is discussed by Mitchell, *The Campaign of the Century*, pp. 187–188; and Douglas Cazaux Sachman, *Orange Empire: California and the Fruits of Eden* (Berkeley, 2007), pp. 205–224.

[54] Those attending the meeting included Asa V. Call, vice president of Pacific Mutual; Byron C. Hanna, California Chamber of Commerce; James L. Beebe, a well-known lawyer; and Sam Haskins of the Merchants and Manufacturers Association. Mitchell, *The Campaign of the Century*, pp. 200–201.

[55] Quoted in Mitchell, *The Campaign of the Century*, p. 140.

[56] Ibid., pp. 261, 311.

Coldwell, founder of the real estate firm Coldwell Banker, to contribute tens of thousands of dollars to the Merriam campaign.

The Hollywood studios were crucial to the anti-Sinclair campaign.[57] Joining the anti-Sinclair crusade were the Hollywood studio bosses. Film director and producer DeMille, who had voted for Roosevelt in 1932, was one of the first Hollywood moguls to come out against Sinclair. Walt Disney called his entire staff together to warn of "the danger of a Communist revolution rolling through California if Sinclair got elected."[58] While Louis B. Mayer was in Paris tending his critically ill wife, his partner at MGM, Irving Thalberg, took charge of the anti-Sinclair campaign. When Mayer returned later that fall, he imposed a tax of one day's pay on every employee as a contribution to the Merriam campaign. Other studios followed, creating what was reputed to be a $500,000 anti-Sinclair fund.[59] Down the street at the Melrose studio, producer Samuel Goldwyn mobilized his staff against Sinclair. The studios opened up their parking lots to allow registration tables to drum up support for Merriam.[60] Newspaper reports began to appear that the studios planned to leave Hollywood if Sinclair were elected.

Typical of the anti-Sinclair directors was W. S. Van Dyke, a former Marine known for his adventure films such as *Tarzan the Ape Man* and the well-received *The Thin Man* (1934), based on novels written by Dashiell Hammett, who joined the Communist Party a few years after the film's debut. Although Van Dyke was a political conservative, he had voted for Roosevelt in 1932. He joined screenwriter Joseph Mankiewicz, who was to have an exceptionally long career in Hollywood as an Academy Award–winning director, in organizing the MGM branch of the Young Crusaders, an anti-Sinclair group. The Young Crusaders undertook biweekly radio broadcasts satirizing Sinclair. Mankiewicz's involvement in the Young Crusaders group surprised many in Hollywood because he was a well-known liberal Democrat. Mankiewicz and Van Dyke shared a fear of Sinclair's election, but few actors came out for Merriam. Sam Jaffe and Mexican American actor Leo Carrillo were exceptions.

At the same time, Hollywood mobilized other forces. Billy Wilkerson's *Hollywood Reporter*, an insiders' daily often seen as a mouthpiece for MGM, kept up a barrage of anti-EPIC articles warning that a Sinclair election would

[57] Greg Mitchell maintains that the Hollywood studios hated Sinclair even before 1934, even though MGM paid Sinclair $25,000 for the rights to his novel *The Wet Parade* (1931). A close examination of Sinclair's papers reveals a steady correspondence between Sinclair and Louis B. Mayer before and after the election. See, e.g., Upton Sinclair to Louis B. Mayer, December 4, 1931, Box 36; and Louis B. Mayer to Upton Sinclair, May 21, 1942, Box 48, Sinclair Papers. Mayer and other studio heads might have disliked Sinclair's politics, but they were not going to let politics interfere with business.

[58] Steven Watts, *The Magic Kingdom: Walt Disney and the American Way of Life* (Boston, 1997), p. 225.

[59] This figure is cited in Hill, *Dancing Bear*, p. 83.

[60] The role of the studios is discussed by Mitchell, *The Campaign of the Century*, pp. 206–227, 340.

surely ruin the motion picture industry.[61] Meanwhile, MGM assigned talented screenwriter Carey Wilson to the Merriam campaign to create and narrate short anti-Sinclair films. Wilson worked with director Felix Feist, Jr. to film a series of shorts to be shown in movie theaters across California. Especially destructive were their pseudo news reports, *California Election News*, which depicted Sinclair supporters as bums, criminals, and nuts. In one episode, in a voice-over, Carey Wilson declared that "Your Inquiring Cameraman interviewed thirty [men] who said they were on their way to California to spend the winter and remain there permanently if the EPIC plan went into effect."[62] Actors using foreign accents were used in fake anti-Sinclair newsreels. In some theaters where the films were shown, EPIC supporters tried to shout down the movies, and fights erupted between EPIC supporters and opponents, but the damage had already been done. Anti-Sinclair opposition placed brochures on doorsteps all over the state just before the election, and Hearst inserted anti-Sinclair materials into home-delivered newspapers.

Sinclair created his own problems. Although he was an adept campaigner, especially when on stage with his running mate Sheridan Downey, local EPIC clubs were often at factional war with one another. Sinclair paid little attention to working with regular Democratic Party organizations or trying to coordinate EPIC clubs with local Democratic clubs. As screenwriter Rob Wagner reported after talking with Sinclair on the phone one evening, "he seemed utterly bewildered." He concluded that Sinclair was a "swell propagandist, but a bum executive."[63] Caught up in the enthusiasm of having won the Democratic nomination, Sinclair made political mistakes. Instead of selecting Senator McAdoo's law partner William C. Neblett to head the state Democratic Committee, Sinclair appointed EPIC supporter Culbert Olson.[64] An angry Neblett turned on the Sinclair campaign. Later McAdoo would also. As a result, the party split into Democrats for Merriam and Democrats for Haight.

Meanwhile, Merriam proved to be better on the campaign trail than his opponents expected – or than later historians have portrayed him.[65] Republicans understood that more was needed to defeat Sinclair than just right-wing clichés. As a result, the 1934 Republican state platform called for more unemployment relief, collective bargaining rights for labor, a thirty-hour work week and six-hour work day, and consideration of a national social security program. Merriam enthusiastically endorsed the platform and called a special session to implement relief measures. An experienced politician, Merriam understood that Californians in the midst of an economic depression wanted

---

[61] Mitchell, *The Campaign of the Century*, pp. 290–291.
[62] Quoted in Mitchell, *The Campaign of the Century*, pp. 500, 499–505.
[63] Robert Wagner to Frank Scully, October 8, 1934, Sinclair Papers, Box 39.
[64] Robert E. Burke, *Olson's New Deal* (Berkeley, 1953).
[65] For example, Mitchell in *The Campaign of the Century* consistently portrays Merriam as a reactionary buffoon.

action. He proved to be a pragmatic conservative, willing to accept New Deal–type policies without losing the support of his conservative backers.[66]

On election day, Sinclair was trounced. Merriam won 1.1 million votes to Sinclair's 879,537. Haight got 302,519 votes. Sinclair won twice as many wards in Los Angeles as his opponent, although not enough to overcome the Merriam vote in the northern and rural parts of the state. In San Francisco, Merriam piled up 110,000 votes to 85,000 for Sinclair. Sinclair could take some consolation in that he received twice the number of votes of any previous Democratic candidate running for governor in the history of California. Surprisingly, Sinclair did not drag the other Democrats down with him. McAdoo won reelection to his U.S. Senate seat; moreover, Democrats increased their representation in the state assembly from twenty-five to thirty-seven, and, in the forty-seat senate, from five to eight.

Studio mogul Mayer was jubilant. He threw a giant election night party at the Hollywood nightclub Café Trocadero, with a guest list included Irving Thalberg, Carey Wilson, Sam Goldwyn, and Harry Cohen. Dropping by were Howard Hughes, Clark Gable, Helen Hayes, Edward G. Robinson, Gloria Swanson, and Groucho Marx. Mayer declared, "The voters of California have made a fearless choice between radicalism and patriotism."[67]

Elected to the governorship in his own right, Merriam secured legislation creating a State Emergency Relief Administration, which made California eligible to receive federal unemployment relief. As the state budget swelled, Merriam obtained passage of a state income tax and raised corporate, estate, and sales taxes. Merriam ran head-on into lobbyists in the state when he called for taxes on liquor, oil, and other minerals. In 1938, the Democrat Culbert Olson won the governorship, but his victory proved short-lived. Republicans came roaring back in 1942, under Earl Warren.

Merriam's election in 1934 marked the end of the EPIC movement. Sinclair believed that the remnants of EPIC were taken over by communists. Making a promise to his wife, he never entered politics again. He felt betrayed by communists to his left and by Roosevelt Democrats to his right. The viciousness of right-wing Republicans did not surprise him at all. As a socialist, he expected as much.

The studios had helped defeat Sinclair, but they faced consequences for their strong-arm tactics with their employees. Many resented being forced to give up one day's pay to support Merriam, whom they considered a reactionary Republican. At MGM, writers Sam Marx, Frances Goodrich, and Albert Hackett refused to support Merriam. Over at Warner Brothers, screenwriter John Bright, known for his script *Public Enemy* (1931), starring James Cagney, refused to pay the tax. Cagney claimed that he refused to give Jack Warner a contribution. The others who were forced to go along resented the political pressure, and this resentment helped foster the union movement within the

[66] Putnam, *Modern California Politics*, pp. 21–22.
[67] Quoted in Mitchell, *The Campaign of the Century*, p. 535.

studios. The studios' methods seemed to impart new life to the SWG and provoked a new attempt to organize screenwriters.[68]

ANTIFASCISM, A SOVIET AGENT, AND MOBILIZATION

The studios' assault on Sinclair in 1934 appears, in hindsight, an example of political overkill – blanket bombing to kill a nonexistent threat. The intimidation used by the studios in their anti-Sinclair campaign, the forced contributions to the Merriam campaign, and the sheer arrogance of the studio executives proved critical in the mobilization of the left within the industry. Salary reductions for studio employees, including writers, in 1930 had already stirred employee resentment, despite the fact that these cuts were restored after the studios began making money again. Further anger came when studios tried to thwart unionization within the guilds and technical unions. Tensions worsened in Hollywood at a time when the national political climate was swinging to the left with the rise of organized labor and a general sentiment within intellectual circles that capitalism had failed. The rise of fascism in Europe intensified this swing to the left among intellectuals. The Hollywood artistic community – screenwriters, directors, cartoonists, and others – were caught up in the rising leftist tide.

The SWG reflected this new militancy among Hollywood writers. The SWG was founded in 1933, but got off to a slow start. At its first meeting were John Howard Lawson, Lester Cole, John Bright, Sam Ornitz, and Robert Riskin; many of these writers had or would develop Communist Party connections. An attempt to merge the SWG with the Author's League of America and the Dramatist League, two organizations based on the East Coast – erupted into what one historian later described as a Hollywood "writers' war."[69] The Author's League and the Dramatist League were viewed by their opponents as having close Communist Party ties. Supporting the merger were John Lawson, Sam Ornitz, Dorothy Parker and her husband Allan Campbell, John Bright, and Lillian Hellman. Shortly before announcing the merger, Lawson also announced that he had joined the Communist Party.

Opposing the merger were the so-called horsemen of the apocalypse because they increasingly saw the world in apocalyptic ways. The opposition included Patterson McNutt, screenwriter for Shirley Temple's *Curly Top* (1935); his older brother William Slavens McNutt, a prolific screenwriter of films including *Lives of a Bengal Lancer* (1935); James Kevin McGuinness, who began work in Hollywood in the 1920s; Howard Emmett Rogers, who was credited with twenty-three screenplays by 1935; and John Lee Mahin, another prolific writer known for his script for *Scarface* (1932). These merger opponents shaped the

[68] Ibid., pp. 394–395.
[69] Nancy Lynn Schwartz, *The Hollywood Writers' Wars* (New York, 1982); and Saverio Giovacchini, *Hollywood Modernism: Film and Politics in the Age of the New Deal* (Philadelphia, 2001).

Hollywood Right as it emerged. Opposition to fascism in the 1930s tended at first to blur differences between the left and the right,[70] but the fight within the SWG brought politics into sharper relief.

After a number of twists and turns that included the establishment of a studio-backed Screen Playwright Guild in 1936, intervention by the National Labor Relations Board resulted in recognition of the SWG as the writers' legal representative in 1938. At the same time, the battle to form unions in other parts of the film industry shaped Hollywood politics over the next two decades. Political divisions were not simply a matter of union versus non-union, although most studio heads opposed unions. Many actors, writers, and directors who emerged as leaders of the Hollywood Right supported unions, and the move to the right on part of many of these actors came gradually. For example, Ronald Reagan and John Wayne, two actors who came to symbolize the postwar right, did not declare themselves as conservatives until after the Second World War. Reagan, as is well known, was a liberal Democrat into the early 1950s, and Wayne appears to have been apolitical throughout the 1930s.

Hollywood became increasingly politicized in the 1930s for a variety of reasons: the sense that capitalism had failed, the attraction of Franklin Roosevelt and the New Deal, union struggles, the rise of fascism in Europe, and the perception that socialism was working in the Soviet Union. There was also the guilt that came with making huge sums of money when many were unemployed. Although progressive causes attracted growing numbers of political activists, Hollywood remained mostly what it always was – a town concerned with making movies, making profits, and making careers. Politics took a back seat for most people in Hollywood.

There were those in Hollywood who were politically committed. As the global economic depression continued and fascists came to power in Europe, political involvement intensified. The most politically committed in Hollywood were communists. They were few in number, however, and being a member of the Communist Party was a transitory state for many. Members came and went. The rigors of party discipline, changes in party line (which were frequent), and simple dilettantism encouraged exodus from the party. The Communist Party in Hollywood was never large, although communists exerted a disproportionate influence in some unions, including the SWG, the Cartoonist Union, and some of the technical unions. Yet, even as a few became converts to communism, political tensions were not evident when it came to making movies. For example, director Victor Fleming, a macho right-winger who gained fame for films such as *Captain Courageous* (1937), *Wizard of Oz* (1939), and *Gone with the Wind* (1939), worked extremely well with Communist Party member dalton Trumbo. The two even grew to like one another personally, even though they had

[70] Giovacchini, *Hollywood Modernism*, p. 2.

diametrically opposed political perspectives. What they shared in common was making movies – and money.[71]

It was understandable why many progressives joined the Communist Party in the 1930s with the rise of fascism in Europe. Antifascism brought communists, fellow travelers (those close to the party), New Deal liberals, and progressives of many stripes together in a campaign to raise political consciousness about the fascist threat. The Communist Party was at the forefront of antifascism in the mid-1930s, and antifascists expressed principled opposition to Hitler and his Nazi government in Germany while providing a recruiting tool for the party. This tie to the Communist Party was evident in the formation of the Hollywood Anti-Nazi League (HANL) in 1936. Playing a leading role in organizing the HANL was Otto Katz, a Soviet-trained agent who came to Hollywood to mobilize progressive antifascist opinion in Hollywood.

Czech-born Katz became a communist in the 1920s, while living in Berlin. He worked closely with Willy Münzenberg, the cultural organizer for the German Communist Party (both Katz and Münzenberg were later to die as enemies of the Stalinist state).[72] Katz became a well-known figure in theatrical and artistic circles in Berlin, where he became associated with a wide array of progressive writers, artists, and theatrical people including director Fritz Lang, playwright Bertolt Brecht, and actresses Salka Viertel and Marlene Dietrich. Münzenberg hired Katz for his film company, which premiered *The Battleship Potemkin* in Berlin. Through the party, Katz was sent to the Soviet Union for training as an agent.

Katz arrived in New York with his wife in late 1935, operating under the assumed name of Rudolph Beda, an antifascist freedom fighter. In New York, he met composer Hans Eisler, who was later a major Soviet intelligence agent in the United States. Katz then traveled to Hollywood, where he connected with Fritz Lang, who was about to begin filming *Fury*, starring Spencer Tracy and Sylvia Sidney. A German refugee, Lang, through the large Hollywood European expatriate community, had become active in the antifascist movement. After arriving in Hollywood, Katz introduced Lang to screenwriter Sam Ornitz, a member of the Communist Party who later became one of the blacklisted Hollywood Ten.

Katz became a darling of Hollywood's liberal intelligentsia. Although a few associated with antifascism were committed to the party, most were dedicated liberals outraged and frightened by the rise of fascism in Germany. Only a few knew Katz was a communist or a secret Soviet agent. Working through the German refugee community in Hollywood, Katz made contact with actor Peter Lorrie and directors William Dieterle, Billy Wilder, and Ernst Lubitsch. He reconnected with Marlene Dietrich to extend his social network to include

[71] Bruce Cook, *Dalton Trumbo* (New York, 1977), p. 146.
[72] For anti fascism in Hollywood, Giovacchini, *Hollywood Modernism*, pp. 81–87; and for Jonathan Miles, *Otto Katz: The Nine Lives of Otto Katz* (New York, 2010); for Münzenberg, see Stephen Koch, *Willi Münzenberg and the Seduction of Intellectuals* (New York, 2004).

actresses Greta Garbo and Norma Shearer, as well as Charlie Chaplin and Fredric March. Comedian Groucho Marx joined the crowd. Paramount scriptwriter Tess Slesinger and actor Lionel Standler hosted parties for Katz. With the support of Dorothy Parker, Katz arranged a series of private parties and fundraisers to aid the antifascist cause. This laid the groundwork for a mass antifascist meeting in the spring of 1936 that gathered twelve hundred people at the Hollywood Women's Club to hear featured speaker James Cagney and recently arrived Prinz Hubertus zu Löwenstein denounce fascism. Donald Ogden Stewart, a recent convert to the communist cause, hosted the first meeting that gave rise to the Hollywood Anti-Nazi League. Serving on the executive committee were composer Oscar Hammerstein, actor Fredric March, and screenwriter Dorothy Parker.

The declaration of the Popular Front in the Soviet Union in the spring of 1934 called for communist parties to form alliances with noncommunist progressives in a war against fascism. This was a reversal of Soviet and communist policy, in which noncommunist progressives were denounced as "social fascists," that is, apologists for capitalism, which ultimately led to fascism. In the twists and turns of Soviet policy, the call for a popular front against fascism encouraged communists to join liberals in forming organizations against fascism. In the United States, this new policy meant that the Communist Party no longer saw Franklin Roosevelt and the Democrats as "social fascists" but as potential allies in the coming struggle against fascism.

The Anti-Fascist League became a hotbed of political activism. Huge meetings were called, attracting thousands of people who came to hear speakers such as actors Fredric March, Eddie Cantor, and Gale Sondergaard, and composer Oscar Hammerstein on "The Menace of Hitler." Comic star George Jessell performed a satiric radio play, "Four Years of Hitler," written by screenwriter Dudley Nichols and director Herbert Biberman (another of the Hollywood Ten). In their enthusiasm, only a few worried about Communist Party involvement in the HANL. Director Ernst Lubitsch quickly disassociated himself from the league when it became apparent to him that it was a communist enterprise.[73]

The outbreak of civil war in Spain in the summer in 1936 further intensified the fight against fascism. Across Europe, Canada, and the United States, volunteer international brigades organized and went to Spain to fight fascism. Support for antifascist republicans in Spain became such a popular cause in Hollywood that appearances required a show of sympathy for the republicans in Spain, whether genuine or not. For example, director John Ford claimed that he had bought an ambulance for the anti-Franco forces although his actual financial contribution was minimal.[74] Some, however, were more serious. Shortly after

---

[73] For the founding and activities of HANL and Lubitsch's concerns of party infiltration, see Miles, *Otto Katz*, on which this discussion of HANL relies heavily.

[74] Bob Ford to John Ford, September 30, 1937; John Ford to Bob Ford, September 1937; note for files, September 1937 (n.d.), Box 1, John Ford papers, Lilly Library.

the outbreak of fighting, Katz left the States for Spain. He was actively involved with Soviet secret police and armed forces in the suppression of accused Trotskyists and anarchists in Spain, even though these groupings were aligned with antifascist republicans.[75] At the same time, Katz continued his role in agit-prop (communist nomenclature for agitation-propaganda). He raised money for the People's Front, at one point wiring Fritz Lang in Hollywood, "LARGE AMOUNT OF MONEY URGENTLY NEEDED FOR HELP MEDICAL SUPPLIES SPAIN STOP PLEASE DO EVERYTHING IN ORDER TO RAISE IT. . . ."[76]

Katz's greatest contribution to anti-Franco propaganda came with his involvement in the making of *The Spanish Earth*, a pro-republican documentary film narrated by American author Ernest Hemingway. Released in 1937, the film drew large audiences across the country and in Europe. At a time when most audiences had not experienced watching actual violence, *The Spanish Earth* shocked viewers with the violence perpetrated by Franco forces against civilians. Planning for the film began in the United States when a group calling itself Contemporary Historians Inc. gathered in New York to organize the project. Contemporary Historians included author John Dos Passos, poet Archibald MacLeish, and playwrights Clifford Odets and Lillian Hellman. The group also included novelist Ernest Hemingway, who fashioned himself a kind of communist.[77] They laid the groundwork for documentary director Joris Ivens and cameraman John Fernhout to shoot *The Spanish Earth*, and Hemingway was brought in to narrate the film. The film premiered in the United States at an exclusive gathering at actor Fredric March's house. Three hundred theaters and union halls scheduled the film. The film's greatest propaganda coup came on July 8, 1937, when *The Spanish Earth* was screened in the White House. The film did not change Roosevelt's declared neutrality toward the Spanish conflict, but it did rally antifascist forces in the States and Western Europe.[78]

Katz's involvement in the United States was not over. In 1939, he returned to the United States to continue work. Evidence suggests that part of his assignment was the elimination of Whittaker Chambers, a former American communist spy

[75] For Katz's involvement in Spain, see Miles, *Otto Katz*, pp. 166–199. On Soviet repression of left opposition in Spain, see Ronald Radosh, Mary Habeck, Grigory Sevostnov, *Spain Betrayed: The Soviet Union in the Spanish Civil War* (New Haven, CT, 2011); Stanley Payne, *The Spanish Civil War, the Soviet Union, and Communism* (New Haven, CT, 2011); and Payne, *The Spanish Civil War* (New York, 2012). Readers will find Payne especially informative on the complex relationship of the Soviet Union and the republican government in Spain.

[76] Quoted in Miles, *Otto Katz*, p. 168.

[77] At this point, Dos Passos was a member of the Communist Party. After a visit to Spain where he learned of Stalinist atrocities against left opponents, Dos Passos broke with communism. This ended his long friendship with Ernest Hemingway, who defended Soviet actions in Spain, including complicity in the murder of Dos Passos's college classmate, Jose Robles. Stephen Koch, *The Breaking Point: Hemingway, Dos Passos, and the Murder of Jose Robles* (New York, 2006). For Katz's involvement in *The Spanish Earth*, see Miles, *Otto Katz*, pp. 200–204.

[78] Miles, *Otto Katz*, pp. 200–209.

who had gone underground shortly before Katz's arrival. Via an introduction through Thomas Mann, a prize-winning German author living in exile in the United States, Katz met Supreme Court justice Felix Frankfurter. Katz, in turn, was introduced by Frankfurter to Franklin Roosevelt's son, James, then an executive with MGM and later a member of Congress from Los Angeles. Katz and his wife traveled to Hollywood to work with James Roosevelt in raising $15,000 for the antifascist cause.[79]

Antifascism mobilized the Hollywood Left and expressed genuine, legitimate fears about the fascist threat in Europe. It also became a means of denouncing conservative opponents by accusing them of harboring pro-fascist sentiments. The proudly anticommunist Hearst media conglomerate became an early target of organized antifascist protest beginning in 1935.[80] Hearst was a natural target for the anticommunist left. His newspapers consistently voiced anti-Soviet and anticommunist criticism. In 1934, Hearst instructed his movie production company, Cosmopolitan, to begin making anticommunist films.

Anticommunism was not a common theme in 1930s movies, but in 1935 four anticommunist films appeared in theaters: *Together We Live* (Columbia), *Oil Lamps for China* (Warner Brothers), *Fighting Youth* (Universal), and *Red Salute* (United Artists). *Fighting Youth* and *Red Salute* were set on college campuses, warning of the dangers of communist subversion of youth. In *Red Salute*, a young coed named Drue Van Allen, played by Barbara Stanwyck, falls for a young activist and begins to spout the communist line. To counter these newsreels and anti-Sinclair propaganda, the Student League for Industrial Democracy, a left-wing campus group, organized protests that brought out hundreds of high school and college students. By the summer of 1935, the call to boycott Hearst publications, newsreels, and feature films had a national following. *The Daily Worker*, the official organ of the Communist Party, urged progressives to "take prompt measures to prevent the appearance in neighborhood houses of current anti-working class films ... as well as to send protests to the producers in Hollywood to help defer or stop production of some of the forthcoming ones."[81] Undergraduates at Princeton University and Amherst College demonstrated against Hearst News outside local theaters, denouncing the newsreels as "offensively militaristic and fascist propaganda."[82]

Sometimes any association with Hearst could cause problems. Such was the case for the most popular and most highly paid film star of the 1930s, Gary Cooper, in an incident that seems rather bizarre today. In 1935, Cooper joined with fellow actor Ward Bond and screenwriter Arthur Guy Empey to form a

[79] Ibid., pp. 223–224.
[80] Especially useful for this discussion of Hearst is Louis Pizzitola, *Hearst Over Hollywood: Power, Passion, and Propaganda in the Movies* (New York, 2002).
[81] Quoted in Pizzitola, *Hearst Over Hollywood*, p. 348. For the anti-Hearst boycott, see pp. 335–348.
[82] Ibid., p. 334.

riding club, the Hollywood Hussars, allegedly with the sponsorship of William Randolph Hearst. No doubt the riding club had political overtones in a year of labor turmoil in San Francisco. Organized along the lines of a military unit, the Hussars had a medical detachment, a signal corps, a motorcycle section, and its own military police and intelligence troops.[83] Empey explained to the *Motion Picture Herald* that the Hussars were "armed to the teeth and ready to gallop on horseback within an hour to cope with any emergency menacing the safety of the community, fights or strikes, floods or earthquakes, wars, Japanese 'invasions,' communistic 'revolutions' or whatnot." Cooper reinforced this political character of the club when he added, "Americanism is an unfailing love of country; loyalty to its institutions and ideals; eagerness to defend it against all enemies; undivided allegiance to the Flag; and a desire to secure the blessings of liberty to ourselves and posterity." He concluded, "Therefore Americanism is the foundation upon which we are building the Hollywood Hussars."[84] Americanism and patriotism were clear code words that signaled a person's allegiance to the political right.

The Hollywood Hussars was modeled on an earlier club, the California Light Horse Regiment, organized in 1933 by the British-born popular character actor Victor McLaglen. The California Light Horse Regiment included a riding parade club, a polo-playing group, and a precision motorcycle contingent. McLaglen brought a pugnacious spirit to his regiment. He had begun his career as a prizefighter, then, after serving in the Irish Fusiliers in the First World War (becoming head of the military police in Baghdad), he became a leading man in British and American silent films. As a former boxer and soldier, McLaglen was full of bluster. He told the Associated Press that his regiment was organized to promote the values of Americanism. "Sure, we're organized to fight. We consider the enemy anything opposed to the American ideal, whether it's an enemy outside or inside these borders. If that includes the communists in this country, why, we're organized to fight them, too." Soon, McLaglen's organization had clubs in Pasadena, Long Beach, and Oakland. In December 1934, McLaglen led his riders to Hearst's *Examiner* building and then on to the American Legion's Olympic Stadium, where he gave a speech on "America for Americans." McLaglen's rhetoric offered an easy opportunity for the Hollywood Left to attack him as a fascist. He denied the charges of fascism, declaring he was "a patriot of the good old-fashioned American kind."[85] These expressions of patriotism and counter-charges of fascism did not hurt McLaglen's film career. Two years after the formation of the California Light Horse Regiment, McLaglen's acting career took off when director John Ford cast him as the

---

[83] Alan L. Gansbergt, *Little Caesar: A Biography of Edward G. Robinson* (Lanham, MD, 2004), p. 73.

[84] Quoted in Anthony Slide, "Hollywood's Fascist Follies," *Film Comment*, 27:4 (July 1991), pp. 63–67.

[85] Ibid., p. 63.

lead character in the tragic tale of an Irish Republican Army informer, *The Informer* (1935).

Empey was a man of the right; McLaglen's actual politics are less clear, but what Empey and McLaglen shared was a background as soldiers. Following the sinking of the British cruise ship *Lusitania* in 1915, Empey, an American citizen, joined the Royal Fusiliers Gun Company in England. Wounded at the brutal Battle of the Somme, in which more than a million casualties were recorded on both sides, Empey returned to the United States, where he enlisted in the American army. Following the war, Empey wrote his best-selling memoir *Over the Top*, later made into a film in which he starred. He wrote other screenplays, but became best known for his pulp and science fiction. Stocky, sharp-spoken, military in bearing, he presented an easy target for charges of fascism by the contemporary left. Later authors repeated these charges.[86]

Gary Cooper also presented a natural target because of his high visibility as Hollywood's most popular and highly paid actor. Any accusation of his involvement in fascist activity would inevitably draw publicity. Furthermore, Cooper was one of Hollywood's most outspoken Republicans. A son of a Montana Republican judge, Cooper remained steadfast in his allegiance to the Republican Party and his deep opposition to Roosevelt and the New Deal. He had voted for Calvin Coolidge in 1924 and Herbert Hoover in 1928 and 1932. When he joined the Hollywood Hussars in March 1934, he set himself up for journalist Carey McWilliams's accusation that he was involved with a fascist group.

So, were the Hollywood Hussars fascists? There is little evidence that either the California Light Regiment or the Hollywood Hussars were anything more than social clubs in a Southern California culture given to polo playing and parades. Polo was one of California's most popular sports in the 1920s and 1930s. It was a rich man's sport, but polo clubs such as the Hollywood Hussars abounded throughout the state. Furthermore, horse clubs could be found marching in every parade in Southern California. Contrary to the braggadocio of Empey that the Hollywood Hussars were prepared to intervene in labor upheavals, the club's charter specifically forbade involvement in labor disputes. Historian Garry Wills, who reexamined claims of crypto-fascism in McLaglen's and Empey's groups, concluded that these clubs did little more than attend charity events. The Hussars liked to dress up in handsome uniforms

---

[86] For example, author Nancy Lynn Schwartz describes Empey's Hollywood Hussars as "a reactionary vigilante army preparing, with the help of gun-toters like [James] McGuinness, Victor McLaglen, and Ward Bond, to do a little housecleaning in their community – their targets, preferably, anyone slightly pink." Schwartz, *The Hollywood Writers' Wars*, p. 205. Omitting the word "fascist" and describing a "sort of only-in-Hollywood operation," historians Larry Ceplair and Steven Englund discuss the Hollywood Hussars in militaristic terms in *The Inquisition in Hollywood, Politics in the Film Community, 1930–1960* (New York, 1980), p. 97.

and enjoy the male companionship that came with horseback riding and military drills.[87]

The charges of fascist involvement forced Cooper to publicly resign from the club. Warned by his agent that this kind of publicity might hurt his popularity with his fans, Cooper left the Hussars. He had only been a member of the Hussars from March to June 1935, but the fear of damaging his career forced him to distance himself from the club. Cooper was not free from later charges of fascist sympathies, however. Along with other prominent Southern California conservatives, including Hearst and his mistress Marion Davis; Harrison Chandler, publisher of the *Los Angeles Times*; sugar mogul Adolph Spreckels; movie czar Will H. Hayes; and studio executive Walt Disney, Cooper attended a number of events that were denounced as promoting fascism. The events included a meeting with Georg Gysling, the German consul general in Los Angeles; a reception for Mussolini's son Vittorio on October 2, 1937; and a reception for SS General the Duke of Saxe-Coburg-Gotha on April 5, 1940. As Cooper's biography notes, these meetings were "ill-advised, even foolish," but occurred before the United States entered the war and were seen as merely social events.

The most vicious accusation of Cooper's alleged fascist sympathies concerned his meeting with Albert Goering, brother of Nazi leader Hermann Goering, in 1939. This meeting led to charges by film historians of Cooper's pro-Hitler stance.[88] Left out of the story is that Cooper traveled to Germany in 1939 to accompany his father-in-law Paul Shields, a Roosevelt supporter, on a U.S. mission to investigate German finances. Albert Goering was staunchly anti-Nazi. He was spared from SS arrest because of his relationship with his brother. Cooper's trip to Germany to witness Nazi power firsthand frightened him. He returned to America to warn about the dangers of Nazi Germany. He told the press that "There's no question in my mind that those people want to have a war. They're determined to be a world power and want war."[89] In warning about Nazi Germany's pursuit of world power through war, Cooper broke with William Randolph Hearst and other isolationists who believed that America could keep out of the European war.

ENTERING THE WAR

Hearst's anticommunist and isolationist views were linked to a general belief that communists were agitating for an interventionist foreign policy in order to

---

[87] Garry Wills, *John Wayne's America* (New York, 1997), p. 205; Jeffrey Meyers, *Gary Cooper: American Hero* (New York, 2001), pp. 203–207.

[88] Charges of Cooper's alleged fascist sympathies, as well as Errol Flynn's pro-Nazi stance, are found in Charles Higham, *Errol Flynn: The Untold Story* (New York, 1980); and Charles and Roy Mosely, *Cary Grant: The Lonely Heart* (New York, 1989), p. 87. The claim that Flynn was a Nazi spy is refuted by Tony Thomas, *Errol Flynn: The Spy Who Never Was* (New York, 1990) and Jeffrey Meyers, *Gary Cooper*, pp. 204–206.

[89] Quoted in Meyers, *Gary Cooper*, p. 206.

protect the interests of the Soviet Union. For many isolationists such as Hearst, the Soviet Union posed an equal, if not greater, threat than did Nazi Germany. Many anticommunists saw a war between Germany and the Soviet Union as a good thing – "Let them kill one another off." As a consequence, anticommunism and isolationism became increasingly intertwined by the late 1930s.[90]

In late August 1939, the world of Hollywood politics appeared to turn upside down with the announcement that the Soviet Union and Nazi Germany had signed a nonaggression treaty. Shortly after the pact was signed, Germany invaded Poland from the West, followed by an attack from the East by the Soviet Union. The Stalin-Hitler Pact signaled a major shift in communist parties throughout the world, leaving progressives stunned. In the United States, the Communist Party switched from its popular front against fascism to peace activism. This was captured in the slogan "The Yanks Are Not Coming." For those true believers who had denied or defended Stalin's purges in the 1930s (later revealed to have taken millions of lives), the Stalin-Hitler Pact was explained away through a dialectical understanding that accommodation with Nazism was a necessity to prepare for an inevitable global war against capitalism. The party's new antiwar position placed it in a bizarre de facto alliance with pacifists and isolationists.

As the Communist Party made some inroads in the film industry (however exaggerated by the party or its opponents), Hollywood became an easy target for political grandstanders. In 1940, the House Committee for the Investigation of Un-American Activities, chaired by Martin Dies (D-Texas), decided to look into communism in Hollywood. The committee was the brainchild of Dies and New Jersey Democrat Samuel Dickstein. Their initial focus was largely right-wing subversion, but when the committee began to pay greater attention to the American Communist Party, Dickstein broke with it. (Later, with the release of documents from Soviet and U.S. intelligence archives, it was revealed that Dickstein was in the pay of the Soviet Union to promote antifascism.)[91] The committee's turn to an examination of alleged communist subversion reflected growing anticommunist sentiments within the American public and the committee's general concern with the issue, as well as the political hay that could be made from investigating it. In January 1940, the Gallup Poll reported that 70 percent of Americans thought it more important to investigate communism than Nazism.[92] For some committee members, such as J. Parnell Thomas (R-New Jersey), the committee was a way to link the New Deal with the communist program.

---

[90] An excellent discussion of noninterventionist and anticommunist sentiment is found in Justus D. Doenecke, *Storm on the Horizon: The Challenge to American Interventionism, 1939–41* (Lanham, MD, 2003).

[91] John Earl Haynes and Harvey Klehr, *Venona: Decoding Soviet Espionage in America* (New Haven, CT, 2001).

[92] Cited in August Raymond Ogden, *The Dies Committee: A Study of the Special House Committee for the Investigation of Un-American Activities, 1938–1944* (Washington, DC, 1945), p. 179.

In summer of 1940, Dies, conducting a one-man, closed-door hearing in Beaumont, Texas, heard former party organizer John L. Leech report that communists had infiltrated Hollywood. He provided a list of forty-two actors and actresses, producers, and directors whom he claimed were affiliated with the party. Dies decided to carry his investigation to Los Angeles.[93] Dies and Hollywood had tangled already. In 1938, a well-known authority on American communism (albeit sometimes loose with his facts), J. B. Matthews observed that careless or indifferent citizens were often used by the party in its propaganda. He cited as an example a telegram signed by actors Clark Gable, Robert Taylor, James Cagney, and child star Shirley Temple to the French communist newspaper *Ce Soir* on its first anniversary. He warned that these actors were not communists, but they had been used by the left for its own purposes. Immediately after the testimony, the liberal press jumped on the statement, accusing the Dies Committee of claiming that Shirley Temple was a communist. Secretary of Interior Harold L. Ickes guffawed that the Dies committee had found "dangerous radicals there led by little Shirley Temple."[94]

Being made a national laughingstock by the liberal press might have dissuaded a more temperate man from going anywhere near Hollywood again, but Dies was anything but judicious. He was, as described by the *New Republic*, an intransigent Texan, "physically a giant, very young, ambitious, and cocksure."[95] He was out for publicity. In August 1940, Dies traveled to Los Angeles, where his subcommittee heard testimony from James Cagney, Humphrey Bogart, Fredric March, and others. Dies declared that he had concluded that none of these witnesses was a communist. Dies's next step was to continue executive sessions in New York to look at stage actors. He exonerated other actors; he reserved judgment in the case of actor Lionel Stander, however.

Not much came from the Dies committee in terms of serious investigation, but these hearings provided ammunition to his opponents, who painted a picture of reactionary intimidation of artistic and political freedoms. At the same time, the Dies hearings encouraged other political opportunists, such as California state legislator Jack Tenney, to launch investigations into communism in the movies. These investigations attracted little support from Hollywood, including the Hollywood Right. There were exceptions: studio head Walt Disney, who confronted a violent strike by his cartoonists in 1941, encouraged Tenney's investigation into communism in Hollywood.[96]

---

[93] Die's investigation into Hollywood is discussed by Ogden, *The Dies Committee*, pp. 64–65 and 212–213; and William Gellermann, *Martin Dies* (New York, 1944).

[94] Quoted in Martin Dies, *The Martin Dies Story* (New York, 1963), p. 106. Much of J. B. Matthews's testimony can be found in *Odyssey of a Fellow Traveler* (New York, 1938). Also, Ogden, *The Dies Committee*, pp. 64–65; and Gellermann, *Martin Dies*, p. 100.

[95] Quoted in Ogden, *The Dies Committee*, p. 47.

[96] Larry Ceplair and Steven Englund, *Inquisition in Hollywood: Politics in the Film Industry, 1930–1960* (New York, 1980), pp. 157–158; Richard Schickel, *The Disney Version* (New York, 1969), pp. 209–216.

Hollywood drew the wrath of isolationists as well as anticommunists. Isolationist sentiment was not popular in Hollywood, and the large number of Jews in the film industry generated intense and understandable hatred of Hitler. The outbreak of war in Europe drew many in Hollywood to rally in support of England in its perilous struggle against Nazi Germany. Hollywood began producing films sympathetic to England and pro-interventionist in sentiment, with Warner Brothers taking the lead in this effort. This pro-interventionist sentiment was by no means universally shared in Hollywood, however. Dalton Trumbo's emotional antiwar novel *Johnny Got a Gun* captured the antiwar position found in Hollywood and much of the nation when it appeared in 1939. Many isolationists saw Hollywood as a hotbed of pro-war fever trying to spread war sickness to the rest of the country. Inevitably, Hollywood came under attack from isolationists.

Leading the charge was journalist John Flynn, a former *Nation* columnist who had turned against Roosevelt's New Deal and what he saw as the administration's conspiracy to bring America into war. In the summer of 1941, Flynn decided to target the movie industry.[97] After contacting well-known isolationists in the Senate including Burton Wheeler (R-Montana), Gerald Nye (R-North Dakota), and others associated with the noninterventionist America First Committee, Flynn orchestrated an open attack on Hollywood. Senator Nye took to the airways denouncing the studios as "gigantic engines of propaganda." Senator Bennett Champ Clark (D-Missouri) introduced a resolution calling for an investigation into the Big Eight studios. In the August hearings, Flynn identified fifty movies that "constitute deliberate propaganda." The studios fired back in full force, hiring former Republican presidential candidate Wendell Willkie, reportedly at a cost of $100,000, to defend them. Willkie told the press that his clients were happy to admit that in the current conflict they favored Great Britain over the Nazis. Then he declared that the real issue was whether the government should control the content of films. In the midst of these hearings, the issue of anti-Semitism erupted when aviation hero and leading noninterventionist spokesman Charles Lindbergh warned that the Jewish-controlled media were promoting war with Germany. Charges of anti-Semitism placed the isolationist movement on the defensive, from which it never recovered.

Hollywood producers caught criticism from all sides: the isolationist right claiming that Hollywood Jews were making pro-interventionist movies and the left who believed not enough was being done to fight fascism. These attacks created a complicated environment that studios had to navigate – one easily misunderstood by contemporary critics and later historians. The irony in isolationist charges that Hollywood moguls were producing pro-war propaganda was Hollywood's acceptance of Hitler's censoring of American movies released in Germany. Anxious to protect the huge German market for American films, Hollywood studio executives sought to accommodate Nazi movie policies, even

---

[97] For a superb account of Flynn, see John E. Moser, *Right Turn: John T. Flynn and the Transformation of American Liberalism* (New York, 2005), especially pp. 134–137.

while despising Hitler and Nazism. Here we see Hollywood greed for profits overcoming politics. There was a strange relief in the party of these true believers when Hitler launched his attack on the Soviet Union in June 1941. Less than six months later, the United States became allied with the Soviet Union in a war against Nazi Germany. The Second World War reunited the American left, as liberals and communists joined together in the struggle to defeat fascism. The war allowed many anticommunist liberals to overlook the despotic nature of communism, the blindness of party followers, and the malleability of party principles. There were a few in Hollywood who were less sanguine about the communist presence in Hollywood. They bided their time before launching an attack on their opponents. What began as a small dust devil grew into a twister that swept all before it aside, leaving destruction and tragedy.

CHAPTER 2

Anticommunism Comes to Hollywood

History, as it has been written, portrays the Hollywood Red Scare that came to the film industry after the Second World War as the dark days of Hollywood. Reputations were destroyed, lives tragically disrupted, and many careers ended by the blacklist. The story of repression, hysteria, and betrayal in those scoundrel days of the late 1940s and the 1950s has been sympathetically told and retold in haunting detail in popular and scholarly histories, novels, movies, and film documentaries. This narrative frequently presents the apologists of Stalinist totalitarianism as the protectors of freedom, while Hollywood anticommunists are rendered as representatives of repression.

This received story portrays Hollywood anticommunists – most notably popular actors such as Gary Cooper, Robert Taylor, John Wayne, and Ronald Reagan – as narrow-minded right-wingers. As the mother of well-known actress Ginger Rogers, Lela Rogers, a founding member of the Motion Picture Alliance, a Hollywood anticommunist group formed in 1944, told House Un-American Activities Committee (HUAC) in its executive session in March 1947, we were "blasted all over, being called fascist, anti-Jew, and anti-union." Being *anticommunist* in liberal Hollywood was not easy either, apparently.

Behind the allegations, the denunciations, the blacklist, and the naming of names there rests a larger story – the emergence of the Hollywood Right and the reshaping of the California Republican Party. Anticommunism forged the Hollywood Right. Their involvement in the anticommunist fight in Hollywood is worth retelling, with the understanding that the larger story is about the restoration of the Republican Party in California.

CALIFORNIA REPUBLICANS: SEEKING WASHINGTON

While the anticommunist issue absorbed the hard-core Hollywood Right, many Republicans in the film industry were more concerned about electing their candidates to political office than they were with rooting out communists in the studios. Many, if not most, of those in Hollywood who participated in Republican campaigns on the local, state, and national levels would not have chosen "anticommunist" to describe their politics. They were Republicans first. This did not mean that they did not take anticommunist positions, especially during the postwar period, as the Cold War between the United States and the Soviet Union heated up. Even in 1947, when Congress launched an investigation into communist involvement in the film industry, many within the Hollywood Right believed that the communist problem in Hollywood unions and the studios had been addressed already, and they testified as such before HUAC. Some hardliners on the Hollywood Right, however, disagreed, believing studio executives were blind to the problem. These hardliners tended to get the publicity.

Political activism among Hollywood Republicans manifested itself intermittently before the Second World War, mostly during presidential campaigns. In 1936, Hollywood Republicans rallied to presidential nominee Alf Landon. Hollywood had its own take on the ineffectual Landon campaign that, by November, clearly was a loser. Critiquing a Landon campaign film shown in theaters at the start of the campaign, the generally conservative *Hollywood Citizen* reported that the film opened with "what probably was the Topeka department of sanitation band playing 'Drink to Me Only with Thine Eyes.'" This was followed by a caption, "A busy day in the executive office," which showed an uncomfortable Landon behind a desk, thumbing his suspenders and occasionally nodding his head. Rumor was that Cecil DeMille was involved in the film, something the producer adamantly denied.[1]

DeMille, who had voted for Roosevelt in 1932, had turned quickly away from the Democrats largely because of their economic program. Although DeMille devoted most of his time to making movies, he became active in the Republican Party. In 1936, he joined Louis B. Mayer as a state elector, and he was a delegate to the 1936 Republican National Convention, pledging to support favorite son Earl Warren, who was then district attorney in Oakland.[2] DeMille was convinced that Republicans had "more than a chance – we will win if we turn our minds, our resources, and determination to victory." Landon proved to be a disappointment.[3] When he won the 1932 governor's race in Kansas, a devastating election year for most Republicans, party insiders saw Landon as the natural candidate to challenge Roosevelt in 1936. It later turned out that Landon's success in 1932 was largely due to his Democratic rival, a huckster who ran for office because he was irate that government had banned his manufactured product, a cure for male impotence based on goat testicle extract.

[1] "Alf Landon Movie Wows Em," *Hollywood Citizen News*, June 9, 1936.
[2] Minutes of the Meeting of the Southern California Delegates to the Republican Program Committee, April 25, 1938, DeMille Papers, Box 80; Cecil B. DeMille, Memo to Paramount Productions, May 28, 1936, Box 79.
[3] Cecil B. DeMille, Memo to Paramount Productions, May 28, 1936, DeMille Papers, Box 72.

Roosevelt out-campaigned, out-flanked, and out-spent Landon, who, by the end of the campaign, was flailing at New Deal socialism.

In 1937, DeMille caught the political bug and decided to explore a serious effort to make a bid for the U.S. Senate. His plan was well-conceived: first, set up an organization in Southern California, then duplicate this organization in Northern California with the support of Earl Warren. Once these organizations were established, DeMille proposed, he could win the support of the State Republican Committee. He began speaking to Republican groups throughout Southern California, warning that Americans should fear the totalitarian state. "[O]nly united forces spread through every city and county and the state and throughout the nation can save us perhaps from the invasion of the barbarian...." He contacted major donors and key Republican leaders in New Orleans, Atlanta, New York, and Boston. He raised money and won the support of prominent California Republicans, including conservative Ed Shattuck, deputy assistant attorney in Los Angeles and president of the California Republican Assembly. He attracted other important supporters to his Draft DeMille Committee, including Cleave Jones, a key political operative for *Los Angeles Times* owner Harry Chandler. The well-connected Southern California lawyer Murray Chotiner agreed to handle public relations for the committee. Robert L. Craig, director of the Republican National Committee in Southern California, and Leo Anderson, chairman of the Los Angeles County Republican Party, signed on to the effort.[4] DeMille was certain that sentiment was growing in the California Republican Party to the effect that "if the Republican Party is going to exist in California," he alone could "save the situation."[5]

The insurmountable problem DeMille faced was that the Republican establishment did not believe he was electable. As one Republican insider told DeMille's contact, "the picture industry is bad with labor and your man is not strong enough in the South." Others told him that unless he got the support of the *Los Angeles Times* and all of the Republican organizations, he could not win. After this bracing feedback, DeMille's assistant humorously advised that he would prefer "our plan years ago for an ambassadorship to Bali with me as first assistant." In the early summer of 1938, DeMille announced that, although many people had urged him to run, he had decided that he would have more influence making movies than he would in the U.S. Senate. He threw his support behind Philip Bancroft, a prominent walnut grower and son of the prominent Californian historian Hubert Bancroft. Writing to Bancroft, DeMille declared that "It is unbelievable that the greatest system of government ever conceived

---

[4] Other prominent members of the Draft DeMille Committee included lawyer and chair of the LA County Republican Party Roger Anderson; Franklin Donnell, who was well connected in southern California financial circles; Luther Anderson, treasurer for the State Central Committee; Wallace Moyer, a financial contact for industrial groups; and other active members within the LA Republican Party and the Republican Assembly. Memorandum, December 28, 1937.

[5] Memorandum, November 27, 1937; Speech to California Republican Assembly, January 26, 1938; Robert Craig to William Pine, January 19, 1838, DeMille Papers, Box 80.

and established in the world . . . could have gone so far astray as it has gone in the hands of theorists and ruthless opportunists."[6]

The midterm election of 1938 left California Republicans in dismay. Philip Bancroft lost the senate race to former Sinclair supporter Sheridan Downey, 54.4 percent to 44.7 percent. The governor's race was won by another leftist Democrat, Culbert L. Olson, who beat incumbent Frank Merriam by nearly 8 points. Not only did the Democrats win these offices handily, both Olson and Downey ran as avowed New Dealers. (Downey was actually tied to California oil interests, but he presented himself as a populist.) What made matters worse for California Republicans was that, nationally, Republicans made major gains in the House and Senate for the first time since 1930. California Republicans took solace that Earl Warren won his race for state attorney general, after winning primaries in both major parties through the state's unique system of cross-filing (see Chapter 1).

While set back in California, Republican gains across the country in the midterm election of 1938 imparted hope to the GOP that they might be able to win the presidency in 1940. Until the Second World War started in Europe, no one predicted that Roosevelt would run for a third term. Republicans nominated a handsome, articulate corporate executive, Wendell Willkie, as their nominee. Willkie won the nomination as a dark horse candidate, but, once he received the nomination, Republicans gave him their enthusiastic support. In Hollywood, actor/dancer George Murphy headed up efforts to rally Republican stars to the Willkie cause, noting that "the other side has no difficulty getting its stars out."[7] The Hollywood Left mobilized inevitably for Roosevelt. They seized on a leaflet circulated by silent film star and Republican Mary Pickford that warned that Jews were going to be voting en bloc for Democratic candidates. This was used as further evidence of anti-Semitism within the Hollywood GOP.[8] Meanwhile, in New York, novelist and screenwriter Ayn Rand gave her heart and soul to the Willkie campaign. This was to be Rand's first and last direct involvement in a presidential campaign, but in the summer of 1940, with Nazi Germany and the Soviet Union allied, Rand feared that a dictatorship was possible in the United States. When Roosevelt decided on a third term, Rand concluded that 1940 might be the last election in American history. Rand, who had moved to New York with her husband (an actor who failed to make it big in Hollywood) to get closer to New York publishers, threw herself totally into the Willkie campaign, leading a research team and then taking to the stump. She spoke on street corners, leafleted coffee shops, and worked in a run-down old theater that fellow

---

[6] Cecil B. DeMille to Philip Bancroft, June 14, 1938, DeMille Papers, Box 342.

[7] George Murphy to Hedda Hopper, telegram, October 22, 1940, Hedda Hopper Papers, Academy of Motion Picture Archives, Murphy file.

[8] This story is related by Edward G. Robinson's biographer, Alan L. Gansberg, although the specific wording of this leaflet is not quoted. Alan L. Gansberg, *Little Caesar: A Biography of Edward G. Robinson* (Lanham, MD, 2004), p. 199.

conservative Republican and movie star Gloria Swanson had rented to show campaign films for Willkie. After each film, Rand took to the stage to speak on behalf of her candidate. During the campaign, she became good friends with Swanson, and met as well with a number of leading conservative magazine editors, journalists, and intellectuals. When Willkie lost, she became indignant, flaying Willkie for backpedaling during the campaign on his commitment to free market capitalism.[9]

Following the disappointments of the 1938 and 1940 elections, Republicans in California threw their energies into state politics by promoting the political advancement of Earl Warren. Warren, who had served as district attorney of Alameda County in northern California before becoming attorney general in 1938, appealed to a broad political spectrum of voters. Warren played up his ethnic heritage as the son of a Swedish immigrant family, and he worked his Masonic connections and cultivated fellow Berkeley alums. In college, Warren had played in the Cal Band with Gordon Sproul, who went on to become the president of the University of California.

Progressive and conservative Republicans each found something to like in Warren. Warren's political roots were in the Progressive movement in California. As district attorney, he cleaned up gambling, bootlegging, and government corruption. He led the Republican attack on Sinclair in 1934, which earned him respect among both the tough-minded politicos and the conservatives within the Republican Party.

At the same time, Republicans were out to ensure that incumbent Olson was not going to win a second term. Olson's open alliance with organized labor infuriated Republicans and conservative Democrats in his own party. Many Democrats had southern roots and drawls, especially among the "Okies" in the Central Valley, and Irish Catholic Democrats also tended to be conservative. Olson's pardon of Tom Mooney, who had been convicted of a terrorist bombing twenty years earlier on admittedly circumstantial evidence, incited the right to organize a recall effort.[10] DeMille backed the Olson Recall Committee by sending in his political associate Robert Craig, whose name appeared on the organization's letterhead.[11] When Warren challenged Olson for the governorship in 1942, DeMille and others in Hollywood joined the campaign. DeMille gave at least $1,200 to the Warren campaign, as well as donating to other Republican candidates.[12] Actor Leo Carrillo, known for playing stereotypical Hispanic parts in the movies, organized "Loyal Democrats for Warren" and spoke throughout the state on Warren's behalf, often to Mexican American

[9] Rand's involvement in the Willkie campaign is discussed in Anne C. Heller, *Ayn Rand and the World She Made*, pp. 130–133.

[10] For a sympathetic account of Olsen that portrays him as more moderate, see Robert E. Burke, *Olsen's New Deal for California* (Berkeley, 1953).

[11] Olson Recall Committee, July 1, 1940, DeMille Papers, Box 354.

[12] Receipt for $100.00, October 20, 1942; Receipt for $200.00, June 5, 1942; and Gladys Rosson to DeMille, June 6, 1942, DeMille Papers, Box 99.

audiences.[13] Warren's landslide victory for governor over Olson, beating his opponent by more than 300,000 of the nearly 2 million cast votes and winning by 16 points in the popular vote (57 to 41 percent), convinced California Republicans that their dreams of placing one of their own, a Californian, in the White House (or at least in the vice presidency) was not farfetched – if not in 1944, then perhaps in 1948. In 1940, California became the fifth most populous state; by 1950, it was second only to New York.

As California Republicans looked to taking the national political stage, many party national and state leaders were chagrined to see the communist issue in Hollywood gaining national attention, especially when a group of hard-core anticommunists encouraged Congress to investigate pro-Soviet propaganda in the motion picture industry.

HARDLINERS MOBILIZE THE MOTION PICTURE ALLIANCE

As the Second World War drew to a close, not all Hollywood Republicans were of one mind about communists. Most of the studio moguls, for example, were willing to ignore the issue as long as it did not prevent them from making money. Even many actors, such as Republican Robert Montgomery, who had battled the communist faction within the Screen Actors Guild, believed that this was an issue best handled internally by the union. However, there were hardliners who believed that communists in Hollywood were part of an international conspiracy, directed by the Soviet Union, to take over Hollywood. These hardliners came together in 1944 to form the Motion Picture Alliance for the Preservation of American Ideals. They represented a small minority voice in the Hollywood community, but this tiny organization's roar echoed in the halls of Washington, D.C. – and HUAC came to town to investigate communist influence in the motion picture industry.

The Motion Picture Alliance (MPA) was formed with the avowed purpose of fighting communists within the industry.[14] The Alliance met once a month at the American Legion auditorium on Highland Avenue to hear anticommunist speakers such as former communist Louis Budenz. For many who joined the MPA, the organization was more a publicity machine than an action organization.[15] Membership was an amalgam of anticommunists of diverse types. As the *New Leader* summarized the founding of the MPA, the organization was composed of "case-hardened Republicans and some case-hardened Democrats; there are people who have elevated President Roosevelt to a least a junior

[13] Leo Carrillo to DeMille, n.d., DeMille Papers, Box 99.
[14] Those associated with early organization of the MPA included Clarence Brown (MGM), George Bruce (MGM), Eddie Bussell (MGM), Borden Chase (Paramount), Ralph Clare (Local 3999), Carl Cooper (IATSE), and Walt Disney (Disney Studio).
[15] Louis Pizzitola, *Hearst Over Hollywood: Passion and Propaganda in the Movies* (New York, 2002), p. 411.

partnership in Heavenly Days, Inc., and people who have cordially demoted him to a senior membership in the rival firm. New Dealers and anti–New Dealers; a pair who call themselves Catholic Socialists and some who go right on voting for Norman Thomas [perennial presidential candidate for the Socialist Party]."[16]

Anticommunism was not new to Hollywood, but, until the formation of the MPA, communism in the film industry faced little organized political opposition. Conflicts between communist and noncommunist factions had been primarily union affairs. Those who formed and later joined the MPA were an odd lot, a group made up of people with diverse personalities, ages, and occupations within the film industry. What they shared was Hollywood movie making and anticommunist politics. The two were not the same. Most MPA members appeared more concerned about their careers and their personal lives, with politics taking a backseat to their focus in life. In this sense, they typified Hollywood film culture. They were affluent, mostly hard-working, some hard-drinking, and all career-driven. Their lives for the most part did not revolve around politics. They said this over and over in their correspondence, public statements, and later memoirs. They accused the opposition – the communists – of dedicating their lives to politics, and they resented this. As the war drew to a close and the Red Army reached Berlin, many within the MPA had become increasingly obsessed with politics – in this case anticommunist politics. This obsession mirrored the heightened anxiety of conservatives around the country concerning the Soviet Union's emergence as a world power bent on global domination.

Even before the end of the war, conservatives warned that the Soviet Union posed a threat to world order. Tensions between the Soviet Union and the United States had begun to worsen even before Franklin Roosevelt's death in April 1945. They deteriorated rapidly after the war when Roosevelt's successor, Harry Truman, witnessed the Soviet Union's brazen suppression of political opposition in Poland. The Soviet Union dominated coalition governments in Bulgaria and Hungary. In China, a full-scale civil war erupted between the nationalist government of Chiang Kai-shek and communists led by Mao Zedong. In February 1948, communists ruthlessly seized power in Czechoslovakia (today the Czech Republic), a Soviet takeover that shocked many in the West. The coup in Czechoslovakia confirmed Truman's worst perceptions of Soviet intentions, and these events propelled the United States and the Soviet Union into a Cold War that lasted for the next forty years. As the Cold War abroad began, anticommunists – conservatives and liberals – launched attacks against communist influence at home. Although membership in the Communist Party remained small, its influence in some unions, student groups, and veterans' organizations and among a few intellectuals presented anticommunists with a serious challenge. Anticommunists were divided on what to do about this problem: some simply wanted to expose communists for what they were, whereas others wanted to

---

[16] "Double Cross in Hollywood," New Leader, July 15, 1944, p. 119.

implement more repressive measures. Divisions were seen within the noncommunist left, as well as the anticommunist right.

Although small, the MPA attracted immediate media attention when America's leading actors, such as Gary Cooper and Robert Taylor, and lesser known actors, such as Ward Bond (who often played the sidekick in John Ford movies) enlisted in the cause. Over the next several years, other immensely popular actors joined the organization, including, to name a few, Clark Gable, Spencer Tracy, Cary Grant, and Barbara Stanwyck. Dancer Ginger Rogers and her mother Lela Rogers (a former U.S. Marine and screenwriter) joined the Alliance. Well-known character actors Adolphe Menjou and Charles Colburn were active members. The fiercely anticommunist novelist and screenwriter Ayn Rand was an early member. Rand handled much of the publicity in these early years, writing press releases declaring that "the purpose of Hollywood's communists is to corrupt our moral premises by corrupting non-political movies . . . making people absorb the principles of collectivism by indirection and implication."[17] Before she resigned from the MPA in early May 1947 over a minor dispute, Rand contributed to an early and widely distributed Alliance pamphlet, "Screen Guide for Americans," in which she instructed movie producers to promote free market, pro-business, and pro-American films. Rand's anticommunism was easily matched by that of the influential Hollywood columnist for the *Los Angeles Times*, Hedda Hopper, who secretly cooperated with the U.S. Federal Bureau of Investigation (FBI) in reporting suspected communists. Hopper was a powerhouse in Hollywood because her column was read daily by millions of readers who looked to her for inside-studio gossip and her take on current movies.[18]

Critical to the MPA were a group of screenwriters who had battled what they perceived as a communist takeover of the Screen Writers Guild (SWG) in the 1930s. These writers formed the core of the Alliance. By 1945, the anticommunist faction within the SWG appeared defeated, convinced that its present board was about two-thirds communists or fellow travelers. As one screenwriter wrote to former president Herbert Hoover, "You know yourself how hard it is to pin a party membership on most of them, but you also know that watching them react over a period of years you can associate them with the Reds to your own conviction by watching them shift and sway with the Party line." The writer noted that the opposition within the SWG was not well organized, adding that

---

[17] Quoted in Axel Madsen, *Stanwyck* (New York, 1994), p. 246.

[18] For two excellent biographies of Rand, see Anne C. Heller, *Ayn Rand and the World She Made*; and Jennifer Burns, *Goddess of the Market: Ayn Rand and the American Right* (New York, 2009). Heller spends more time on Rand's career in Hollywood. For Hopper, see Julia Frost, *Hedda Hopper's Hollywood: Celebrity, Gossip and American Conservatism* (New York, 2011). Frost is highly critical of Hopper's right-wing politics.

"The Pinkos seem to have no social life other than cell meetings. They are bread, butter, liquor, and sex to the Reds."[19]

Screenwriters within the MPA included anticommunist SWG activists Rupert Hughes, James Kevin McGuinness, Howard Emmett Rogers, Borden Chase, John Mahin, and Morrie Ryskind. The oldest of the group was Rupert Hughes, who, after serving as a lieutenant in New York's famous "Fighting Sixty-Ninth" during the Spanish American War, had risen in New York newspaper circles. He came to Hollywood in the 1920s, gaining fame as both a screenwriter and the author of a multivolume biography debunking George Washington.[20] In 1941, at the age of sixty-eight, he enlisted in the National Guard and then helped form the California State Guard. He was a quirky, self-declared atheist, but hated world government, communism, and fascism.[21] Rupert was the uncle of Howard Hughes, Jr., who made a fortune in oil drilling and the aviation industry. Howard emerged as a major movie producer in Hollywood with his Academy Award–winning comedy, *Two Arabian Nights*, his big-budget ($3.2 million) aviation film *Hell's Angels* (1930), and the controversial gangster film *Scarface* (1932).

McGuinness was basically the driving force behind the Alliance. A charming, handsome, hard-drinking Irishman who liked to slip into brogue when talking to Irish drinking pals, McGuinness arrived in Hollywood in 1927 with a high reputation in literary circles.[22] He had served as a writer for the prestigious *New Yorker*'s "Talk of the Town" column. He was a snob, married to a baroness, and a born leader. He wrote the story that became the Marx brothers' classic comedy *A Night at the Opera* (1935), which Morrie Ryskind, also a founding member of the MPA, turned into a screenplay. McGuinness was joined in his fight against progressives by the equally conservative Howard Emmett Rogers, a master of suspense writing employed by MGM since 1932.

Rogers reputedly had a gun with two silver bullets in it, one for his wife and one for himself in case of a communist takeover. Borden Chase, a novelist before he came to Hollywood, was notorious in left-wing circles for his rabid "red-baiting." Chase was an especially easy target for the left. He was accused of being a "notorious womanizer" who had married his stepdaughter, divorcing her mother (his wife) supposedly after she caught them together in bed.[23] John Lee Mahin loved guns as well, lining his study with rifles. He was the youngest in

[19] James McGuinness to Westbrook Pegler (n.d. 1945), "Communist Infiltration, 1954–63 File," Westbrook Pegler Papers in Herbert Hoover Library.

[20] Insight into Hughes is found in Edward Dymytrk, *Odd Man Out: A Memoir of the Hollywood Ten* (Carbondale, IL, 1996), p. 45; and a full biography, James O. Kemm, *Rupert Hughes, A Hollywood Legend* (Beverly Hills, CA, 1997).

[21] For a discussion of the fight within the SWG, see Nancy Lynn Schwartz, *The Hollywood Writers' Wars* (New York, 1982), especially pp. 61–72. For Hughes, see Kemm, *Rupert Hughes*.

[22] Randy Roberts and James S. Olson, *John Wayne: American* (New York, 1995), p. 331.

[23] Bernard Gordon, *Hollywood Exile or How I Learned to Love the Blacklist: A Memoir* (Austin, TX, 1999).

the anticommunist SWG faction, but he was equally conservative in his politics and prolific in his writing.[24] He did not receive credits for his work on *The Wizard of Oz* (1939), but his earlier films, *Red Dust* (1932), starring Clark Gable and Jean Harlow, and *Scarface* (1932), were considered masterpieces of the time.

Morrie Ryskind was new to the anticommunist cause. In the 1930s, he had fought McGuinness, Rogers, and Hughes in the SWG. Ryskind got his start in theater, collaborating with George Kaufman and George Gershwin. In 1933, Ryskind won the Pulitzer Prize for his *Of Thee I Sing*, a Gershwin musical. In Hollywood, he worked on a number of Marx brothers' films, including such farces as *The Cocoanuts* (1929), *Animal Crackers* (1930), and *A Night at the Opera* (1935). He was nominated for Oscars for writing *My Man Godfrey* (1936) and *Stage Door* (1937). A longtime member of the Socialist Party, he aligned himself with the progressive wing of the SWG and played a leading role in fighting for recognition of the union. In 1934, he supported Upton Sinclair, publicly opposing studio-enforced donations to the Merriam campaign. In the late 1930s, he raised money for the Loyalists during the Spanish Civil War. By 1940, Ryskind had moved to the right, opposing a third term for Franklin Roosevelt. He wrote the campaign song for Republican nominee Wendell Willkie.

His political move to the right continued as he became friends with former communist writers Max Eastman and John Dos Passos, as well as conservatives such as former New Dealer Raymond Moley and rabid anticommunists Ayn Rand and Suzanne La Follette. He took particular offense at two pro-Soviet films produced during the Second World War, *Mission to Moscow* (1943) and *Song of Russia* (1944). He was not alone in viewing these films as part of a communist propaganda campaign within the industry. Studio heads producing these films were naïve, he thought, but the screenwriters who worked on these films knew what they were doing. They were conscious apologists, he believed, for the Soviet Union.[25]

Clark Gable, one of America's most popular actors, joined the MPA, although his participation in the organization appears minimal. Gary Cooper, Hollywood's highest paid star, took pride in his membership in MPA. Sam Wood, the president of MPA, directed Cooper in *Pride of the Yankees* (1942) and *For Whom the Bell Tolls* (1942), both of which earned Cooper Academy Award nominations for Best Actor. The latter film was based on the novel by Ernest Hemingway, well known for his support of leftist, popular-front causes. *Pride of the Yankees* cast another right-winger, Walter Brennan, who appeared

[24] An insightful interview of Mahin is found in "Interview with John Lee Mahin," Pat McGilligan, *Backstory: Interviews with Screenwriters of Hollywood's Golden Age* (Berkeley, 1986, pp. 241–266).
[25] Morrie Ryskind and John H. M. Roberts, *I Shot an Elephant in My Pajamas: The Morrie Ryskind Story* (New York, 1994), pp. 169–171.

in close to seventy films by the end of his career. Brennan kept his politics out of the public eye until the 1960s, but he was a rabid anticommunist. Clark Gable, who had joined the Alliance in the spring of 1944, spoke for the general patriotism of the group when he declared at an early Chamber of Commerce banquet for the Alliance in 1945, shortly after his release from the Army Air Corps, "I recently left a place [the army] where there are no communists or Anti-Semites ... and I hate to see anything like communism enter into the home front."[26]

Many of the screenwriters and actors worked for MGM, which gave rise to rumors that Louis B. Mayer was behind the formation of the MPA. Writer Ayn Rand, one of the founding enlistees of the Alliance, later wrote that she thought Louis B. Mayer was behind the establishment because "the real purpose was not to fight communism in Hollywood, but to have a front so the press of the country would not accuse Hollywood of being Red."[27] Given that most of the Alliance's founding members came out of MGM, with the single exception of Walt Disney, this rumor had some legs to run on. If Louis B. Mayer, head of MGM, wanted the MPA to be simply a PR front for the studio, he got more than he bargained for.

Others said that William Randolph Hearst, the newspaper magnate whose coverage of a film could make or break it at the box office, was the driving force behind the MPA. Actor Adolphe Menjou and his wife were frequent guests of Hearst's and his mistress Marion Davies at their mansion, and James McGuinness had helped rewrite a Davies script for *A Divided Heart* (1936) at Hearst's Cosmopolitan Films at MGM. This was enough for some to see a Hearst-MPA connection. Hearst newspapers reported widely on the MPA, although these rumors of Hearst involvement remain unconfirmed.[28] Those involved in forming MPA did not need Hearst. They knew one another professionally and socially, having worked on many films together. Most of the screenwriters involved in the MPA had developed a tight bond during factional fights within the SWG. Directors such as King Vidor and Sam Wood were well known in Hollywood for their conservative politics and knew one another from working at MGM.

Most major studio moguls did not associate themselves with the MPA, viewing the Alliance as too right-wing for their tastes. No studio head wanted a congressional investigation into Hollywood – with one major exception: Walt Disney. Disney was moderately conservative in the early 1930s, coming out against Sinclair in 1934. He was not alone among studio heads in this regard. He turned into a crusader, however, when cartoonists went out on a five-week strike in 1941. The strike was bitter, ending in a forced settlement; Disney was

---

[26] Quoted in Schwartz, *The Hollywood Writers' Wars*, p. 204.
[27] Quoted in Robert Mayhew, *Ayn Rand and Song of Russia: Communism and Anti-Communism in 1940s Hollywood* (Lanham, MD, 2005), p. 78.
[28] Pizzitola, *Hearst Over Hollywood*.

convinced that communists were behind the strike. Disney's view ignored work-ing conditions in his studio, but there was no doubt of communist influence within the cartoonists' union. Of course, not every striking cartoonist was a communist, but by this point Disney was unwilling to make fine distinctions. He was a natural for the MPA.[29]

Roy Brewer, president of the International Alliance of Theatrical Stage Employees and Motion Picture Machine Operators (IATSE), which represented movie technicians, stage hands, and movie projectionists, brought a critical component to the Alliance: anticommunist unionists. Brewer, former head of the Nebraska State Federation of Labor, came to Hollywood in 1945, to take over a union rife with corruption and organized crime connections. He came to Hollywood a liberal Democrat, but how anticommunist he was when he arrived is not clear. In his battle against rival Conference of Studio Unions, which was alleged by some to be communist controlled, Brewer emerged as one of the leading voices denouncing communist infiltration in the film industry. Violent jurisdictional strikes in 1945 and 1946 between the two unions occurred in this highly charged political environment. In this pitched battle between the two unions, Brewer accused Herb Sorrell, head of the Conference of Studio Unions, of being a member of the Communist Party. Brewer, once a liberal Democrat, became a founding member of the Alliance.[30]

Sam Wood, head of the Alliance, admired William Randolph Hearst, although Hearst described himself as a conservative Democrat and Wood became a Republican. Hearst's father had been a Democratic senator from California, and the son played a powerhouse role in Californian and national politics for decades. Hearst loathed Roosevelt for being a liberal, for raising taxes on the rich, and for failing to stay out of the Second World War. Wood believed that communists were a profound threat to American democratic values, and he carried a black notebook in which he carefully took down names of suspected party members.[31] After working as an assistant to Cecil B. DeMille in silent films, he became a director at Paramount Studios, where he churned out two or three films a year, working with stars such as Gloria Swanson in *Bluebeard's Wife* (1923). In 1927, Wood joined MGM, where he directed an extraordinary range of films including the Marx brothers' *Night at the Opera* (1935) and *Day at the Races* (1936), *Kitty Foyle* (1940), *The Devil and Miss Jones* (1941), *Pride of the Yankees* (1941), and *For Whom the Bell Tolls* (1942). Although Groucho Marx and his brother Harpo were Hollywood

[29] Disney biographies are numerous, but among the best are Steven Watts, *The Magic Kingdom: Walt Disney and the American Way of Life* (New York, 1998) and Neil Gabler, *Walt Disney: The Triumph of the American Imagination* (New York, 2007). Disney is negatively depicted in Marc Eliot, *Walt Disney: Hollywood's Dark Prince* (New York, 1993).

[30] For an in-depth, although at times untrustworthy account of these union wars, see Gerald Horne, *Class Struggle in Hollywood 1930–1950* (Austin, TX, 2001).

[31] Larry Ceplair and Steven Englund, *Inquisition in Hollywood: Politics in the Film Industry, 1930–1960* (New York, 1980), pp. 209–210.

liberals and despised Wood's politics, their willingness to work with him in the mid-1930s shows how money and movie success trumped politics.

At the same time, Wood associated with many of the actors and writers who became founding members of the Alliance. For example, Sam Wood helped reshape Ginger Rogers's career from a dancer in Fred Astaire movies to a dramatic actress in *Kitty Foyle* (1940). Playing a heartbroken and emotionally torn working-class girl unable to break into mainline Philadelphia society, Ginger Rogers won an Oscar as Best Actress for her performance. She was not the only conservative actor to win an Oscar nomination under Wood's direction: Charles Colburn, another founding member of the MPA, received a nomination as Best Supporting Actor in another Wood-directed film, *The Devil and Miss Jones*, a comedy about a wealthy New York department store owner who goes undercover as a shoe clerk to identify labor agitators, only to discover that his employees have legitimate complaints. The film starred Robert Cummings, a popular film star in the 1930s and '40s, who later made a successful transition to television sitcoms. Although not associated with the Alliance, Cummings was a conservative Republican.

The MPA had a single goal: the weeding out of communists within the film industry. Convinced that communists were in control of the SWG and the technical guilds in the Conference of Studio Unions, the leaders of the MPA called on studio heads to address the communist problem, convinced as they were that these studio heads were not taking the communist problem in the industry seriously enough. Members of the Alliance maintained that communists wanted to gain control of Hollywood through the unions in order to propagandize America and the world through movies. Alliance members held that Hollywood films scripted by communists were full of sly innuendo about corrupt politicians and greedy businessmen in materialistic America, and they believed that pro-communist screenwriters and directors inserted pro-Soviet lines into their films. Alliance members insisted that such material was more than typical New Deal and prowar rhetoric, that it rose to the level of overt political commentary designed to erode, albeit gradually, traditional American democratic values. At their first meeting at the Beverly Hills Wilshire Hotel, with about 100 people in attendance, the Alliance told the press that the organization stood "in sharp revolt against the rising tide of communism, fascism, and kindred beliefs that seek by subversive means to undermine and change the American way of life."[32]

The MPA espoused a vision of American individualism, and the opening paragraphs of the Alliance's founding principles captured the militancy and intent of the organization: "We believe in, and like, the American way of life: the liberty and freedom which generations before have fought to create and preserve; THE FREEDOM TO SPEAK, TO THINK, TO LIVE, TO WORSHIP,

---

[32] "M.P. Alliance Formed to Fight Subversive Forces," *Hollywood Reporter*, February 7, 1944; "Four Speakers Set in Anti-Red Series," *Hollywood Reporter*, January 29, 1947.

TO WORK, AND TO GOVERN OURSELVES AS INDIVIDUALS, AS FREE MEN [emphasis in original]; the right to succeed or fail as free men, according to the measure of our ability and our strength." None of us are "joiners" or "go to meetings types," Wood told the curious press. The organization had been formed, as Wood put it, because "those highly indoctrinated shock units of the totalitarian wrecking crew have shrewdly led the people of the United States to believe that Hollywood is a hot bed of sedition and subversion."[33]

Although of a single mind in their anticommunism, Alliance members were divided on questions such as whether the Communist Party should be legally banned and communists blacklisted in the industry. Later in the 1950s, some members, such as Cecil B. DeMille, Ward Bond, and Adolphe Menjou, supported Senator Joseph McCarthy in his crusade to root out communists in government, while others, such as John Lee Mahin, saw him as an "ass" and "a fool" who damaged the anticommunist cause.[34] The formation of the MPA showed that Hollywood was dividing itself into two camps. In 1944, the anticommunist camp was soft, and the communist camp was in turmoil as party line changed again, rejecting popular-front cooperation with liberals in favor of a new hardline position predicated on a world clash between the forces of progress (the Soviet Union) and the forces of reaction and imperialism (the United States and Great Britain).

Immediately after the formation of the MPA, the left lashed out at this organization and those members who joined it. Robert Taylor, who served briefly as president of the MPA following Wood's death from a heart attack shortly after the HUAC hearings, recalled that attacks on the organization by the left were malicious. Anyone associated with the Alliance, Taylor declared, was attacked as "Fascist, anti-Semitic, or whatever other dastardly epithet the Stalinists and their dupes chose to apply."[35] Charges of anti-Semitism hit a particularly soft spot because Jews were a major influence in Hollywood. Alliance members pointed out that six members of its executive committee were Jewish, but there was often-repeated gossip that key figures in the organization, including Walt Disney, King Vidor, and Adolphe Menjou, were anti-Semitic. Menjou was particularly outspoken in denying this allegation, and although there is no evidence to support this accusation, his critics were quick to point out that the foppish character actor had accepted a personal invitation from Adolph Hitler to attend the 1936 Berlin Olympics. Morrie Ryskind, who was Jewish, took particular umbrage at the charge that the MPA was anti-Semitic. He wrote to the *Saturday Review of Literature* to counter an attack piece playwright Elmer Rice had written in this leading literary journal. Replying

---

[33] Quoted in Schwartz, *The Hollywood Writers' Wars*, p. 264.

[34] "John Lee Mahin," in McGilligan, *Backstory*, p. 122.

[35] "President Robert Taylor's Message, *The Vigil*, March 1949, in Hedda Hopper's Papers, Motion Picture Academy, File 3870; similar complaints were heard from other Alliance members. For example, John Mahin recalled, "Oh yeah, a lot of people called us fascists, anti-Negro, anti-Jewish, and anti-labor." Interview with John Lee Mahin, in McGilligan, *Backstory*.

to one of the nation's best-known playwrights of his day (Rice is little remembered today), Ryskind said that he would be "a sucker to go around joining anti-Semitic organizations." Ryskind, whose first language was Yiddish, refused at one point in his career to return to the Algonquin Hotel in New York after the manager told him, "I don't like to see more than two Jews sitting at one table."[36]

Ethnic slurs, it might be noted, pervaded Hollywood culture in these years – and were used by Jews, Irish, Italians, and WASPs. Director John Ford's correspondence, for example, is full of teasing his lawyer about being Jewish, even while recommending to friends undergoing a divorce to get a good Jewish lawyer. At the same time, what is surprising in the correspondence of both communists and anticommunists is the absence of anti-black sentiment or slur. This does not mean that there was no racism in Hollywood. There was. But what this suggests is that racial slurs toward blacks were too impolite to be put into writing. There was a paternalism toward African Americans in Hollywood, and blacks in the 1930s were relegated mostly to stereotypical roles. Hollywood's sensibility toward race, ethnicity, and anti-Semitism underwent rapid change during the Second World War.

There were ironies worth noting in this changing sensibility toward race. In 1945, as the war was drawing to a close, black actor/dancer Lincoln Perry, whose stage name was Stepin Fetchit, the first African American to receive a film credit, wrote director John Ford pleading for film work. Perry told Ford that he had been forced to play in black clubs in Chicago and was not making a go of it. He lamented, "you'd think I was the one who started this war. I've been doing awful." Ford wrote Darryl Zanuck to ask if he could cast Perry in a film he was making on Wyatt Earp. Zanuck replied, "No one has laughed longer and louder at Stepin Fetchit than I have, but to put him on the screen at this time would I am afraid raise terrible objections from colored people." Zanuck added that Walter White and the National Association for the Advancement of Colored People (NAACP) singled Perry out as an example of "the humiliation of the colored race." Zanuck asked Ford if he really wanted to take a chance of political attack by hiring Perry. The answer was no. A year later, Perry declared bankruptcy.[37]

The attack on the newly formed MPA was immediate, well-coordinated, and massive. At the forefront of the attack was the Council of Hollywood Guilds and Unions, which called an emergency conference in late June 1944 that drew approximately 1,000 delegates from 17 guilds and unions to the Women's Club of Hollywood. Invective against the Alliance was vociferous and vicious. Speakers included prominent members of the Hollywood Left. Leading the charge was Herbert Sorrell from the Conference of Studio Unions, a fiery

---

[36] Morrie Ryskind, "Strictly Personal," *Saturday Review of Literature*, December 23, 1944; Ryskind, *I Shot an Elephant in My Pajamas*, p. 51.

[37] Stepin Perry to John Ford, February 16, 1945; John Ford to Darryl Zanuck, February 4, 1946; and Darryl Zanuck to John Ford, February 6, 1946, February File 1946, Ford Papers, Box 1.

speaker who minced no words in denouncing his opponents as fascists, red-baiters, and anti-Semites. Joining him on the platform was Sidney Buchman, a screenwriter and Communist Party member, best known for his Oscar-winning screenplay *Mr. Smith Goes to Washington* (1941) as well as *Mr. Jordan* (1941). Ironically, Buchman got his start in Hollywood working on Cecil B. DeMille's *Sign of the Cross* (1932). Others joining the attack included fellow travelers (those sympathetic to the party) such as screenwriter Mary C. McCall, good liberals such as producer Walter Wagner, president of the SWG Emmett Lavery, and novelist James Hilton (*Lost Horizon*, 1932, and *Goodbye Mr. Chips*, 1933). Actress Rita Hayworth, director Orson Welles, and producer Dore Schary sent special messages in support of the conference.

Conference speeches and resolutions immediately appeared in print in a thirty-three-page pamphlet, *The Truth about Hollywood*, that was distributed throughout the Hollywood Left community. The speeches reflect the outrage and fear felt in the left with the formation of the MPA, and only a few, such as Emmet Lavery's and Dore Schary's, could be described as tempered. A few examples capture the temperament of the conference: Walter Wagner attacked the MPA as sowing "disunity between America and her Allies; disunity within America between races, classes, and creeds." Sidney Buchman warned that the formation of the MPA threatened democracy itself. Herb Sorrell declared that the MPA was simply a front for the "open shop" and that behind the MPA's wrapping itself in the American flag was hidden "a black shirt or a brown shirt, or two."[38] A special report and resolutions passed by the conference reveal a more pointed political attack.

The special report offered by the conference's research committee alleged direct links between members of the MPA and fascists. It was guilt by association. Howard Emmett Rogers and Lela Rogers, as well as six unnamed members of the Alliance, the report noted, had given speeches before the war to the isolationist Los Angeles America First Committee and Mothers of America. Members of Mothers of America included such people as "Mrs. Elizabeth Dilling, now on trial for sedition," and "T. W. Hughes, whose books are distributed by the Aryan Book store." Speakers accused Lela Rogers as being directly tied to American fascists such as Gerald L. K. Smith, Herman Schwinn, and Fritz Kuhn. The ideals offered by the MPA "differ not too greatly from the proclaimed aims of the first National-Socialist Party in this country – that is to say, the Nazi Party." If this was not damning enough, the report warned that the MPA was "anti-Negro," "anti-Semitic," and "anti-labor."[39] The concluding resolution of the conference pledged that it would "combat all groups or individuals seeking to disseminate anti-labor doctrines or propaganda

---

[38] Walter Wagner, "The Meaning of the Attack"; Sidney Buchman, "To the Front Office"; Herbert K. Sorrell, "To the Workers in the Offices, on the Stages, and the Back Lots," *The Truth about Hollywood* (Hollywood, CA, 1944), pp. 8–10; pp. 14–15; pp. 15–17.

[39] "Bill of Particulars," *The Truth about Hollywood*, pp. 21–29.

encouraging racial discrimination or religious intolerance, during and after the war."[40] The Second World War was about to end. Another war, however, was about to begin.

LIFE IN THE PARTY

To understand the ferocity that both sides brought to this war, it is necessary to understand what it meant to be a communist in Hollywood in the 1930s and 1940s. Scholars remain divided as to the nature of the Communist Party, specifically what it meant to be a rank-and-file member.[41] Many who joined the party were idealists who believed that capitalism had failed, leaving in its wake fascism, imperialism, militarism, and profound racial, ethnic, and labor injustices. In 1930s America, it was easy to be a declared liberal, and for many a leftward step, albeit a large one, to the Communist Party, either as member or fellow traveler, was not difficult. Membership in the party was usually a short-lived experience.[42] The maximum number of comrades in Los Angeles County at any one time was estimated at 4,000, with about 300 members in the film industry. This estimate is probably low, but the Communist Party in Southern California was not large.[43] After an initial wave of enthusiasm bordering on a nearly religious experience for some, members became gradually disillusioned with the demands of party discipline, the commitment of time, and the shifting party lines. A member joining the party in 1939 and staying through 1941 might have attended antifascist rallies in the early summer of 1939, only to shift with the new party line that followed the Stalin-Hitler Pact in late August 1939. This meant joining antiwar rallies to keep America out of war and working with pacifists and isolationists. Within two years, after Hitler invaded the Soviet

---

[40] "Action Taken: Denunciation and Repudiation of the Motion Picture Alliance," *The Truth about Hollywood*, pp. 30–32.

[41] Similar debates are found in the scholarly literature over whether rank-and-file members understood the full meaning of Stalinism in the Soviet Union, China, Italy, France, and England. A good beginning in this literature is Theodore Draper's cutting review of Maurice Isserman, *Which Side Were You On? The American Communist Party in the Second World War* (Urbana, Il 1982) in the *New York Review of Books*, May 9, 1985, and Isserman's reply, September 26, 1985. Insightful on party life is Vivian Gornik, *The Romance of American Communism* (New York, 1979). For a view of disciplined party membership, see Bert Cochran, *Labor and Communism: The Conflict that Shaped American Unions* (Princeton, NJ, 1977). For a sympathetic account of rank-and-file idealists, see Ellen Schrecker, *Many Are the Crimes* (Princeton, NJ, 1999).

[42] Figures from the CPUSA reveal the rapid turnover in membership: in August 1939, a senior party official presented to the Communist International three measures of membership in the United States. The largest, 80,000, were "enrolled" members. These were persons who had joined the party and continued to be carried on its membership rolls. The next largest, 66,000, were "registered" members, persons who that year had joined a local unit of the party. The final figure, 46,000, were "dues-paying" members. The year 1939 recorded the largest membership in the party. Harvey Klehr, John Earl Haynes, and Kyrill M. Anderson, *The Secret World of American Communism* (New Haven, CT, 1996), p. 72.

[43] Horne, *Class Struggle in Hollywood*, p. 20.

Union, party members were called on to denounce pacifists and isolationists and demand that the United States join the war effort. As good gnostics, well-educated party members held the secret knowledge, in this case Marxist dialectics, that enabled them to understand the teleological sweep of history in which abrupt party shifts could be explained. For those less-informed party members and outsiders, changes in party lines looked like flip-flops, and party apologists seemed nothing more than circus acrobats in pink tights.

During the Second World War, when a "popular front" brought liberals and communists together to defeat fascism, joining the Communist Party was easier emotionally. Party ranks in the United States swelled during the Second World War, with fellow travelers easily outnumbering the less than 50,000–60,000 party members. The party's shift away from the popular front in 1944 forced many to reconsider their membership. Following the swings in party line proved unbearable except for the most committed members, and this was especially the case for Hollywood writers.

Those who joined the party in Hollywood did so for many reasons, and to suggest that some in Hollywood did so only out of guilt presents too easy an explanation. A screenwriter such as Dalton Trumbo, who was making $3,000 a week or $70,000 a script in 1946, might have felt guilt, but, in the 1930s, there were more important reasons for joining the party. Many writers turned to the Communist Party during the fight to organize the SWG in the 1930s. While some writers made huge salaries, most writers were relatively poorly paid at a time when studios were making outsized profits as audiences flooded into movie houses to find relief from the worries of the Great Depression. For some, like John Howard Lawson who headed the Hollywood Communist Party, it was a matter of commitment and power. Lawson joined the party in 1934 and became close friends with Mike Gold, a journalist who was one of the cultural czars of the party in New York. Lawson came to the party from an upper-class background – private schools, good college, and tours of Europe. He had a distinguished career as a Broadway playwright. As head of the Hollywood section, Lawson proved a rigid party hack who insisted that party line be adhered to without question. He was an oyster-like man, crusty, ragged-edged, irritated within – but he offered few pearls. He enforced discipline, expelling those who did not conform or those not willing to undergo a nearly paranormal experience of ritualized self-criticism at party sessions lasting hours, sometimes even days. His son later described his father as "an aloof, very, very angry and driven man."[44]

Lawson's verbal attacks on political opponents, both within and outside the party, could be brutal. In a debate over the Stalin-Hitler Pact in 1939, Lawson

---

[44] John Lawson, "An Ordinary Life," in Judy Kaplan and Linn Shapiro, *Red Diapers: Growing Up in the Communist Left* (Chicago, 1998). Lawson's ideological rigidity is captured by his sympathetic biographer, Gerald Horne, *The Final Victim of the Blacklist: John Howard Lawson, Dean of the Hollywood Blacklist* (Berkeley, 2006).

told an audience of 700 who had gathered at the Hollywood Hotel that "We don't want to see the blood of young Americans spilled all over Europe because of an imperialist war." Howard Rogers rose from the audience to challenge Lawson: "A few years ago you told me that you were satisfied to have communism come to the United States even if it brought with it great bloodshed. Now you are crying that you do not wish to have the blood of one American spilled on European soil. I cannot reconcile your two points of view. What happened to you?" Lawson's brazen reply cut him short: "You have just heard a first class demonstration of Red-baiting by a first class Red-baiter."[45]

For Yale University–educated Donald Ogden Stewart, joining the party was close to a religious experience. He recalled in his memoirs that, by the mid-1930s, he was rich and bored. His life as a screenwriter, when he was not writing, allowed him to be on his tennis court every afternoon and in a bar every evening. Dinner guests included Clark Gable, Sam Goldwyn, and Fred Astaire. He realized something was missing, so, at the age of forty-one, he arranged for a friend to drop him off at the Marion Yacht Club near New Bedford on the coast of Massachusetts. He was set ashore with a typewriter, without a dinner jacket, and with some Marxist books and magazines such as *The New Masses*. His reading convinced him that he, too, was a communist. "The Soviet Union was the country," he wrote, "where the underdog had taken power into his own hands and I wanted to be on the side of the underdog.... And over in the corner of my imagination, behind the worker, there crouched an image of a little man who needed my help – the oppressed, the unemployed, the hungry, the sharecropper, the Jew under Hitler, the Negro." He returned to Hollywood, joined the party, and eventually divorced his wife and married Ella Winter, the widow of muckraker Lincoln Stephens, who was also a communist. He took up the antifascist cause, working with dedicated communists such as playwright Clifford Odets (*Waiting for Lefty*, 1935), young novelists such as fellow traveler Irwin Shaw, and devoted liberals such as Hollywood movie star Fredric March. Like many converts, Stewart proved more orthodox than the orthodox. Only later in life, while still a progressive, he confessed that "The one big mistake of which I was guilty was that I linked my philosophy too rigidly and too naïvely with the Soviet Union and particularly Stalin."[46]

Ring Lardner, Jr., another member of the Hollywood branch, also later confessed his obdurateness when it came to Stalin and the Soviet Union. After joining the Communist Party in the 1930s, he recalled, "I treated every piece of antagonistic writing about the Soviet regime with the automatic skepticism that I might have applied to an argument in favor of the Inquisition or reincarnation."

---

[45] Testimony of Howard Emmett Rogers, May 15, 1947, House Un-American Activities Committee, Executive Sessions 1947, National Archives, Box 2, RG 233.

[46] Donald Ogden Stewart, *By a Stroke of Luck! An Autobiography* (London, 1973), pp. 215 and 294. For a brief summary of Lardner's political career, see Patrick McGilligan, "Ring Lardner, Jr.," in Patrick McGilligan and Paul Buhle, *Tender Comrades*, pp. 404–415.

Lardner joined the party at the urging of Budd Schulberg, a screenwriter and son of a pioneering Hollywood producer, while working on the script for *A Star Is Born*, released in 1937. As a party member, Lardner found his life filled with attendance at two to five events per week. Assigned to a special unit of screen-writers, actors, directors, and script readers, he attended separate organization and educational meetings of his branch, unit, and union faction, as well as meetings with close sympathizers of the SWG. There were meetings of the Guild, the Hollywood Anti-Nazi League, the Motion Picture Artists Committee for Spanish Democracy, and, during the Second World War, the Hollywood Writers Mobilization and Russian War Relief. Serving as a dedi-cated communist was a full-time job for those who could endure it.[47]

Being a communist meant following the party line as dictated by party leaders. This proved too much for some intellectuals, especially when this policy reached the point of absurdity. Such was the case of Budd Schulberg, the son of a privileged Hollywood family. His father was an executive at Paramount and his mother a movie executive. The Schulberg household was liberal, and both parents were sympathetic to the Soviet Union. Following graduation from Dartmouth College, Schulberg traveled to the Soviet Union, where he became enraptured with the Soviet "experiment." He returned to Hollywood as a screenwriter and joined the Communist Party. He became a leading activist in the SWG. By the late 1930s, Schulberg had begun to drift away from the party. The signing of the Stalin-Hitler Pact did not help, but his problems went deeper. They were artistic. When parts of the novel he was writing, *What Makes Sammy Run?*, began to appear as short stories, Hollywood party czar Lawson instructed Schulberg that he needed party permission to write the novel. Lawson insisted that the novel be vetted through the party, specifically Richard Collins, another screenwriter, and cultural czar Mike Gold in New York. Schulberg fled California, traveling with his wife Jingee to Vermont, where he finished the novel.

The novel captured the career of the coarse and shallow Sammy Glick as he rose through the studio system to become an executive. After reading it, Mayer flew into a rage, believing it to be about him. For communists, it seemed proletarian enough – at first. Initial response in the party's newspaper, *Daily People's World*, on April 2, 1941, was to praise the novel as "the great Hollywood novel." In a lengthy review, Charles Glenn raved, "Schulberg has written a bold and daring work." He opined, "Schulberg must be considered an important 'comer' ... an author to be watched." The realization that the novel failed to convey the oppression of Hollywood workers came only slowly. Schulberg was being watched by party bosses, and they understood that Schulberg was a renegade. Glenn quickly got the correct message, and just three weeks later, he retracted his review without flinching. He declared that he had "dashed" off his review, but, after reflection and "constructive

[47] Ring Lardner, Jr., *I'd Hate Myself in the Morning* (New York, 2000), pp. 97–99.

self-criticism," he now understood that the work failed utterly to capture the struggle of workers and writers against producers. Instead, the novel presented only a gaudy, anti-Semitic stereotype of Hollywood. He warned that this kind of novel could only play into the hands of "Fascist critics of Hollywood" who were looking for "filthy propaganda weapons" to attack Jews. Hollywood, he said, was not about "gin and sex." Instead, the real story of Hollywood, the one Schulberg did not write, was "the trade union struggles ... to keep democracy alive and to bring peace to the world." Democracy, of course, needed to be of a certain party variety.[48]

Schulberg's break with the party is easily understood. More perplexing is that so many stuck by the party. Being a Hollywood communist reflected confused idealism combined with rigid ideology. Hollywood anticommunists presented their opposition in Manichean perspective: us against them, the Children of Light against the Children of Darkness. Communist activity in the film industry paid off, though. As a well-disciplined organization with a small but committed membership, communists used secret party cell meetings to dominate and control the SWG, the cameramen's union, the sound men's outfit, the laboratory technicians, the costumers, the script-writers union, and studio editors. Party members drew suspicion from the leadership if they associated too frequently with outsiders. As a result, communists naturally socialized mostly with other members or fellow travelers. These informal gatherings, as much as formal party meetings, enabled communists to plan and script their roles to control union meetings. Because membership in the party was secret, to such a degree that even party members might not know who was in other units (or cells), allegations of control were based largely on circumstantial evidence.[49]

The major goal of the party in Hollywood was to dominate the unions, including the SWG. Within each union, this meant taking a militant line, gaining, where possible, high-level positions within the union and agitating for politically correct positions. In the popular front period in the 1930s and early 1940s, the distinction between a communist line and a New Deal liberal position was often hard to discern. Indeed, during the Second World War, the Communist Party of the United States, disbanded itself as a party in 1944, declaring itself to be the Communist Political Alliance (CPA). The CPA continued to function as a disciplined party but did not run its own candidates challenge the Democratic Party.[50]

---

[48] Charles Glenn, "Novel: The Story of a Hollywood Heel," *Daily People's World*, April 2, 1941; and Charles Glenn, "Hollywood Vine," *Daily People's World*, April 24, 1941.

[49] On this point of communist control of Hollywood unions, see Herbert Aller, *The Extortionists* (Beverly Hills, CA, 1972); and for a view that "control" was a myth, see Gerald Horne, *Class Struggle in Hollywood*.

[50] The best books on the American Communist Party remain Theodore Draper, *The Roots of American Communism* (New York, 1957); and *American Communism and Soviet Power* (New York, 1960), but new information about the party derived from Soviet archives is found in Haynes and Klehr, *The Secret World of American Communism*. A valuable study of factionalism

Communist screenwriters did not conspire to write entire movies promoting the Soviet Union, portraying capitalism as failed, businessmen as bad, politicians as corrupt, or workers as oppressed. They did not need to conspire. These sentiments were shared in the 1930s by the American public. For most Americans, unregulated capitalism had failed. Businessmen were greedy, and politicians were corrupt. What communist screenwriters tried to do was sneak in a scene here and there, or even just one line in a dialogue, that reinforced progressive views. John Charles Moffitt, who broke with the party, testified in an executive session of HUAC that a Hollywood party branch boss instructed him, "Try to get five minutes of Left Wing doctrine into any expensive scene, a scene involving crowds, or a large set, or an important set. This way it won't be cut."[51]

The issue of pro-Soviet or communist propaganda in Hollywood films proved to be a misguided accusation used by HUAC in 1947 and by some members of MPA as a ploy to garner publicity. Although Hollywood during the Second World War produced a few overtly pro-Soviet films, such as *Song of Russia* and *Mission to Moscow*, the vast majority of films produced during the war were designed to entertain and promote American patriotic values. *Mission to Moscow* was an apology for Stalinism – as was Joseph Davies's book by the same title – but the intention of both the movie and the book was to persuade the audience that Americans could work with the Soviets. America was allied with the Soviet Union in the war against fascism, and this alliance should be maintained. Most anticommunists within the film industry, stars such as Ronald Reagan, Robert Montgomery, and George Murphy, dismissed charges of Soviet propaganda in film making and sought to disassociate themselves from the wild-eyed members of the MPA.

What everyone on the Hollywood Right did agree on was a problem of communist involvement in the unions. For studio heads and pro-industry actors such as Reagan, the communist issue had been addressed, or was being addressed, in 1947. In other words, the issue of communism in the film industry was a labor union issue. It was not about pro-Soviet films. The struggle to form the SWG in the 1930s opened the first wounds in the movie industry. The Second World War and the unified fight to defeat fascism masked factional divisions. The issue of communist influence within the film industry erupted with full virulence with industry strikes in 1945 and 1946, which featured violence, death threats, and physical intimidation. The pustular communist debate infected the entire Hollywood community.

---

within the party is found in James R. Barrett, *William Z. Foster and the Tragedy of American Radicalism* (Urbana, IL, 2001). The need for a full biography of Earl Browder, the head of the American Communist Party during the popular front period, remains, but a start is found in James Ryan, *Earl Browder: The Failure of American Communism* (Tuscaloosa, AL, 2008).

[51] John Charles Moffitt, May 13, 1947, Records of the United States House of Representatives, House Un-American Activities Committee, Executive Sessions 1947, National Archives, Box 12, RG 233.

Tracing the factionalism that rose within the SWG presents an exercise in taxonomy. The basic history is simple: following wage cuts for screenwriters imposed by the studios, screenwriters organized the new SWG in 1933 under the newly enacted National Recovery Administration (NRA) code. The committee drafting the charter for the organization included men and women with diverse political views within its 173 charter members.[52] What brought the screenwriters together was a union commitment. Most screenwriters did not make much money in 1934; the majority earned less than $4,000 a year (still a good Depression-day salary), although only 10 percent earned more than $10,000 a year. Forming a union meant taking on the studios, and the movie moguls immediately launched a campaign of intimidation and firing against the union.

Even while under attack, the union was already divided on the issue of communist involvement within its ranks. In November 1934, Lawson announced that he had joined the Communist Party. By May 1936, an anticommunist faction, led by James McGuinness and Howard Emmett Rogers, had emerged in the SWG. "[W]e found out who was really running the thing, with Lawson and his minions," anticommunist and founding MPA member John Lee Mahin recalled. "We went cloak-and-dagger, and we found out that all the heavy, leading hard-working guys in the Guild were members of the Party. We sent guys to meetings. Frankly we spied on them."[53] The split came quickly. In May 1934, after an attempt at reconciliation, two SWG board members, Morrie Ryskind and Bert Kalmar, resigned, soon followed by 125 writers. They formed a rival organization, the Screen Playwrights. Mahin was elected its first president. The Playwrights won contractual union recognition by the studio heads, leading the SWG to denounce their rivals as "producers' stooges." The quick recognition given to the Playwrights by the major studios gave weight to these charges. A knife could not have cut through the tension felt by writers as they encountered one another at work. Eyes were averted in halls, sharp words exchanged in meetings, and each group separated to their own tables in studio cafeterias. Only after National Labor Relations Board elections in 1939 did the SWG become the recognized union. Although the majority of voting screenwriters opted to be represented by the SWG, the Playwrights had restricted their membership to well-established authors. As a consequence, the Playwrights group came into the election with one arm tied behind its back.[54]

Communist factions emerged less visibly in the Screen Actors Guild (SAG), so factional tensions there were less apparent at first. Formed in 1933, the SAG quickly grew from a few hundred members to several thousand.[55] The formation

---

[52] The committee to draft SWG work rules included Samuel Ornitz, Jane Murfin, Rupert Hughes, Oliver H. P. Garret, Robert Riskin, S. N. Behrman, and John Bright. See Schwartz, *The Hollywood Writers' Wars*, pp. 21–25.

[53] John Lee Mahin, Interview, McGilligan, *Backstory*, p. 2.

[54] Schwartz, *The Hollywood Writers' Wars*; and Horne, *Class Struggle in Hollywood*.

[55] A fine piece of scholarship on SAG is found in David F. Prindle, *The Politics of Glamour: Ideology and Democracy in the Screen Actors Guild* (Madison, WI, 1989).

of the SAG appeared less threatening to producers, perhaps because they perceived most actors as underpaid working stiffs. It helped that William Randolph Hearst, although generally anti-union, despised movie moguls for having stifled his attempt to build his mistress, Marion Davies, into a star. In addition, he believed that the industry was rapidly moving toward monopolization, with studios controlling movie houses, so the "battle is now on between these gigantic spiders of monopoly to see which one will eat up the others."[56]

More important, the party developed a strong presence within the studio workers' unions through the Conference of Studio Unions (CSU), an international union belonging to the AFL Brotherhood of Carpenters and Joiners. The CSU represented carpenters, painters, cartoonists, and set decorators. Herb Sorrell, a militant union leader with ties to the Communist Party, headed the CSU in Hollywood. The CSU directly challenged the rival craft union, the International Alliance of Theatrical Stage Employees (IATSE), which had a history of corruption tied to Al Capone and Frank Nitti's Chicago mob. In 1934, the Chicago mob installed George Brown as IATSE president to work with a former gang enforcer William "Willie" Bioff. In May 1941, Brown and Bioff were finally indicted on charges of federal racketeering. At that point, the IATSE brought in Roy Brewer to clean up the union.[57]

THE WAR FOR DEMOCRACY: REPUBLICANS FOR THOMAS DEWEY

America's entry into the Second World War following the Japanese attack on Pearl Harbor in December 1941 tamped down sharp political differences as Hollywood rallied to defeat the Axis powers. This was to be a war for democracy, and all sides rallied to the cause. Partisan politics did not disappear, and, for Hollywood Republicans, the presidential contest of 1944 pointed to new ways for stars and moguls to join forces during a political campaign. The communist issue in Hollywood was no longer center stage, at least in the first years of the war. Only as the war drew to a close would the issue reappear, this time with a vengeance. The release of pro-Soviet films such as *Song of Russia* and *Mission to Moscow* lit a slow fuse among MPA supporters, but the explosion finally came with industry strikes in 1945 and 1946 that brought violence, fear, and intractable division.

With the outbreak of the war, leading stars and screenwriters rushed to enlist in the military. Many were not obligated to go to war, but they did. Film star David Niven, a Scot, at the age of thirty-one joined a Highland regiment, expecting to die in the war.[58] Director John Ford joined the Navy at the age of forty-seven to organize a photographic unit that would later see action in the

---

[56] Quoted in Pizzitola, *Hearst Over Hollywood*, p. 252.
[57] John Cogley, *Report on Blacklisting: Movies* (New York, 1972), pp. 47–53.
[58] David Niven to John Ford, March 1940, 1940 File, John Ford Papers, Box 1.

Pacific, in Italy, and at D-day. As one regular Navy man wrote to a commanding officer about Ford, "It is beyond my comprehension and possibly yours why a man earning in excess of a quarter of a million dollars a year would be not only willing, but anxious, to throw that overboard."[59] Ford, however, was not the only patriot in Hollywood. Robert Taylor received a commission in the Navy; Ronald Reagan enlisted as an officer in the Army. The military employed these actors mostly in making propaganda films, but Jimmy Stewart and Clark Gable in the Army Air Corps insisted on flying military missions. Stewart flew twenty missions as squadron commander.[60] The Hollywood Left joined up as well. Henry Fonda joined the Navy because he did not want to be seen as a phony patriot. Screenwriters Michael Wilson and Michael Blankfort joined the Marines; Budd Schulberg enlisted in the Navy. Others joined the Army fighting in Europe.[61] The war brought a unity to Hollywood not seen since the 1920s.

One of the great later ironies of this outpouring of patriotism in Hollywood was that actors John Wayne and his sidekick Ward Bond – both of whom came to personify and embrace American nationalism – did not enlist. Ward Bond was in his forties by the time America entered the Second World War, but Wayne was in his mid-thirties and in good health. Their mentor John Ford had enlisted and would be wounded in action. Wayne kept writing Ford to tell him that he was going to enlist and asking for advice on how to become a Marine or a Seebee (he played both parts in his war films). The problem was that Wayne did not try very hard to join the military, possibly because his acting career had finally taken off. After playing bit parts, Wayne had won acclaim for the Ford-directed *Stage Coach* (1939). At the same time, he left his wife and two kids. His wife came from a well-established Southern California Catholic family, and she was friends with the Catholic wives of Bob Hope and Gary Cooper. This was upper-crust Los Angeles Catholic culture, and Wayne did not like the uptight atmosphere. Ford's wife was also Catholic, and she found Wayne's behavior disgusting. She wrote her husband in 1943, "Things are in bad shape at the Wayne House. Duke wants a divorce. Josie [Wayne's wife] is terribly broken up. My candid opinion is that he has gotten too big for his britches.... With all the problems in the world, I think Duke could find something more important than tail to think about. It's quite sickening."[62] While Duke and Ward Bond, who also left his wife at this time, were preoccupied with their careers and sex, more high-minded Republicans looked to prevent Roosevelt from winning a fourth term in 1944.

Republicans believed that Thomas Dewey was the candidate best positioned to regain the White House in 1944. Dewey had rocketed to national fame in the

[59] Lt. Commander Jack Bolton to Admiral Calvin T. Durgin, August 13, 1941, 1941 File, Ford Papers, Box 1.

[60] Donald Dewey, *James Stewart* (Atlanta, GA, 1996).

[61] Larry Ceplair and Steven Englund, *The Inquisition in Hollywood: Politics in the Film Community, 1930–1960* (New York, 1980), p. 179.

[62] Mary Ford to John Ford (July 1943), April–June 1943 File, Ford Papers, Box 1.

mid-'30s when, as special prosecutor, he took on organized crime in New York City. Working closely with New York reform mayor Fiorello Laguardia, a liberal Republican, Dewey brought down major crime figures including Dutch Schultz and Mafia chieftain Lucky Luciano. At the same time, he successfully pursued the indictment and conviction of Richard Whitney, the former head of the New York Stock Exchange, for embezzlement. Although Dewey lost the race for governor against Democratic incumbent Herbert H. Lehman, he won his second bid for the governor's mansion in 1942. As governor, he cut taxes, increased state support for education, and raised salaries for state employees while cutting the state debt. Inspired by Dewey's accomplishments, screenwriter Rupert Hughes wrote a sympathetic biography of Dewey, whom he had gotten to know over the years. Based on extensive research, the biography presented a dramatic narrative of Dewey as a man of courage.

Hughes was joined by in Hollywood in his support for Dewey. Once Dewey won the party's presidential nomination in 1944, Hollywood Republicans rallied to the Dewey cause. The list of Hollywood luminaries endorsing Dewey was impressive. Film star Lionel Barrymore served as master of ceremonies. Producer Cecil B. DeMille chaired the election committee, bringing his immense organizational skills to the campaign, as well as deep pockets and financial connections.[63] As the campaign between Roosevelt and Dewey heated up, the Hollywood Committee organized a spectacular mass rally for Dewey that filled the Los Angeles Coliseum, a classical outdoor stadium built for the Olympic Games in 1932. An estimated 93,000 fans turned out to see their favorite actors take the stage, among them Don Ameche; comedians Gracie and George Burns; and movie stars Gary Cooper, Irene Dunn, Clark Gable, Cary Grant, Fred McMurray, George Murphy, Raymond Massey, Adolphe Menjou, Ray Milland, William Powell, Ginger Rogers, and Barbara Stanwyck. Producer David O. Selznick gave a rousing speech. It was the grandest evening that Republicans had enjoyed in Hollywood since the days of Herbert Hoover.

---

[63] Others in Hollywood who signed on to the Hollywood for Dewey campaign included producers Harry Cohn, Frank Freeman, Walt Disney, Charles Koerner, Eddie Mannix, Francis Marion, David O. Selznick, Leon Schlesinger, and Darryl Zanuck; directors Sam Wood, Mark Sandrich, Preston Sturges, Howard Hawks, and King Vidor; screenwriters included James Caine, Morris Ryskind, and Borden Chase. The list of actors was extensive, including Edward Arnold, Wallace Beery, William Bendix, Janet Blair, Donald Crisp, Frank Craven, Ray Collins, Charles Coburn, Leo Carillo, Richard Dix, Brian Donlevy, Francis Dee, Lee Garmes, Lillian Gish, Ruth Hussey, Porter Hall, Gloria Holden, Al Johnson, Otto Kruger, Joel McCrae, Jeannette MacDonald, Constance Moore, Raymond Massey, Mary Pickford, Rosalind Russell, Ann Southern, Gene Tierney, and Claire Trevor. Suggested speakers were Ginger Rogers, Jeanette MacDonald, Gene Tierney, Rupert Hughes, Edward Arnold, Joel McCrea. Barbara Stanwyck, Leo Carillo, and Howard Hawks. Cecile B. DeMille, Hollywood for Dewey, October 18, 1944, Cecil B. DeMille Papers, Box 212; List of Speakers for Governor John Bricker; and Mass Meeting Hollywood for Dewey, Strategy Session, October 5, 1944, Cecil B. DeMille Papers, Box 11.

Although Roosevelt rallied voters and won his fourth term to office, Dewey had come closer to winning than had any other Republican in the last twelve years, polling 46 percent of the popular vote.

In 1944, Republican spirits were higher than ever. With Roosevelt's death in April 1945, Harry S. Truman came into the White House, and the Democratic lock on the White House appeared fragile. Few, even within the Democratic Party, thought Truman up to the job. In 1946, Republicans gained control of both houses of Congress for the first time since 1928. Indeed, Americans seemed fed up with, as one Republican put it, "long haired men and short haired women" bureaucrats in Washington running their lives. In California, Earl Warren captured both major party nominations and easily won reelection.

Americans looked forward to resuming their lives. The Second World War had ended, and America was at peace – except in Hollywood, where another war was about to break out, beginning with a massive and violent labor strike in the movie industry in 1946, followed a year later with HUAC coming to town to call communist witnesses to account for their activities. The Second World War had brought unity to Hollywood. The irony of peacetime Hollywood was that it entered into an unforgiving war that left the city divided and forever haunted.

PHOTO 1 Republican presidential candidate Wendell Willkie in 1940 and producer Cecil
B. DeMille *Academy of Motion Picture Arts and Sciences Library* (date unknown).

PHOTO 2 Movie mogul Walt Disney testifying before the House Un-American Activities Committee (HUAC) in 1947. *Academy of Motion Picture Arts and Sciences Library* (date unknown).

PHOTO 3 Screen writer and novelist Ayn Rand who testified before the House Un-American Activities Committee (HUAC) in 1947. She was a founding member of the anticommunist Motion Picture Alliance (MPA). *Academy of Motion Picture Arts and Sciences Library* (date unknown).

ADOLPH MENJOU - Metro *Goldwyn* - Mayer   AM-3

PHOTO 4 Character actor Adolphe Menjou, a founding member of the Motion Picture Alliance (MPA) and ardent anticommunist in Hollywood. *Academy of Motion Picture Arts and Sciences Library* (date unknown).

PHOTO 5 Actor Robert Montgomery testifies before the House Un-American Activities Committee (HUAC) in 1947. He believed that the communist problem in Hollywood had been taken care of by the time of the hearings. He played an important role in rallying Hollywood to the Republican cause. *Academy of Motion Picture Arts and Sciences Library* (date unknown).

PHOTO 6 Robert Taylor and his wife Barbara Stanwyck before their divorce. Both were active Republicans. Taylor had hopes of running for public office and spoke often at Republican rallies. *Academy of Motion Picture Arts and Sciences Library* (date unknown).

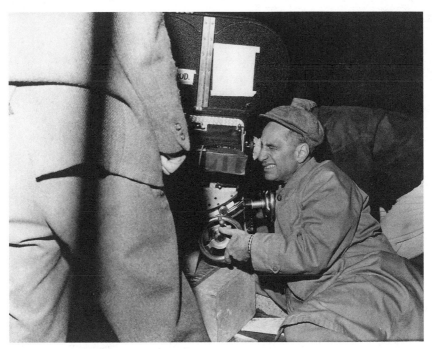

PHOTO 7 Director Elia Kazan, a former member of the Communist Party, who repudiated his past affiliations. He gained fame for directing *On the Waterfront* (1954), which won twelve Oscars. *Academy of Motion Picture Arts and Sciences Library* (date unknown).

CHAPTER 3

The Red Scare Hits Hollywood

At 10:30 A.M., Monday October 20, 1947, in Washington, D.C., the first public hearings of the House Un-American Activities Committee (HUAC) investigating communism in the film industry opened. Television cameras, newspaper reporters, radio announcers, and a standing-room-only crowd filled the Caucus Room of the Old House Office Building. A battery of nine newsreel cameras lined the room. Overhead, a great crystal chandelier lit the room, its ordinary bulbs replaced by high-intensity lamps. On the right side of the room stood a control panel and other broadcasting equipment. Loudspeakers of a public address system amplified every sound. On the rostrum were three microphones. Additional microphones had been placed on the witness table, and several more stood on chief investigator Robert Stripling's table. The public waited in long lines to get into the hearing room. The nation's capital was giddy with excitement as it awaited the parade of Hollywood glitterati standing in the wings for their cue to appear.[1]

J. Parnell Thomas, Republican from New Jersey, chaired the hearings. A short, red-faced man with sparse gray hair, he was known for his political grandstanding. As a member of the Dies Committee in the 1930s, he emerged as a persistent voice trying to link Roosevelt's administration to a larger communist conspiracy. Republican leaders, including presidential hopeful Thomas Dewey and the Speaker of the House Joe Martin, had tried to persuade Thomas to call off the hearings, but Hollywood was too much of a publicity lure for Thomas to pass up. When he entered the hearing room, cameramen asked him to rise and make his entrance again. They placed a pillow on the seat of his chair to make sure he sat high enough to be captured on film.

---

[1] This description is drawn from "The Hollywood Hearings," chapter I, author unknown, found in the House of Un-American Activities Committee, Executive Sessions (1947), Records of the U.S. House of Representatives, National Archives, RG 253, hereafter cited as HUAC papers (1947).

The first week of the hearings brought "friendly" witnesses, those sympathetic to the hearings, film stars including Ronald Reagan, Gary Cooper, Robert Taylor, and Adolphe Menjou; screenwriter and novelist Ayn Rand; and leading Hollywood producers, directors, and studio executives. As the week drew to a close, the media was in a complete frenzy as the ten former and active communists were called to testify. Of the ten "unfriendly" witnesses – John Howard Lawson, Dalton Trumbo, Albert Maltz, Alvah Bessie, Samuel Ornitz, Herbert Biberman, Ring Lardner Jr., Adrian Scott, Edward Dmytryk, and Lester Cole – eight were screenwriters. Dmytryk was a director and Scott a producer. These witnesses became known as the Hollywood Ten.

Until the ten unfriendly witnesses took the stand, the national media had been critical of HUAC's investigation into alleged communist influence in the film industry. Lead editorials in the *New York Times* and the *Washington Post* blasted the proceedings. News articles about the hearings focused on the appearance of preening celebrity witnesses, foolish statements made by the "friendlies" (e.g., when Walt Disney mistakenly called the League of Women Voters a communist front), and the inability of HUAC to prove that explicit communist propaganda had been inserted into Hollywood films. In the media's eye, the first round had gone against the Committee and its friendly witnesses.

The ten "unfriendly" witnesses who followed presented the Hollywood Left at its worst – arrogant, intolerant, and out of touch with mainstream America. The Hollywood Ten refused to answer basic questions as to their political affiliations or union membership, pleading free speech under their First Amendment rights. This was the first time this right was asserted in a congressional hearing; the U.S. Supreme Court later rejected it. (It was not until late 1951 that the idea of pleading Fifth Amendment rights in a congressional hearing was first asserted in a hearing by a mobster whose criminal lawyer knew about the use of the amendment in criminal cases.) By refusing to answer questions in 1947, the witnesses appeared to be hiding something. Of course, they were trying to hide a great deal, under orders from their party attorneys to stonewall the hearings. Communist leaders believed that the public would sympathize with the witnesses if the committee could be seen as hounding them. The public instead found the witnesses' behavior repulsive. Even more alienating to the general public listening on their radios and watching on their new television sets in 1947 were the belligerent denunciations of the hearings as undemocratic and as a first step toward fascism in America. Comparisons between Nazi Germany and the United States, after fighting a war against Hitler, simply did not wash with the American public.[2] For communists, party line dictated that postwar America was headed toward fascism; the HUAC hearings confirmed this Marxist perspective.

---

[2] Second World War movies are discussed by Clayton R. Koppes and Gregory Black, *Hollywood Goes to War: How Politics, Profits, and Propaganda Shaped World War II Movies* (Berkeley, CA, 1998).

This Communist Party defense strategy backfired both legally and politically. For one thing, HUAC investigators had accumulated huge amounts of material on each of the unfriendly witnesses showing Communist Party involvement and often including exact party card identification numbers. After witnessing the performance of the unfriendlies at the hearings, many liberal supporters, including Humphrey Bogart and his wife Lauren Bacall, retreated to Hollywood and quickly distanced themselves from the entire business. Director Billy Wilder captured liberal sentiment in his reputed quip: "Of the Unfriendly 10, only two had any talent; the other eight were just unfriendly."[3]

Suddenly, in the second week of hearings, Thomas announced that the committee was in recess, and he promised to resume the hearings at a later date. Exactly why the hearings were canceled is not clear, but they never resumed under Thomas.

THE END OF THE POPULAR FRONT

Any understanding of the 1947 hearings must begin with two events: changes in the Communist Party line in 1945 that declared the end of the popular front, and a second strike by studio unions in 1946. These two events set the backdrop for the HUAC hearings in 1947. Communists were involved in the strike, both as union activists and strike supporters, although the head of the striking Conference of Studio Unions, Herbert Sorrell, was never confirmed as a communist. He was close to the party, and a good deal of circumstantial evidence was produced that suggested he might have been a party member, but, whatever the true case, he showed a strong independent streak that belied a disciplined party member.

In 1945, the Communist Party in the United States once again shifted political lines. Following the dictates of the Soviet Union, then under the leadership of Stalin, communist organizations throughout the world repudiated the popular front alliance with liberals and social-democrats that had existed throughout the Second World War, taking instead the view that the United States and Britain were capitalist and imperialist enemies of the Soviet Union.[4] This change in party

---

[3] Wilder's quip is often quoted. See, for example, Thom Anderson, "Red Hollywood," in Frank Krutnik, Steve Neale, Brian Neve, *Un-American Hollywood: Politics and Film in the Blacklist Era* (New Brunswick, NJ, 2007); Victor S. Navasky, *Naming Names* (New York, rev. edition, 2003), p. 80; and Bernard F. Dick, *Radical Innocence: A Critical Study of the Hollywood Ten* (Lexington, KY, 1989), p. 10. Both Navasky and Dick take issue with the accuracy of Wilder's observation.

[4] The literature on Stalin's foreign policy at the outset of the Cold War has grown since the collapse of the Soviet Union. A good point of entry into this literature is Vladislav Zubok and Constantine Pleshakov, *Inside the Kremlin's Cold War: From Stalin to Khrushchev* (Cambridge, MA, 1997); Vladislav Zubok, *A Failed Empire: From Stalin to Khrushchev* (Chapel Hill, NC, 2008); and Jonathan Haslam, *Russia's Cold War: From the October Revolution to the Fall of the Wall* (New Haven, CT, 2011).

line mandated the purging of party leaders throughout Europe and the United States who had promoted the popular front. In the U.S. Communist Party, Earl Browder, who had symbolized the popular front during the Second World War, quickly came under attack for having betrayed the principles of Marxist-Leninism and was ultimately expelled from the party.

A full-scale attack on "Browderism" began within the party in spring 1945. The scale of this attack was evident at the Special Party National Convention of the Communist Party called in July 1945. Key speeches and reports from this convention were later published in a book, *Marxism vs. Revisionism*, edited by William Z. Foster, who replaced Browder as General Secretary of the Party.[5] This book became the study guide for local and unit meetings to eradicate Browder revisionism in the party. William Z. Foster, Browder's longtime rival within the party, led the attack, and others joined the flailing. Writing the Foreword to *Marxism vs. Revisionism*, party hack Max Weiss declared that the fatal mistake of Browderism was that it rejected "Lenin's analysis of imperialism as the final stage in the development of capitalism . . . and advocacy of the theory of ending the epoch of imperialism." Weiss declared that the postwar reconstruction of Europe was "insoluble under capitalism" and that American capitalism, facing the crisis of "monopoly capitalism," was "strong, greedy, and aggressive." Foster seconded this attack.[6] This change in party line, predicated on the threat of fascism in America, had serious consequences within the Communist Party and, more important, for the legal strategy in response to the HUAC hearings in 1947. When screenwriter-director Abraham Polonsky first heard of the change in party line away from the popular front, he stood up at a party meeting to denounce it as absurd. He was immediately threatened with expulsion. Like most others in the party, he fell into line.[7]

A few weeks following Browder's expulsion from the party, screenwriter Albert Maltz felt the full, brutal weight of the new party line. In early 1946, Maltz published an invited response to the role of the writer within the party for the communist *New Masses*. In his essay, "What Shall We Ask of Writers?" Maltz argued that party intellectuals and writers should not be slaves to "proletarian literature." Instead, they should appreciate literature for its own sake and learn from the great writers such as Fyodor Dostoyevsky, Joseph Conrad, Honoré de Balzac, John Dos Passos, and James T. Farrell. (Recommending John Dos Passos, who had left the party, and James T. Farrell, who had become a

[5] William Z. Foster, Jacques Duclos, Eugene Dennis, and John Williamson, *Marxism vs. Revisionism* (New York, 1946).

[6] Max Weiss, "Forward," p. 4, and William Z. Forster, "On the Question of Revisionism," Report to the National Committee of the Communist Party, p. 37; and Foster, "The Struggle against Revisionism," Report to the Special Convention of the Communist Political Association, July 26–28, 1945, p. 78, in William Z. Foster, Jacques Duclos, Eugene Dennis, and John Williamson, *Marxism vs. Revisionism*.

[7] Saverio Giovacchini, *Hollywood Modernism: Film and Politics in the Age of the New Deal* (Philadelphia, 2001), p. 177.

Trotskyist, really poured salt into the wounds.) To see art only in terms of being a "weapon in class struggle" was, for Maltz, the "vulgarization of the theory of art and placed the writer in a 'strait jacket.'"[8]

Retaliation against Maltz's interpretation of literature, which a few months before would have found favorable reception, came quickly. The first salvo against Maltz came when party cultural commissar Mike Gold published four pieces in the party newspaper, the *Daily Worker*, denouncing Maltz. He wrote that Maltz had been poisoned by living in the "luxury and phony atmosphere of Hollywood." Gold declared that now Browderism was over and that the party was "painfully trying to get back on the Marxist rails of history." Maltz's advice to young writers to tolerate Trotskyites and bourgeois novelists threatened to "derail" the party. Maltz, he concluded was teaching a "terrible confusion."[9] Others joined in vicious denunciations of Maltz. Party novelist Howard Fast castigated Maltz for his lack of proper thinking, while Foster accused Maltz of being a Trotskyite or a Browderite. Threatened with expulsion, Maltz underwent a humiliating self-criticism in which he was forced to repent his wrongheadedness. He declared, "What should be clear is that my article made fundamental errors.... A serious and sharp discussion was required." He added, just so there was no mistaking this point, that "I believe also that my critics were entirely correct in insisting that certain fundamental ideas in my article would, if pursued to their conclusion, result in the dissolution of the left-wing cultural movement."[10]

He was welcomed back into the fold at a mass meeting presented as "Art – The Weapon for the People," held at the Los Angeles Embassy Auditorium. The master of ceremonies was John Lawson, czar of the Hollywood Communist Party, who made the fleet shift away from Browderism to the new hardline position. Speeches were given by Dalton Trumbo and others, including Maltz, all of whom declared themselves in favor of "proletarian" art and against "bourgeois" art. Later, Maltz explained why he relinquished even the appearance of intellectual independence: "I didn't want to be separated from the Movement and all that I held dear."[11]

---

[8] Albert Maltz, "What Shall We Ask of Writers?," *New Masses*, February 12, 1946, reprinted in Kenneth Lloyd Billingsley, *Hollywood Party: How Communism Seduced the American Film Industry in the 1930s and 1940s* (Rocklin, CA, 1998), pp. 290–298.

[9] Mike Gold, "Change the World," *Daily Worker*, February 12, 1946, reprinted in Billingsley, *Hollywood Party*, pp. 299–307. Also, see Larry Ceplair and Steven Englund, *Inquisition in Hollywood: Politics in the Film Industry, 1930–60* (New York, 1980), pp. 233–235; and Patrick McGilligan and Paul Buhle, *Tender Comrades: A Backstory of the Hollywood Blacklist* (New York, 1997).

[10] Albert Maltz, "Moving Forward," *Daily Worker*, April 7, 1946; Billingsley, *Hollywood Party*, pp. 301–307. Quoted in Arthur M. Schlesinger, "The U.S. Communist Party," *Life Magazine*, July 23, 1946.

[11] Albert Maltz, "Interview," in Barbara Zheutlin and David Talbot, *Creative Differences: Profiles of Hollywood Dissidents* (Boston, 1995), p. 35.

This perception that fascism was near dictated the legal strategy that transformed the HUAC hearings into a political event. In 1947, the right to plead the Fifth Amendment to protect oneself from self-incrimination before a congressional hearing had not yet occurred to anyone involved. Instead, the legal team representing the unfriendly witnesses decided to employ the First Amendment right to free speech. Given the political position of the Communist Party in 1947, as it prepared to enter into this projected final struggle that would see the death throes of capitalism, a political defense made perfect sense. By claiming an abridgement of free speech, the witnesses could show the world how superficial the right of free speech was under capitalism. By shouting down HUAC members, they presented themselves as martyrs resisting the forces of repression. But only later, after much pain had been inflicted, did the unfriendly witnesses actually become martyrs.

HOLLYWOOD ON STRIKE

The HUAC hearings came after labor strikes ripped apart the film industry in March 1945 and September 1946. The violence that occurred in these strikes intensified anticommunist sentiments: without these strikes, the subsequent Hollywood Red Scare might not have occurred. Initiated by the left-dominated Conference of Studio Unions (CSU), the strikes divided Hollywood into warring camps. The first strike began when the CSU called out its 10,000 members in protest over a jurisdictional dispute with the International Alliance of Theatrical Stage Employees (IATSE). More than 10,000 workers walked out, embroiling forty-two craft unions in the strike. The specifics of the dispute involved typical rival union infighting – in this case, who represented seventy-seven set decorators – but the strike divided Hollywood, pitting the major studios – Columbia, Fox, MGM, Paramount, RKO, Universal, and Warner Brothers – against the CSU. The strike lasted six months.[12]

The strike divided Hollywood as rival IATSE workers crossed picket lines, as did members of the Screen Actors Guild (SAG). Actors Humphrey Bogart, Susan Hayward, Rosalind Russell, Robert Montgomery, and Leo G. Carroll joined rival union members in also crossing the lines. A few of the stars, sympathetic to the strike, including Bette Davis and Joseph Cotton, refused to become "scabs" and refused to cross the picket lines. Passions rose in the summer of 1945. Violence followed. Ronald Reagan, one of those who did cross the picket line, recalled homes and cars being bombed. After death threats, he took out a gun permit and began carrying a gun. Jane Wyman, Reagan's first wife, remembered that "there was more than one night that she had awakened to see him [Ronnie] holding the gun, sitting in bed having thought he had heard noises in the

[12] Gerald Horne, *Class Struggle in Hollywood, 1930–1950* (Austin, TX, 2001), p. 11.

house."[13] Roy Brewer, head of the rival IATSE, claimed that five homes of those who crossed the picket lines were bombed over the course of that summer.

Violence reached a high point on October 5, 1945, when 300 strikers tried to block the main gate at Warner Brothers. Cars trying to enter studio gates were stopped; some were turned over and drivers beaten. As security guards and Burbank police tried to contain the strikers, calls were sent out to other picket lines for reinforcements, and more than a thousand strikers and their supporters converged on the studio. The Los Angeles police arrived to assist the Burbank police and the studio security guards. A full-scale riot broke out. Later, both sides claimed that their rivals used chains, hammers, and baseball bats to attack them. Warner security guards fired tear gas into the crowd, while studio employees sprayed the strikers with fire hoses. At the end of the day, more than forty injuries were reported, and violence continued over the following week. During the strike, more than 1,000 people were arrested in connection with labor violence.

An uneasy peace settled over Hollywood with the apparent settlement of the strike a month later.

The dispute between studio management and the CSU was by no means over. In early September 1946, the CSU went on strike again when the studios announced that they were giving the IATSE guarantees that their people could fill CSU jobs, and CSU set decorators and carpenters were reassigned to jobs they believed violated their contracts. Violence again characterized the thirteen-month strike that followed. The degree of violence is captured in arrest reports: October 11, 1946, 26 arrested at Technicolor Studios for violation of a court injunction; October 14, 1946, 208 arrested at Columbia Studios; October 26, 1946, 125 arrested; November 15, 1946, 696 arrested at Columbia Studios; and November 16, 1946 an additional 124 arrested. On November 22, 1946, felony indictments were returned against 14 union leaders, including Herbert Sorrell. The bitter end to the strike came in early 1947, in an utter defeat for the CSU. The CSU never recovered.

Opponents of the CSU charged Communist Party involvement in the strikes, but the degree of party involvement remains unclear. State senator Jack Tenney, who chaired the notoriously anticommunist California Senate Committee on Un-American Activities, told Governor Earl Warren that the strike was a spearhead of the "long range Communist strategy to control [the] motion picture" industry. Reagan, who had been elected president of the SAG, concluded as well that the strike was part of the "Soviet effort to gain control over Hollywood and the content of its films."[14] Former SAG presidents George Murphy and Robert Montgomery concurred with these charges. Reagan had reached his conclusion after trying to mediate the second 1946 strike as elected head of a special SAG committee. He and his committee held meetings over the next seven months with

---

[13] Quoted in David E. Prindle, *The Politics of Glamour: Ideology and Democracy in the Screen Actors Guild* (Madison, WI, 1988), p. 49.

[14] Both the Tenney and Reagan quotes are found in Horne, *Class Struggle in Hollywood*, p. 4.

representatives from Sorrell's CSU painters' union. In September, a SAG delegation headed by Reagan and consisting of George Murphy, Edward Arnold, Dick Powell, Walter Pidgeon, Jane Wyman, Robert Taylor, and Gene Kelly traveled to the American Federation of Labor (AFL) convention in Chicago to try to bring peace to Hollywood. Reagan concluded that the CSU did not want to settle the strike unless Roy Brewer's IATSE was completely destroyed.

Approximately 350 members signed a petition asking for a meeting to discuss SAG's policy of opposing the strike, which resulted in a mass meeting at the Hollywood Legion Stadium in early October, which more than 1,800 actors attended. At the rally, Reagan was at his best. Speaking without notes, he presented a clear and persuasive account of SAG's failure to mediate the strike.[15] Although Reagan did not talk about what he saw as communist influence in the strike or factionalism within SAG, it was apparent that his views had moved toward Brewer's. At the beginning of the strike, Reagan had rejected Brewer's perspective that communists were behind the strike; however, confronted by his failure to mediate the strike and by the factional opposition within SAG, Reagan gradually came to share Brewer's anticommunist position.[16]

Fed up with communist influence in his union and Hollywood, Reagan, joined by his wife Jane Wyman, arranged a meeting in early 1947 with Federal Bureau of Investigation (FBI) agents in Los Angeles to discuss their suspicions of people who they believed were carrying out communist work in the guild. Reagan and his wife claimed that they believed two coordinated communist "cliques" were operating within SAG, one headed by actress Anne Revere, known for her supporting roles, and another by actress Karen Morley, whose career was in decline by the late 1940s. Both Revere and Morley pleaded the Fifth in later HUAC hearings. Of the individuals mentioned by the Reagans, the Los Angeles FBI office confirmed the following as "being or having been members of the Communist Political Association or the Communist Party": Anne Revere, Howard DaSilva, Howland Chamberlain, Karen Morley, Dorothy Tree, and Larry Parks.

The full extent of communist involvement in the CSU is difficult to determine precisely. Sorrell, head of the CSU, was accused of being a member of the party by his opponents, but evidence for this allegation remains largely circumstantial. In its ninety-three-page report, "Communist Infiltration: Motion Picture Industry" (1947), the FBI presented a party card under the name of "Herb Stewart" whose signature was "positively identified" as being that of Herbert K. Sorrell, even though the report stated that the Los Angeles Bureau had "no documentary evidence of membership on the part of Sorrell" in the party or the Communist

---

[15] "Actors Urged to Cross Lines: Scores of Stars at Legion Stadium Rally Applaud SAG Board's Recommendation," *The Hollywood Reporter*, October 3, 1946; Alan L. Gansberg, *Little Caesar: A Biography of Edward G. Robinson* (Lanham, MD, 2004), p. 127.

[16] Prindle, *The Politics of Glamour*, p. 47; and Horne, *Class Struggle in Hollywood*, p. 210. For insight into the Brewer-Reagan relationship, see John Meroney, "Left in the Past," *Los Angeles Times Magazine*, February 2, 2012, http://www.latimesmagazine.com/2012/02/left-in-the past. html.

Party of America (CPA) since 1938.[17] (The Communist Party encouraged members to use party names rather than real names in all party work.) Charges of communist affiliation were brought against Sorrell in the Los Angeles Central Labor Committee, but the subsequent trial came to an indecisive end.[18]

Communist involvement was, however, evident in a number of the CSU-affiliated unions. The Los Angeles FBI reported to Washington in 1947 that the Communist Party in Hollywood was especially well placed among "the union and cultural organizations."[19] The FBI reported that party members held leadership positions in the Film Technicians Union, the Set Decorators Union, the Painters Union, the Carpenters Union, the Screen Story Analysts Guild, and the Studio Carpenters Union.[20] If a communist presence in some of the CSU-affiliated unions was evident, then Sorrell acted independently from the party because the 1945 strike came at a time when the Communist Party was still pursuing a wartime policy of union–management collaboration that involved a no-strike pledge. As a consequence, when the CSU went out on strike in 1945, the Communist Party did not take an active part in the strike, and, indeed, at first denounced it. The West Coast party daily *People's World* maintained that there was no excuse for any kind of strike in the midst of the war. Only in July, when the repudiation of Browder's alleged revisionism occurred and with the war in Europe over, did the party issue a call to support the strike.[21]

Defenders of the CSU, then and later, saw the strikes of 1945 and 1946 as class warfare that pitted a militant trade union against studio management that had aligned itself with a red-baiting rival union, the IATSE.[22] However one stands on the nature and degree of influence of the Communist Party within the CSU, the Hollywood strikes set the context for HUAC coming to town in 1947.

THE DESTRUCTIVE FOIBLES OF THE HOUSE UN-AMERICAN ACTIVITIES COMMITTEE

Although the HUAC hearings in 1947 have been correctly seen by later historians as destructive to the careers of those accused of being communists – the

---

[17] Federal Bureau of Investigation, "Communist Infiltration into the Motion Picture Industry" (1947), File Number: 100–138754, Serial 251x1, Pt. 7, p. 73, released through Freedom of Information and Privacy Acts. The FBI's move into Hollywood is recounted in John Sbardellati, *J. Edgar Hoover Goes to the Movies: The FBI and the Origins of Hollywood's Cold War* (Ithaca, NY, 2012).

[18] John Cogley, *Report on Blacklisting: Movies* (New York, 1956, reprint, 1972), p. 67.

[19] Federal Bureau of Investigation, "Communist Infiltration into the Motion Picture Industry," (1947), File Number: 100–138754, Serial 251x1, Pt. 7, pp. 18.

[20] Ibid., pp. 61, 62, 65–73.

[21] The change in party positions is recounted in Federal Bureau of Investigation, "Communist Infiltration into the Motion Picture Industry" (1947), File Number: 100–138754, Serial 251x1, Pt. 7, pp. 67–68.

[22] This perspective is articulated by Horne, *Class Struggle in Hollywood*.

Hollywood Ten – the foibles of the congressional interrogators and defendants were readily apparent at the time.[23] If the hearings had not had such painful consequences for the "unfriendly" witnesses – as well as for many of the "friendly" witnesses (usually left out of the histories of this period) it would have been a comedy.

The Republican Party leadership tried to prevent the hearings for fear of how they would play politically. Shortly before the hearings opened, Governor Thomas Dewey of New York, the 1944 presidential nominee, phoned J. Parnell Thomas, chairman of HUAC, to try to persuade him to call off the Hollywood hearings. Dewey argued that the Hollywood film industry was already experiencing a financial "crisis" because England had imposed a high excise tax on imported films. Dewey, who was looking toward the 1948 presidential election, also feared a possible backlash by the public who would see the hearings as a Republican witch hunt. To bring home the message, Dewey told Thomas that *Los Angeles Times* publisher Harry Chandler had requested that the hearings be called off. Shortly after Dewey phoned, Thomas received a phone call from the new Speaker of the House, Joseph Martin (R-Massachusetts), following up on Dewey's request.

Thomas refused both men. Thomas told Dewey and Martin that "we were not amateurs at this, and while there was always a danger of unfavorable things happening, I did not look for much trouble." He added that his investigation had revealed that "there was a large amount of infiltration of communism in the motion picture industry."[24] Thomas's past performance on the HUAC committee in the 1930s imparted little confidence that the hearings were not going to turn into a fiasco. While serving on the Dies Committee, Thomas had consistently played the role of a grandstander given to making wild charges. He had tenuously tried to link the New Deal to communism, which presented an easy target of ridicule for the Roosevelt administration. And there were other issues that created concern about the hearings. The expressed goal of the hearings to investigate communist propaganda into Hollywood films was amorphous. What exactly constituted propaganda? Given that the Soviet Union was America's ally in the Second World War, how could prowar propaganda be distinguished from pro-Soviet propaganda? This was a thorny issue that would be raised in the hearings and later by historians.[25] To prove communist influence in film meant proving that communists were involved in writing the scripts, which meant bringing forth circumstantial evidence and subjective

---

[23] The effects of the Red Scare are conveyed in Patrick McGilligan and Paul Buhle, *Tender Comrades* (New York, 1997).

[24] J. Parnell Thomas, Memo, September 6, 1947, House Un-American Activities Committee, RG 23253, Box 12.

[25] For a case that communist propaganda had been inserted into films, see Ronald Radosh, *Red Star Over Hollywood: The Film Colony's Long Romance with the Left* (San Francisco, 2007); Billingsley, *Hollywood Party*; and Bob Herzberg, *The Left Side of the Screen: Communist and Left Wing Ideology in Hollywood, 1929–2009* (Jefferson, NC, 2011).

interpretation. Scripts were collective projects, often written by many screen-writers, edited by directors, and with substantial parts left on the cutting room floor. Communist screenwriters did try to inject favorable portrayals of the Soviet Union, caricature businessmen and politicians, and depict workers as heroic. They were encouraged to do so by cultural czars such as John Lawson, but proving this in a congressional hearing was not an easy task.[26]

From the outset, the HUAC hearings faced a public relations problem tied directly to the nature of the hearings themselves. By calling hostile witnesses, HUAC entered new territory. The ground rules for calling unfriendly witnesses before the committee – and their refusal to answer questions – raised unprece-dented issues of whether charges of "contempt of Congress" could be brought against them. The refusal to allow witnesses to present their statements publicly inevitably led to shouting matches between the witnesses and Thomas that turned the hearings into a circus. This might have played to the unfriendly witnesses' benefit if they had pursued a different defense strategy.

Unfortunately, the unfriendlies undertook a legal strategy based on the con-stitutional principles of free speech embodied in the First Amendment and a larger political strategy to reveal to the American people the threat of fascism in America. In this way, the legal claim of free speech was integral to the political goal of fighting fascism. Transforming legal trials into political trials was a well-used tactic of the left. It had been seen in the Sacco and Vanzetti trial in the 1920s and in the Scottsboro Boys case in the 1930s. The object of a political defense was to win in the court of public opinion, and not simply in the legal courts. The consequence of turning the hearings into a political case became quickly evident, as unfriendly witness followed by unfriendly witness denounced the hearings as fascist. These denunciations were more than rhetorical: unfriendly witnesses were being literal in their accusations of fascism. The new party line dictated by the Soviet Union was that the ruling classes in the United States and Great Britain would turn to imperialism and fascism to protect their privileges in the last stages of capitalism. The HUAC hearings were used in an attempt to confirm this prediction.

Although the political defense strategy failed, the specific legal defense based on First Amendment rights made sense at the time. A defense based on the Fifth Amendment – the right not to incriminate oneself – before a congressional committee was as yet untried. In any case, membership in the Communist Party in 1947 was not illegal. Given the backlash caused by the unfriendlies' unruly behavior in the hearings, the strategy of answering questions, even of

---

[26] If "propaganda" had been inserted into some films, it was minimal. As screenwriter and hardline anticommunist John Lee Mahin observed, the threat was not in the movies. If communist propaganda did get into a film, it was "so innocuous it did not mean anything." The threat, he said, was to the screenwriters as an organization: "We had to watch every step, and we did not want to. There was no threat to pictures." "John Lee Mahin," in Pat McGilligan, *Backstory: Interviews with Screenwriters of Hollywood's Golden Age* (Berkeley, CA, 1986), p. 280.

present and past progressive political affiliation, while denying any effort to promote explicit Soviet or communist propaganda would have arguably placed the Thomas hearings on the defensive and made it look like a witch hunt. Although some historians concluded that it was just this, in fact, the defense strategy did not win in the court of public opinion and, at the end of the day, unfriendlies went to jail for contempt of Congress.[27]

At the time, the Hollywood Right found laughable irony in the "free speech" defense, given the party's record on this issue. Two notable incidents belied the communists' claims to be defenders of free speech. The first came during the Second World War, at the height of the popular front in a debate between liberal Alexander Meiklejohn and Earl Browder over free speech for fascists. Writing in the communist periodical *New Masses* in 1943, Meiklejohn accused communists of denying free speech to anyone the party declared as "fascist." Browder did not deny the charge. He replied, "Of course, we demand the suppression of American fascists! We fight for the complete, merciless, and systematic destruction of fascism in all its aspects everywhere." Browder argued that racism and anti-Semitism were reflections of fascism. Novelist Howard Fast echoed Browder's position, writing that, of course, free speech should be denied to fascists: "Take Voltaire's old epigram, 'I do not agree with what he says, but I will defend to the death his right to say it.' How often has that been quoted, and what arrant nonsense it is!"[28]

The second incident occurred in 1946, involving another issue of free speech. Gordon Kahn, managing editor, and Dalton Trumbo, editor of the Screen Writers Guild's (SWG) official publication, *The Screenwriter*, rejected an article by anticommunist screenwriter Richard Macaulay. In his piece, Macaulay took on an essay written by Alvah Bessie. In rejecting the piece, Trumbo wrote to Macaulay, "It is difficult to support your belief in 'the inalienable right' of man's mind to be exposed to any thought whatsoever, however intolerable that thought might be to anyone else. Frequently such right encroaches upon the right of others to their lives. It was this 'inalienable right' in Fascist countries which directly resulted in the slaughter of five million Jews."[29]

Prior to the Washington hearings that began in October 1947, HUAC investigators collected extensive files on each of the witnesses, friendly and unfriendly. For unfriendly witnesses, this meant extensive FBI reports of party and popular front involvement, which entailed reports of party membership from FBI informants. Allegations of party membership were not based only on participation in

---

[27] For hostile interpretations of the HUAC hearings, see Reynold Humphries, *Hollywood's Blacklists: A Political and Cultural History* (Edinburgh, 2008); and John Joseph Gladchuk, *Hollywood and Anticommunism: HUAC and the Evolution of the Red Menace, 1935–1950* (New York, 2007).

[28] Robert Mayhew, *Ayn Rand and Song of Russia: Communism and Anti-Communism in 1940s Hollywood* (Lanham, MD, 2005), p. 87.

[29] Quoted in Cogley, *Report on Blacklisting*, p. 67. The Screen Writers Guild Archives in Los Angeles unfortunately is missing issues of *The Screenwriter* in these years.

popular front activities, a tactic frequently employed by popular anticommunist writers or groups such as the American Legion in their campaigns to root out communists. Congressional investigators also took particular care in doing background checks and interviews with potential friendly witnesses. Investigators were surprised to learn that not all of the friendly witnesses were friendly or desirable. Congressional investigator H. A. Smith, a former FBI agent, offered detailed reports on these friendly witnesses to Robert E. Stripling, a tall Southerner who had climbed from clerk of the Dies Committee to HUAC's chief investigator. Smith's detailed reports on each of the witnesses reveal differences among the so-called friendlies, as well as a few surprises that belie the caricature of the friendly witnesses as hysterical red-baiters.

HUAC investigators understood the land mines that awaited them in the hearings. Smith warned that studio executives were defensive about any intimation that they had made procommunist films and resented the hearings. Samuel Goldwyn told Smith that he felt it unnecessary for him to testify in Washington and that he would not "finger" anyone he thought was a communist. More important, he said, given the nature of the production process, it was impossible for communist propaganda to be placed in a film. He pointed out that the idea for his Oscar-winning film "The Best Years of Our Lives," a disturbing story of veterans returning home after the war and finding it hard to get jobs, came from the War Department. Goldwyn related how an under secretary of war had called him during the making of the film to complain that returning veterans were not getting their jobs back. On hearing this, Goldwyn asked Robert Sherwood, a noncommunist liberal, to write a scene about this problem. Within a day, Sherwood had written the scene as it appeared in the movie.[30]

Eric Johnston, newly appointed head of the film industry trade association, the Motion Picture Association of America (MPAA), bluntly told Smith that HUAC had left a "damaging impression" and that Hollywood was "running-over with communists and communism." Although Johnston was a Republican, he was a moderate businessman who had accommodated himself to the New Deal and organized labor. Johnston had risen to the presidency of the Chamber of Commerce after joining a revolt by younger, moderate business executives who pushed the old conservative wing of the Chamber out of office. During the Second World War, Johnston worked in the Roosevelt administration in a number of positions.[31] Johnston reflected moderate political opinions and the studios' position that the HUAC investigation into communist propaganda in

---

[30] H. A. Smith, Memo, Interview with Samuel Goldwyn, August 6, 1947, Records of the House Un-American Activities Committee, Executive Sessions, RG 253, Box 4.

[31] Fabian Bachrach, "Eric Johnston Dies," *New York Times*, August 23, 1963. An excellent discussion of the film industry's role in Hollywood politics is found in Kathryn Cramer Brownell, "The Entertainment Estate: Hollywood in American Politics, 1932–1972," Ph.D. dissertation, Boston University, 2011.

movies was a misconceived enterprise. He wrote Speaker of the House Martin, "In America, we hold that the individual is a higher power than the state. . . . The sovereign rights and dignity of the individual supersede all else. There is no place in our society for any procedure or practice which cuts away part of those rights. There can be no such thing in America as a half-citizen."[32] Privately, he told unfriendly witnesses before the hearings that they need not fear the industry imposing a blacklist. However, after the public backlash caused by the antics of the unfriendly witnesses in the Washington hearings, Johnston joined the producers' call for a blacklist. Protecting the industry from bad publicity, it turned out, superseded individual rights.

Ronald Reagan, as head of SAG, also took an industry position in the hearings by claiming that the "communist issue" had been addressed. Behind the scenes, Reagan informed Smith that he was "reticent" to testify. He told Smith that he vehemently disagreed with many of the individuals in the Motion Picture Alliance (MPA). Reagan added that he considered Jim McGuinness a "professional Redbaiter" and did not want to be associated with him. After some discussion, Smith persuaded Reagan to testify and convinced him, as the actor put it, that he was "probably wrong" about McGuinness and had perhaps "drawn erroneous conclusions from promiscuous statements made by other individuals."[33]

Although Reagan was initially hesitant to testify, Smith discovered that actor Gary Cooper was eager to appear before the hearings. Cooper told Smith that he was "happy" to appear before HUAC, although he noted that it might cost him "thousands" of dollars, and he was not going to identify any specific people as communists. Smith believed that Cooper would make an ideal witness. He "presents a very excellent appearance and will testify in a smooth, even, soft-spoken, unexcitable manner."[34] (In the hearings, Cooper presented exactly this image, which people mistakenly perceived as reluctance to testify.) Smith was equally confident that Morrie Ryskind was an ideal witness. Smith described him as "very level headed and a brilliant strategist," who could help us "arrange the order of the witnesses."[35] MPA founder Leo McCarey also agreed to testify, but told Smith that he was one of several people who "continually ask the question, 'What are we going to accomplish?'" Smith thought McCarey would make an okay witness, but he was concerned about some of the others.

Smith was impressed, too, with actor Adolphe Menjou, for all his limitations. Smith noted that numerous people had criticized Menjou, stating that "he is such

[32] Eric Johnston to Parnell Thomas, September 29, 1947; and Press Statement, October 26, 1947, Records of the House Un-American Activities Committee, Executive Sessions, RG 253, Box 4.

[33] H. A. Smith, Interview with Ronald Reagan, September 2, 1947, Records of the House Un-American Activities Committee, Executive Sessions, RG 253, Box 6.

[34] H. A. Smith, Memo, Interview with Gary Cooper, September 2, 1947, Records of the House Un-American Activities Committee, Executive Sessions, RG 253, Box 2.

[35] H. A. Smith, Memo, Interview with Morrie Ryskind, Records of the House Un-American Activities Committee, Executive Sessions, RG 253, Box 6.

a rightist that whenever it rains he blames it on the communists, and in turn, if he does not like the sunshine he states the communists are causing too much sunshine." Smith responded to such characterizations as unfair. He was impressed with Menjou's "brilliant memory," but thought the actor had a tendency toward prolixity. Smith recommended going over his testimony with him, and "it should be confined to certain distinct information that he can give."[36] Smith was equally impressed with Ayn Rand, the noted author of *The Fountainhead*. She was, in his opinion, a "very brilliant" woman who understands the Communist Party line. Her major drawback as a witness was her thick accent, and "her appearance is slightly detrimental in that she has a semimannish haircut." Her strength was that she was able to review movies that contained communist propaganda.[37]

More disconcerting for Smith was his interview with Lela Rogers, screenwriter and mother of Hollywood star Ginger Rogers. In closed-session hearings prior to the public hearings in Washington, Lela Rogers had not come off well. Her testimony was rambling, revealing a strong-willed, highly opinionated woman. A single mother, Lela was one of the first women to join the U.S. Marine Corps in the First World War. She was a devout Christian Scientist, whose world revolved around her daughter Ginger and her career. She tended to come across as a crackpot, which she readily admitted.[38] Smith understood that Rogers presented a problem for the committee. He noted that "if we can confine her testimony to brief, concise opinions, she will be of value. However, if she goes off... it will do us more harm, than good."[39] Smith was particularly concerned that Rogers might bring up one of her hobby horses – that communist propaganda was evident in the 1943 film *Tender Comrade*, in which her daughter, playing a working woman sharing an apartment with two other women, declares in the movie that they should "share and share alike – that's democracy." It was a passing line designed to show that the women had learned to live together, but Lela believed it was an overt political message. Given the context in which the line appeared, it was at most a subliminal message that must have sailed over the heads of most in the audience, but Lela Rogers simply could not be persuaded to drop the example. After all, the script had been written by communist Dalton Trumbo and directed by Edward Dmytryk, two unfriendly witnesses. When she testified in the public hearings, she brought up the example once again.[40]

[36] H. A. Smith, Memo, Interview with Adolphe Menjou, September 2, 1947, Records of the House Un-American Activities Committee, Executive Sessions, RG 253, Box 5

[37] H. A. Smith, Memo, Interview with Ayn Rand, September 2, 1947, Records of the House Un-American Activities Committee, Executive Sessions, RG 253, Box 6.

[38] Lela Rogers, Transcript of Testimony before HUAC, May 14, 1947, Records of the House Un-American Activities Committee, Executive Sessions, RG 253, Box 12.

[39] H. A. Smith, Memo, Interview with Lela Rogers, September 2, 1947, Records of the House Un-American Activities Committee, Executive Sessions, RG 253, Box 7

[40] Nancy Lynn Schwartz, *The Hollywood Writers' Wars* (New York, 1982), p. 256.

Before the public hearings in Washington, D.C., in October 1947, J. Parnell Thomas had conducted closed sessions in Los Angeles the previous May.[41] Held at the Los Angeles Biltmore Hotel, the hearings proved to be as leaky as a faucet with a cracked washer. Committee members and witnesses, friendly and unfriendly, gave detailed accounts of their testimony, and these reports created immediate problems for HUAC. The bad publicity generated from these not-so-closed hearings gave second thoughts to witnesses such as actor Robert Taylor about going public with his testimony. In the closed-session hearings, Taylor testified that he had been cajoled into starring in *A Song of Russia* (1944).[42] The film told the story of an American conductor, played by Taylor, on a tour of Russia on the eve of the German invasion of the Soviet Union. The movie depicted Russian villagers living blissfully in Stalin's Soviet Union. Taylor testified in a closed hearing on May 14 in Los Angeles that he believed the film was sheer pro-Soviet propaganda. Reluctant to star in the film, he had been summoned to Louis B. Mayer's office. In attendance at the meeting was Lowell B. Mellett, assistant to Franklin Roosevelt. At the five-minute meeting, Taylor told them he disapproved of large parts of the script. Their response, Taylor testified, was "Well, my God, we are no more communist than you are, but we don't see how this can possibly do any damage and if there is anything communist in it, we will take it out." Taylor believed that his recent commission in the U.S. Navy would be threatened unless he made the film. During the filming, Taylor continued to complain about the script, which had been written by John Wexley, a known communist.[43]

Taylor expected his testimony to be kept secret; after all, the session was closed to the public. Less than twenty-four hours after his testimony, however, J. Parnell Thomas appeared before the press to applaud Taylor's "courage" in revealing that MGM and the Roosevelt administration had made a film that favored "Russian ideologies, institutions and way of life over the same things in our country." Thomas, with typical hyperbole, declared that Taylor's testimony proved "another instance where persons in our government have been aiding and abetting communism even to the extent of getting one of our prominent actors to play a leading role in a picture to which he had already objected."[44]

Taylor hit the roof when he read Thomas's statement. He understood immediately that he had placed his employers at MGM in the terrible position of appearing to have actually made movies full of communist propaganda. This was exactly what Thomas was charging and the studios had been denying. When Taylor was summoned to testify in Washington, he protested. In neatly typed

[41] "House Group Starts Red Probe," *The Hollywood Reporter*, May 9, 1947; "Many Reds Named to Committee," *The Hollywood Reporter*, May 16, 1947.

[42] "Pressured Into 'Son of Russia' Role, Says Taylor," *The Hollywood Reporter*, May 15, 1947.

[43] Transcript of Hearings Held in Los Angeles, May 14, 1947, House Un-American Activities Committee Papers, National Archives, RG 253, pp. 182–191; Linda Alexander, *Reluctant Witness: Robert Taylor, Hollywood and Communism* (Swansboro, NC, 2008), pp. 186–235.

[44] Quoted in Alexander, *Reluctant Witness*, p. 210.

text (Taylor prided himself on his typing skills), he wrote a blistering letter to the committee. He declared that he had testified in Los Angeles under the assurance that his testimony was confidential. Instead, he had been made to look "pretty silly." The hearings proved, he wrote, to be "utterly ridiculous and a waste of time, both for me and the committee." Their only value thus far has been to garner free publicity for Mr. Thomas and his Committee, and, he pointedly added, it is not inherent in my job as a motion picture actor to "aid in the feathering of their nest for them via publicity from my name – a name, by the way, which I have worked God Damn hard to build and maintain without a blemish." He ended his rant by saying that he would go to Washington but "I shall resent every minute of the whole thing. Consider me an unfriendly to the committee." He added, "You'll seldom find a guy who hates Communism as much as I – nor one who is so adamant about not going to Washington to testify."[45] In the end, Taylor testified in Washington, and what he had to say about *Song of Russia* there was much more tempered than what he had said in the closed-session hearings.

Following the closed hearings, which received front-page coverage in the newspapers, the Hollywood Left mobilized to rally public opinion. The HUAC hearings coincided with a massive rally held in the Hollywood Bowl in support of Henry Wallace's campaign to challenge incumbent president Harry S Truman's bid for reelection in 1948. Sponsored by the Progressive Citizens of America, a group affiliated with the Hollywood Independent Citizen's Committee of the Arts, Science and Professions (HICCASP), the rally drew 27,000 people. Originally known as the Hollywood Democratic Committee, the formation of the Hollywood Independent Citizen's Committee reflected the shift in the communist line away from the popular front. By 1947, many in Hollywood came to believe that HICCASP was a Communist Party–dominated organization. In July 1946, James Roosevelt, composer Johnny Green, and actors Olivia de Havilland, Melvyn Douglass, and Ronald Reagan resigned from the organization when it refused to pass a resolution condemning communism. Actors such as Edward G. Robinson stayed in HICCASP.[46] Indicative of a shift in party line away from the popular front, HICCASP threw its support behind the formation of a third-party presidential effort. The highlight of the rally for Wallace at the Hollywood Bowl was a rousing keynote address by actress Katharine Hepburn. The irony contained in the success of the rally is that it encouraged the left to overestimate its popular support.[47] At the time, a big rally meant a lot because the art of polling was still in its infancy. Wallace's subsequent third-party presidential campaign as the Progressive Party candidate received only 1.7 million votes, less than the States' Rights Party

---

[45] Robert Taylor to H. A. Smith, September 23, 1947, Records of the House Un-American Activities Committee, Executive Sessions, RG 253, Box 8.
[46] Gansberg, *Little Caesar*, pp. 118–122.
[47] Schwartz, *The Hollywood Writers' Wars*, p. 255, and Thomas W. Devine, *Henry Wallace's 1948 Presidential Campaign and the Future of Postwar Liberalism* (Chapel Hill, 2013).

candidate. Wallace later said that communist infiltration into the Progressive Party had destroyed whatever chances his campaign might have had. All of this came later. In 1947, though, the Hollywood Left felt a heady assurance that the public was on its side.

The left in Hollywood rose to defend the unfriendly witnesses who had been subpoenaed to appear before HUAC, and a Committee for the First Amendment was formed to bring the case before the public. The first meeting was held in composer Ira Gershwin's home. An advertisement was placed in *Variety* in early October, protesting HUAC. Signed by 150 people, the advertisement read, "We hold that these hearings are morally wrong because: Any investigation into the political beliefs of the individual is contrary to the basic principles of our democracy."[48] Movie stars enlisted to defend what was seen as HUAC's attempt at political intimidation of the film industry. Leading the committee were Humphrey Bogart, his wife Lauren Bacall, Henry Fonda, Danny Kaye, Gene Kelly, Sterling Hayden, Marsha Hunt, and John and Walter Huston. These celebrities flew to Washington to support the unfriendly witnesses.[49]

THE 1947 HUAC HEARINGS INTENSIFY ANTICOMMUNISM

The evening before the hearings opened, nineteen men, including twelve screen-writers, five directors, a producer, and an actor gathered in a room in the Shoreham Hotel to await word from a conference being held in the same building between their lawyers and representatives of the producers. The law-yers included California politician Robert W. Kenny, Bartley Crum, Ben Margolis, Charles Katz, Martin Popper, and Samuel Rosenwein. Representing the producers were Eric Johnston, president of the Motion Picture Association, former U.S. senator from Indiana Paul W. McNutt, and Maurice Benjamin. The attorneys wanted assurance that a blacklist was not going to be imposed. Eric Johnston assured them that they need not worry: "We share your feelings, gentlemen, and we support your position." Kenny replied that Thomas had implied that a blacklist had already been produced. Johnston replied indignantly, "That report is nonsense! As long as I live, I will never be party to anything as un-American as a blacklist, and any statement purposing to quote me as agreeing to a blacklist is a libel upon me as a good American." He added, "Tell the boys not to worry. There'll never be a blacklist. We're not going to go totalitarian to please this committee."[50] When the lawyers returned to the hotel room to report Johnston's words, there was a loud cheer. The nineteen entered the hearings confident of their support from the public and the industry.

---

[48] Quoted in Christopher Bigsby, *Arthur Miller, 1915–1962* (Cambridge, 2009), p. 290

[49] "Stars Flying East Amid Probe Furor," *The Hollywood Reporter*, October 27, 1947.

[50] Unknown Author, "The Hollywood Hearings" (undated manuscript), in Records of the House Un-American Activities Committee, Executive Sessions, RG 253, Box 8.

More than ninety people filled the room on the first day of the hearings. *The Hollywood Reporter* announced that this was the capital's biggest show of the year. Four newsreel companies were assigned to shoot the proceedings, four major radio networks were there to provide live coverage, and space was allotted for 125 reporters.[51] Thomas made a grand entrance at 10:20 A.M., after other members of the committee had already taken their seats, including the newly elected representative from Southern California, Richard Nixon. The eastern sun slanted through the windows to reveal the broadcasting equipment, and loudspeakers for the public address system captured every whisper in the room. First, the producers testified, followed by the friendly witnesses. The last part of the hearings, in which the unfriendly witnesses appeared, turned into what Robert Taylor had predicted: a three-ring circus.

One defense attorneys set the bitter tone for what followed when he rose with a request to "quash" the hearings. Thomas interrupted and told him that unfriendly witnesses were not going to be called until the following week, so the committee would take the motion under advisement. Then, attorney Crum rose to submit a formal motion to end the hearings. A frustrated Thomas declared, "You may not ask one more thing at this time. Please be seated." This was to be war.[52]

The first witnesses called were producers Jack Warner and Louis B. Mayer. Thomas allowed Warner and Mayer to read their statements because they were "pertinent" to the inquiry. Both denied communist propaganda in their films. Warner pointed out that his studio's most controversial film, *Mission to Moscow* (1943), was produced when Russia was an American ally. "If making *Mission to Moscow* in 1942," Warner declared, "was a subversive activity, then the American Liberty ships which carried food and guns to Russian allies ... were engaged in subversive activities. The picture was made only to help a desperate war effort and not for posterity." The committee did not quite buy it, and Warner came in for some tough questioning before Richard Nixon came to his rescue. He asked Warner if his studio had made anti-Nazi films before and during the war, and if the films were made to "protect free speech and the free press in America." Warner answered affirmatively. Then, in a long-winded question, Nixon asked if Warner opposed the infiltration of propaganda by either fascists or communists in the movies. Nixon apologized for the length of the question, to which Warner replied, "It was a good statement; it was the statement of a real American, and I am proud of it." Nixon was there to defend the film industry in Southern California, and he played the same role when Mayer came to testify.[53]

[51] "Red Probe on Today; 50 Called," *The Hollywood Reporter*, October 20, 1947.
[52] U.S. Congress, *Hearings Before the Committee on Un-American Activities* (Washington, DC, 1947), p. 47.
[53] Ibid., pp. 7–53, 69–81.

The so-called friendly witnesses followed. At the time, and later, the friendly witnesses were portrayed as a uniform group, but a close reading of their testimony shows a surprisingly disparate group when it came to the communist issue in Hollywood and what was to be done about it. Some of these differences reflected individuals' relations to the studios, as well as political and ideological differences within Hollywood and the Republican Party. For the press, the Hollywood Left, and much of the American public, either a person supported the Hollywood Ten or did not. It was one side or the other. Studio chiefs caught up in this public relations nightmare created by HUAC, however, held the position that there was no issue of communist propaganda in their films, and any problems of communists in the film industry had been addressed already.

In the first week of the hearings, the studios stuck by their position that communism was not an issue in Hollywood. They were supported by the testimony of Ronald Reagan, Robert Montgomery, and George Murphy. These actors had served (or in Reagan's case were serving) as presidents of the SAG. Murphy, Montgomery, and Reagan believed that the small communist problem in the industry had been addressed by the studios. There was no need for Congress to get involved in an industry problem that no longer existed. *The Hollywood Reporter* summarized their testimony with the headline carried on its front page, "Few Reds in Industry, Say Stars."[54] This is exactly what Thomas did not want to hear.

In his testimony of October 23, 1947, Reagan stressed that he agreed whole-heartedly with Montgomery and Murphy in their previous testimony that much of the publicity around the communist issue made it appear that only a minority had been involved in confronting communists in the industry. Reagan countered this perception by saying that "99 percent of us are pretty well aware of what is going on." Furthermore, "I think within the bounds of our democracy we have done a pretty good job in our business of keeping those people's activities curtailed." He told the committee that, after all, the Communist Party is a legally recognized political party. "On that basis," he emphasized, "we have exposed their lies, when we came across them, we have opposed their propaganda, and ... we have been currently successful in preventing them from, with their usual tactics, trying to run a majority of an organization with a well-organized minority."[55] Reagan suggested that the hearings were unnecessary. Even hard-liner Rupert Hughes declared that he believed communists were on the defensive in 1947 because "they are losing a great many of those fashionable followers who thought it was smart to be communists and who now find it is unpopular and are deserting them."[56]

[54] "Few Reds in Industry, Say Stars," *The Hollywood Reporter*, October 24, 1947.
[55] U.S. Congress, *Hearings Before the Committee on Un-American Activities* (Washington, DC, 1947), p. 217.
[56] Ibid., p. 130.

Murphy and Montgomery also took a softer line than did some of the other friendly witnesses as to whether the Communist Party in the United States should be outlawed. When directly asked this question, Reagan agreed with Murphy that such a decision was a matter for "the government to decide," but "as a citizen I would hesitate, or not like, to see any political party outlawed on the basis of its political ideology. We have spent 170 years in this country on the basis that democracy is strong enough to stand up and fight against the inroads of any ideology." Reagan then equivocated slightly, adding that "if it were proved that an organization is an agent of a power, a foreign power, or in any way not a legitimate political party ... then that is another matter."[57] Reagan's answer, even with his qualification, was hardly hardline.

Surprisingly, some members of the hardline MPA took a similar stance. James McGuinness, whom nobody accused of being soft on communism, declared that "outlawing of a political belief serves no purpose. I don't think a law overcomes an idea." Like Reagan, although more forcefully, he said that if "sufficient evidence" was brought to Congress to show that the Communist Party was acting as an agent of a foreign party, "then it is obligatory to defend the sovereignty and the freedom of the United States" by outlawing the party.[58] Even fervent anticommunist Walt Disney deferred on the issue, telling the committee that he did not think he was qualified to speak on that question. "I feel," he said, joining the other witnesses, that if the party is shown to be un-American then "it ought to be outlawed," but without interfering with the rights of the people.[59] Perhaps such qualifications were a cop-out because many of the friendlies believed that the Communist Party did serve as an agent of a foreign power, but their insistence that this assertion be proved prior to the enactment of any prohibition indicated a genuine concern about the subversion of rights in a democratic society. Adolphe Menjou was totally opposed to outlawing the Communist Party. Declaring that J. Edgar Hoover was a close personal friend, he said that the communists should be brought out into the open. They are now underground, he declared, and "I want to bring them out so we can see who they are."[60] Menjou's position was strategic, concerned with how best to defeat domestic communists.

Others were less qualified in their opinions. Rupert Hughes believed that the Communist Party should be outlawed, although "I reached that decision with great hesitation." Ryskind also believed that the party should be outlawed, but added "I don't know just how you can do it." Robert Taylor did not have any hesitation in declaring that the party should be outlawed, nor did Lela Rogers. They believed the Communist Party in the United States was an arm of a hostile foreign power, the Soviet Union. But the fact remained that, in the 1930s and

---

[57] Ibid., p. 217.
[58] Ibid., p. 135.
[59] Ibid., p. 89.
[60] Ibid., p. 101 (Menjou).

1940s, the Communist Party was a legal political party, and the United States had been an ally of the Soviet Union during the Second World War.[61]

Although the testimony of the friendly witnesses showed a diversity of opinion about the exact nature and current threat of communism in the film industry and differences over whether the Communist Party should be outlawed by Congress – as if the opinions of actors and screenwriters should matter – some of the statements made in the first week of the hearings provided easy targets for the press.

Novelist Ayn Rand, who began her writing career in America while working in Hollywood, came across as strident. Rand appeared on the first day of the hearings to counter the previous testimony by studio head Jack Warner, who vehemently denied the possibility of communist influence in Hollywood movies. Rand's testimony focused on *Song of Russia*. She opened her remarks by noting that the film began with a scene of an American conductor, played by Robert Taylor, giving a concert in America for Russian war relief. He starts, she pointed out, playing the American national anthem, which "dissolves into a Russia mob, with the sickle and hammer on a red flag very prominent above their heads." She said that the scene "made me sick." What the scene conveyed, in her opinion, is that it "was quite all right for the American national anthem to dissolve into the Soviet." The rest of the film showed happy, well-fed peasants played by well-manicured actors. The film suggested that Soviet peasants owned private property, their own tractors, and were prospering. She concluded that the film was pure propaganda, although she noted that she could see how Louis B. Mayer tried to cut some of the propaganda from it. Rand, a refugee from Russia, understood that the film was made during the war, when the Soviet Union was an ally, but she believed *Song of Russia* was deceitful and conveyed a message that "it is all right to live in a totalitarian state. . . . In war or peace or at any time you cannot justify slavery. You cannot tell people that it is all right to live under it and everybody there is happy."[62]

Rand came under tough questioning from Republicans and Democrats on HUAC, particularly John N. Wood (D-Georgia) and John McDowell (R-Pennsylvania). Wood was a segregationist Southerner who was alleged to have been at the infamous hanging of Leo Frank, a Jew falsely accused of raping and murdering a white gentile woman in 1915. Allegations were made that he was close to the Ku Klux Klan in his state. Although anti-Red himself, he went after Rand for not supporting Lend-Lease aid to the Soviet Union in the war. More sarcastic in his questioning was John McDowell, who asked Rand, "Does not anybody smile in the Soviet Union anymore?" Rand answered emphatically, "Not quite that way; no. If they do, it is privately and accidentally."[63] The remark that Russians did not smile anymore projected an image of harshness.

---

[61] Ibid., p. 133 (Hughes); p. 170 (Taylor); p. 187 (Ryskind).
[62] Ibid., pp. 90–92.
[63] Ibid., p. 90.

Lela Rogers came across as foolish. To the dismay of HUAC investigators and even to those on her side, she once again brought up the film *Dear Comrade* as evidence of communist propaganda in Hollywood films. In citing other films reflecting communist propaganda, she pointed to *None but the Lonely Heart* (1944), scripted by Clifford Odets, a member of the Communist Party. The script contained didactic speeches about class differences in England, but Rogers went further. When asked whether communist activity in the film industry was increasing or decreasing, she did not hesitate to reply, contrary to many of the friendly witnesses, "I think their activities are increasing." She added that some of the communist influence had been checked in the last six months by being exposed, but that the American people still believed that a typical communist is "a man with bushy eyebrows and a great huge Russian bear. They can't believe that they could be American citizens.... But they are – and pretty, too."[64] Screenwriter John Lee Mahin later summed up her testimony as "stupid."[65] If Rogers came across as a bit shrill, studio head Walt Disney, another founding member of MPA, presented himself as a soft-spoken, reasonable man – until he described the League of Women Voters as a "Commie front." He later retracted that description, declaring that he meant "League of Women Shoppers," but by that time it was too late.

Disney's testimony was followed by the unfriendly witnesses. By this point, the hearings were becoming a circus. Throngs of nearly uncontrollable fans had turned out to hear Gary Cooper and Robert Taylor appear before the hearings, reinforcing the complaint that HUAC was really about publicity in search of a nonexistent issue – communist propaganda in movies. The final act opened as the unfriendly witnesses appeared on day six, October 27.

The first five days of the hearings proved to be a public relations disaster for Thomas. Newspapers denounced the hearings as a fiasco, and Adolphe Menjou wrote to Clare Booth Luce, wife of *Time* magazine publisher Henry Luce, that he had been presented by the magazine "in a more than a ridiculous fashion."[66] The *Washington Post* editorialized on October 30, just two weeks after the hearings had opened, that Thomas had allowed friendly witnesses to make accusations based on little more than "vulgar gossip grouped in malice or misconception."[67] The liberal magazine *New Republic* a few days later called the hearings a "garish vulgar show" with the friendly glamourous witnesses appearing for publicity with vague inconsequential testimony.[68] This might have been expected from the liberal press, but it was not only the liberal press that saw the hearings as

---

[64] Ibid., pp. 229–237, especially p. 233 (*None But the Lonely Heart*), p. 236 (increasing influence of communists), p. 237 (American views of communists).

[65] "John Lee Mahin," in McGilligan, *Backstory*, p. 280.

[66] Adolph Menjou to Clare Booth Luce, November 1, 1947; Clare Booth Luce to Adolph Menjou, November 5, 1947, Clare Booth Luce Papers, Library of Congress, Box 140.

[67] Memorandum, Criticism Made of Hollywood Hearings, Records of the House Un-American Activities Committee, Executive Sessions, RG 253, Box 5.

[68] Ibid.

going nowhere. Fortunately for Thomas, opinion was about to change – thanks to the unfriendlies. There was a certain irony in that, finally given their chance to appear before the committee to make their case, they turned public opinion against themselves.

The first unfriendly witness was John Lawson, Hollywood communist chieftain. He proved bellicose, unnecessarily inflammatory, and repulsive, except perhaps to the true believer. Lawson began his testimony by asking if he could read his statement. Thomas asked to see it. After reading the first few lines Thomas refused to have it read aloud or inserted in the proceedings. The first line of Lawson's statement called the hearings "an illegal and indecent trial." The friendly witnesses, it declared, were a "parade of stool-pigeons, neurotics, publicity-seeking clowns, Gestapo agents, paid informers, and a few ignorant and frightened Hollywood artists." HUAC, he declared, was seeking to "subvert orderly government and establish an autocratic dictatorship." Thomas was only a tool of "more powerful forces. Those forces are trying to introduce fascism in this country."[69] Thomas's decision not to allow Lawson to read his statement or include it in the official record reveals the tenuous political situation that Thomas faced, as well as his arbitrary conduct of the hearings and the new territory Congress had entered in conducting the hearings.

Determined to fight the forces of American fascism, Lawson refused to answer questions about his association with the SWG on the grounds that his involvement in the union was "outside the purview of the rights of the committee." He continued to shout, "I am an American and I am not at all easy to intimidate." He was gaveled down by Thomas. When asked if he was a member of the Communist Party, Lawson replied, "You are using the old technique, which was used in Hitler's Germany in order to create a scare there." Thomas again gaveled him down, and Lawson again refused to answer, declaring that "I have to teach this committee the basic principles of American . . ." He did not get a chance to complete his sentence, when Thomas, pounding his gavel, declared, "That is not the question. . . . Have you ever been a member of the Communist Party?" Lawson refused to answer the question. Thomas ordered court officers to escort him from the room, but Lawson refused to be silenced: "I have written Americanism for many years, and I shall continue to fight for the Bill of Rights, which you are trying to destroy." Thomas dismissed him as a witness. The crowd interrupted in boos and cheers. As Lawson was escorted from the stand, demonstrators in favor of Lawson stood cheering.[70]

A similar pattern was followed the next day when screenwriter Dalton Trumbo took the stand. Thomas again ruled that Trumbo could not read his

---

[69] John Lawson, "They Want to Muzzle Public Opinion," in *Thirty Years of Treason: Excepts from the Hearings before the House on Un-American Activities, 1938–1968*, ed. Eric Bentley (New York, 1971), pp. 161–165.

[70] U.S. Congress, *Hearings Before the Committee on Un-American Activities* (Washington, DC, 1947), pp. 290–296.

statement, a denunciation of the hearings. Trumbo then tried to introduce more than twenty of his scripts into the record, but Thomas refused, saying that they were too long. When asked if he was a member of the SWG, Trumbo launched into a speech denouncing the committee as "anti-labor." When asked again the same question, Trumbo responded by demanding to know if any committee member had voted in favor of the Taft-Hartley bill. After more back and forth, Trumbo was excused. Before he left, he warned that "This is the beginning ... of an American concentration camp." Demonstrations broke out again, leading Thomas to pound the gavel, declaring "This is typical Communist tactics."[71]

And on it went. Albert Maltz was allowed to read his statement into the record, a statement that ended with, "I would rather die than be a shabby American groveling before men whose names are Thomas and Rankin [a segregationist U.S. congressman from Mississippi], but who now carry out the activities in America like those carried out in Germany by Goebbels and Himmler."[72] Alvah Bessie was allowed to read the opening paragraphs of his statement, which echoed Maltz: "I will never aid or abet such a committee in its patent attempt to foster the sort of intimidation and terror that is the inevitable precursor to a Fascist regime."[73] Samuel Ornitz refused to answer questions and was excused.[74] Director-screenwriter Herbert Joseph Biberman was excused after he accused the committee of trying to end free speech in the motion picture industry.[75] Director Edward Dmytryk and screenwriters Adrian Scott and Lester Cole joined those also dismissed when they refused to answer questions, claiming the hearings were unconstitutional.[76] Ring Lardner, Jr., before he was dismissed, got in the most memorable line when he refused to answer whether he was a member of the Communist Party by saying, "I could answer it, but if I did I would hate myself in the morning."[77] Lardner's line became much quoted, and was seen as a sign of courage. Yet, given the immediate aftermath of the hearings, there was actually much to regret.

After just ten days of hearings, Thomas suddenly announced that he was suspending them. More unfriendly witnesses stood in the wings waiting to be called, and evidence of Communist Party involvement for some of the uncalled witnesses appeared to be more circumstantial. Studio pressure against the hearings, moreover, had continued to build. As soon as Thomas announced the suspension of the hearings, Paul McNutt, representing the film industry, declared that the abrupt end of the hearings "vindicated" the industry's position. McNutt declared that "The committee made serious charges against us. ... The truth is, there are no pictures of ours which carry communist propaganda."

[71] Ibid., pp. 329–340, especially pp. 332 and 334.
[72] Ibid., p. 366.
[73] Ibid., p. 384.
[74] Ibid., pp. 411–412.
[75] Ibid., pp. 413.
[76] Ibid., pp. 459–461 (Dmytryk); pp. 466–467 (Scott); pp. 489–490 (Cole).
[77] Ibid., p. 482.

What should have been more worrisome was McNutt's next statement: "There are communists in Hollywood as in other places. . . . But, so far as Hollywood is concerned, they are a tiny and ineffectual minority."[78]

McNutt's observation was astute. The HUAC hearings in 1947 failed miserably in convincing the public that there was widespread communist propaganda in Hollywood movies. On the other hand, the hearings showed – with help from the unfriendly witnesses – that there *were* communists in the film industry. This created a public relations problem for Hollywood.

BACKLASH TO THE HEARINGS

The first sign that things had not gone well for the unfriendly witnesses was the desertion of the liberals. After the hearings, Humphrey Bogart and most of the other supporters of the Committee for the First Amendment rapidly sought to disassociate themselves from the unfriendlies. Bogart told the press, "I am not a Communist. I am not a Communist sympathizer. I detest Communism." He concluded that his trip to D.C. in support of the unfriendly witnesses was "ill-advised," adding that he was disgusted by Lawson's misbehavior at the hearings. Behind the scenes, he was blunter. He told the defense attorneys that they had "fucked him over."[79]

Worse was to come. On November 21, 1947, an "anti-Red" ticket of the middle-of-the road All-Guild slate swept twenty of the twenty-one offices in the SWG election.[80] Three days later, on November 24, the House of Representatives voted 346 to 17 to cite the ten unfriendly witnesses with contempt for refusing to testify before HUAC. The following day, film executives meeting at the Waldorf Astoria hotel in New York announced the firing of the Hollywood Ten. Although there was some dissent at the meeting over issuing the blanket blacklist, studio executives were anxious to protect the industry from a severe public backlash that appeared to be developing after the hearings. They particularly feared boycotts of films organized by the American Legion. Although some historians have speculated that if studio executives had shown more spine, or if the unions had organized strikes, the blacklist might have been prevented, but given the context of the times – an aroused public, the desertion of many liberals from the cause, and anticommunist sentiment within Hollywood unions – the executives believed they had little choice but to fire the Hollywood Ten.[81]

---

[78] "Industry Upheld, Says McNutt," *The Hollywood Reporter*, October 31, 1947, p. 1 and p. 20.
[79] Gerald Horne, *The Final Victim of the Blacklist: John Howard Lawson, Dean of the Hollywood Ten* (Berkeley, CA, 2006), p. 194; and Ceplair and Englund, *The Inquisition in Hollywood*, p. 291.
[80] "Anti-Reds Sweep 20 of 21 Offices in SWG Election," *The Hollywood Reporter*, November 21, 1947.
[81] Ceplair and Englund, *The Inquisition in Hollywood*, pp. 298, 328–331.

The Hollywood Ten undertook a public relations campaign to rally the public to their side. They launched defense committees, went on speaking tours, and spoke to the press. Behind the scenes, there were divisions. Many expected that any contempt charges would be overturned in the courts. These expectations proved wrong. After being convicted of contempt in early 1948 and after waging an unsuccessful legal battle, the Hollywood Ten began serving prison sentences. While they were in prison, the SAG voted 1,307 to 157 in favor of honoring the new Taft-Hartley Act by requiring officers to sign affidavits denying membership in the Communist Party.[82] Few of the Hollywood Ten found solace as prison martyrs, but some consolation came when, in a strange twist of fate, Lester Cole and Ring Lardner, Jr., found themselves in the Danbury, Connecticut, federal prison with the man who had sent them there, J. Parnell Thomas; he was serving time after being convicted of defrauding the government by putting relatives on his congressional payroll.

The Hollywood Red Scare intensified with the outbreak of the Korean War on June 25, 1950. Beginning in 1951, congressional investigators shifted their focus to the extent of Communist Party membership in Hollywood. From 1951 to 1954, Congress identified 324 persons as communists. In 1951, HUAC issued subpoenas in batches to actors, writers, story editors, screen analysts, producers, and directors. Hollywood reacted to these 1951 and 1952 investigations in a panic; as one reporter said, Hollywood was like a "group of marooned sailors on a flat desert island watching the approach of a tidal wave."[83] The blacklist was extended to the radio and television industry. Aided by lists drawn up by organizations such as the American Legion and consulting firms such as American Business Consultants, publishers of *Counterattack*, and anticommunist publications such as *AWARE*, the media industry blacklisted entertainers, studio technicians, and writers. In 1951, the American Legion national convention instructed the editor of the *American Legion Magazine* to publish all the information about communist associations of people still employed in the film industry. After the misuse of this information by some movie executives, the studios agreed that the American Legion should not serve as a clearinghouse and developed their own policy for ex-communists, noncommunist liberals, and persons innocent of left-wing associations.

During this blacklist period, 1947 through 1960, more than 300 people in the film industry were banned from employment in Hollywood. Another 180-plus found themselves blacklisted in radio and television.[84] For example, Joan Copeland, the actress sister of playwright Arthur Miller, who was accused of being a communist, found work falling off sharply. She recalled that "I did not

---

[82] Prindle, *The Politics of Glamour*, p. 60.

[83] Cogley, *Report on Blacklisting*, pp. 92–95.

[84] David Everitt, *A Shadow of Red: Communism and the Blacklist in Radio and Television* (Chicago, 2007). Also, Thomas Doherty, *Cold War, Cool Medium: Television, McCarthyism and American Culture* (New York, 2003), pp. 7–27.

know why" until she was told that it was because of her brother. She was not alone in her experience. Mildred Dunnock, another actress, discovered that work dried up for her because she was listed in the anticommunist publication *Red Channels*. "I felt contaminated. I felt I had leprosy," she recalled. "I felt I had incriminated my husband, a conventional man."[85]

There was some organizational resistance to the Red Scare in Hollywood. The Screen Directors Guild defeated an attempt by Cecil B. DeMille in 1950 to have the union's elected board sign a loyalty oath. Opposition was organized by directors John Ford and George Stephens at a special membership meeting attended by 600 guild members. When DeMille tried to speak in favor of the resolution, he was booed down. Ford stood up to declare, "My name is John Ford. I make westerns. I don't agree with Mr. DeMille. I admire him, but I don't like him." Director Fritz Lang followed, declaring, hyperbolically and disingenuously to a large degree, "Mr. DeMille, I want you to know that for the first time I am in America, I am frightened – because I have an accent. You made me frightened Mr. DeMille." DeMille's attempt to institute a loyalty oath failed. This was depicted as a victory against the anticommunists, but, actually, those involved in defeating DeMille were, as director Elia Kazan later noted, iconoclasts. They stood for fairness and decency. DeMille believed, with just cause, that he had become persona non grata in the guild.[86]

Resistance to the blacklist and blanket anticommunism often revolved around defending individuals accused of being communists or former communists. This was the case of director Frank Capra, a film director of great distinction who had made documentary films about combat in the war. Capra wrote Ford to complain that he had been denied a government security clearance. Ford was outraged. He angrily wrote the Army, Navy, and Air Force Personnel Security board to tell them he was shocked by the decision, declaring that "Frank Capra and I joined hands in our Guild some sixteen years ago when Commies, Fellow Travelers, and Bleeding Hearts, or whatever you want to call them, tried to infiltrate the Motion Picture Director's Guild." We waged, he continued, a successful fight to keep them out. Ford, known for his temper, was just getting started. He told the board that Capra never protested the HUAC hearing. "Frankly," he said, "I objected to it loudly and vociferously. I'll now go on record as saying I think it was a publicity stunt."[87] Capra received his security clearance.

Others on the right did not have problems with loyalty oaths and the firing of communists. Ayn Rand, noted for her libertarian views, argued that studio

[85] Quoted in Bigsby, *Arthur Miller*, pp. 536–537.

[86] Edward Dymytryk, *Odd Man Out: A Memoir of the Hollywood Ten* (Carbondale, IL, 1996), pp. 147–149; Cecil B. DeMille to Joseph G. Youngerman, November 16, 1951, Cecil B. DeMille Papers, Box 422; Eli Kazan, *A Life* (New York, 1989), pp. 389–393.

[87] John Ford to Army, Navy, and Air Force Personnel Security Board, December 14, 1951; Frank Capra to John Ford, December 19, 1951; Victor W. Philips to Frank Capra, December 14, 1951; John Ford Papers, Lily Library, Box December 1951.

executives had an "inalienable right" to fire communists in their industry. She maintained that "Under the American system a man has the right to hold any ideas he wishes, without suffering any government restraint for it, without the damage of physical violence, bodily injury or police seizure."[88] Studio heads, as private employers, had the right not to employ communists in order to protect the financial interests of their businesses. Rand claimed that the blacklist was a private matter, arranged by private individuals, and not a government-imposed policy.

AFTERMATH

Although they presented a unified front in public, behind the scenes there was growing division within the Hollywood Ten and within the party. Accepting party discipline was always difficult for Hollywood. As the Cold War heated up, the Korean War broke out in the summer of 1950, and anticommunism reached a fever pitch, it became easy to abandon the party. Edward Dmytryk, one of the Hollywood Ten who publicly denounced the party while serving a one-year prison term, related an incident that typified the turmoil in the party. Shortly before he began serving his term, Robert Rossen, director of *All the King's Men* (1949) was called on the carpet by John Howard Lawson. At a meeting held at Maltz's home, Lawson, Alvah Bessie, and Herbert Biberman excoriated Rossen Albert for exposing the evils of dictatorship. Not all dictatorships, Lawson said, were bad. The dictatorship of the proletariat was good, and the one-man rule of Stalin had saved the Soviet Union during the war. Barraged on all sides, finally Rossen had had enough. "Stick the whole party up your ass!" he yelled and walked out of the house.[89] Less dramatic defections were taking place throughout the party in these years. Dmytryk, Budd Schulberg, Richard Collins, and Larry Parks notoriously "named names" in subsequent HUAC and other congressional hearings, but the fact of the matter was that party membership had become intolerable to many by this time. Still, turning over names of former comrades to the FBI and congressional committees was not an easy decision for any of these men. They were denounced as reprehensible by many of their contemporaries and later by scholars and the Hollywood Left. At the time, the choice came down to whether these men should sacrifice their careers and families for a cause and a party they no longer had faith in and genuinely rejected.

For blacklisted former communists, rehabilitation was costly financially and psychologically. The absolute requirement was a private reappearance before HUAC; appearances before the media were optional. Released from prison on November 15, 1950, after filing an affidavit that he had been a member of the Communist Party before he left it in 1945, Edward Dmytryk worked with reporter Richard English in writing "What Makes a Hollywood Communist?"

---

[88] Mayhew, *Ayn Rand and "Song of Russia,"* pp. 80–93.
[89] Dmytryk, *Odd Man Out*, pp. 114–115.

which appeared in the *Saturday Evening Post* on May 17, 1951. HUAC helped arrange for the publication in the conservative *Post*, which gave Dmytryk a public seal of approval. The article drew the wrath of former comrade Albert Maltz, who claimed that Dmytryk actually had not left the party but had gone underground.[90] Similarly, screenwriter Richard Collins published "Confession of a Red Screenwriter" in the *New Leader*, October 6, 1952. There were others as well, and years later, it appeared uncomfortably reminiscent of the habit of "self-criticism" within the Communist Party. But naming names did not necessarily earn respect in the anticommunist camp. Columnist and vice president of the MPA Hedda Hopper resisted having former communists rehabilitated back into the industry, and she remained unforgiving in her views.

Others were less trenchant. When screenwriter Richard Collins, who had helped write *Song of Russia*, revealed names, he became a pariah in Hollywood. He claimed that after his appearance before HUAC in 1951, "No matter which way you went, you didn't get work. I think the studios in the main felt they'd be safer not to hire anybody who was involved in it, no matter which way they went. . . . And I know a lot of them did not work ever again – or at least very little."[91] Actor Ward Bond phoned Collins and his wife to ask how he was doing. He made a similar call to actor Larry Parks and invited him to join him at the SWG meeting. John Wayne also reached out to Parks, inviting him to attend a MPA meeting. As Wayne put it, "Parks was breaking not just with the Party, but all his friends." Wayne believed that Parks needed moral support so other witnesses would be encouraged to break.[92] Few in Hollywood could accuse either Wayne or Bond of being soft on communism – except Hedda Hopper. She publicly rebuked Wayne for his attitude toward former communists. "Duke," she said, "is a little dumb about these things. . . . We must be careful lest we give sympathy to those who do not deserve it – and Parks certainly does not."[93]

A price was paid as well by those who cooperated with Congress. The *New York Times* reported in 1956 that those "cooperative witnesses suffered social ostracism and an informal blacklist by the studios," although evidence of this social ostracism or informal backlash remained on the anecdotal level. Ayn Rand observed that the Hollywood hearings did not hurt famous stars such as Cooper and Taylor. "The real tragedy," she claimed," is what happened to second-rank people, i.e. people like Adolphe Menjou, who after the hearings could not find work and got into financial trouble." Or take Morrie Ryskind, she

---

[90] Richard English, "What Makes a Hollywood Communist?," *Saturday Evening Post*, May 17, 1951; and Dymytryk, *Odd Man Out*, p. 172.

[91] Richard Collins, "Confession of a Red Screenwriter," *New Leader*, October 6, 1952, pp. 7–10; quoted in Mayhew, *Ayn Rand and "Song of Russia*," p. 93.

[92] Cogley, *Report on Blacklisting*, p. 95; Wayne quote in Randy Robert and James S. Olson, *John Wayne: American* (New York, 1995), p. 346.

[93] Emanuel Levy, *John Wayne: Prophet of the American Way of Life* (Lanham, MD, 1998), p. 287; Norm Goldstein, *John Wayne: A Tribute* (New York, 1970), p. 96; and Navasky, *Naming Names*, pp. 371–372.

said: "he has not worked as a [film] writer one day since appearing as a friendly witness." She said that young writers were the most vulnerable, and she offered two examples of such writers who cooperated with HUAC: Fred Niblo Jr., the son of the director, and Richard Macaulay, neither of whom worked again as a screenwriter. Niblo worked as a laborer at Lockheed Corporation in California before he got a job working for the U.S. Information Agency in Southeast Asia.[94] Hopper noted that Jack Moffitt, who testified as a friendly in 1947, failed to get a job afterward. "Figure that one out," she said.[95] No doubt jobs in Hollywood were in decline in the studio system, and a younger generation of writers whose views were closer to the times got jobs. Much of the blacklist was about being outdated and a has-been.

The end of the blacklist came gradually, finally ceasing in 1960, when director Otto Preminger announced publicly that Dalton Trumbo had scripted the forthcoming film *Exodus*. Six months later, Kirk Douglas insisted that Trumbo be given screen credit for writing *Spartacus*. Over the course of the next few years, lawsuits were won against anticommunist publications for falsely identifying some people as communists.[96]

Some of the Hollywood Ten continued to stick with the party. Norma Barzman, the wife of Ben Barzman, recalled that not even the Soviet invasion of Hungary in 1956 changed their loyalty to the party. Indeed, they believed that the Soviet Union was about ready to return to its ideals. Only in 1968, while living in France and witnessing the widespread student upheavals, did they realize the "treachery of the party."[97] Lester Cole also remained in the party. Although he scripted the highly successful British movie *Born Free* (1966), his career in the film industry was limited to this one hit. It left him bitter and envious of writers such as Ring Lardner Jr., who enjoyed great success after the lifting of the blacklist. Cole believed that the difference between him and writers such as Lardner, Schulberg, and Maltz was that they capitulated to the blacklist. These emotions came out when Lardner wrote an op-ed piece for the *New York Times*, "30 Years After the 'Hollywood 10,'" on March 18, 1978. In the editorial, Lardner wrote that American history revealed "a continuous cycle from liberty and repression." This statement itself was enough to arouse Cole's ire. He became enraged by Lardner's statement that "Albert Maltz and I have been free to work in Hollywood more or less when we wanted to. Alvah Bessie and

---

[94] Mayhew, *Ayn Rand and "Song of Russia,"* p. 91.

[95] Hedder Hopper, "Columnist Takes Attacker to Task," August 20, 1953, Hollywood Ten Blacklist File, Hedder Hopper Files, Academy of Motion Pictures Archives.

[96] For insight into the breakdown of the blacklist, see Albert Maltz to the *New York Times*, May 5, 1978, Ring Lardner, Jr. papers, Academy of Motion Picture Arts and Sciences, Folder 5. Also of importance are Cleo Trumbo to Ring Lardner, Jr., May 8, 1991; Cleo Trumbo to C. D. Rhoden, March 6, 1991, Lardner papers, Folder 196.

[97] Norma Barzman, *The Red and Blacklist: The Intimate Memoir of a Hollywood Expatriate* (New York, 2003), pp. 280, 322, and 421.

Lester Cole have not. But it isn't because two aging writers may be blacklisted or graylisted."[98]

Beside himself with anger, Cole wrote Lardner that he had been offended "personally, politically and in all ways." He told Lardner that Maltz, Trumbo, and Lardner had been "free to work" in the industry because they had "performed the required industry ritual publicly confessing" that past associations had been severed. He instead had refused to be "humiliated or degraded." Unlike Maltz or Lardner, who kept fit by swimming in their luxurious pools, Cole wrote, "I keep fit by walking picket lines protesting violations of our civil liberties and unfair labor practices ... and get exercise for my lungs in lusty protest."[99] In a further exchange of letters, Lardner's attempts to ease tensions with Cole proved hopeless. In his final exchange, Cole challenged Lardner's depiction of the Communist Party as "corrupt and foolish." Cole pointedly added that a good communist's task is not to quit. To call the party foolish reflected Lardner's class origins, which were "at odds with those held by persons like myself, of working class origins, of exploited parents and relatives, and comrades who saw party mistakes as reasons to increase the struggle for improvement."[100] Cole's language was that of the 1930s communist – a language of the past that the successful members of the Hollywood Ten, Lardner, Maltz, and Trumbo wanted to forget.

If division and disappointment characterized the Hollywood Ten in the aftermath of the blacklist, the other side did not fare well either. Death came early to many of the leaders of the MPA. Three of the Alliance presidents died in office from heart attacks, including Sam Wood and Jim McGuinness. (The MPA tried to keep McGuinness's name alive by offering a student award in his name at Pepperdine University.) Ward Bond became the third president of the MPA in 1955, only to suffer a massive heart attack in 1960.[101] Others within the MPA said that they could never find work in Hollywood after testifying. Adolphe Menjou was out of work for three years and worked only sporadically after the hearings. Ward Bond made few movies, finding success only in television when his series *Wagon Train* became a hit. Morrie Ryskind claimed that he was whitelisted in Hollywood. He went on to found the right-wing publication *Human Events*. Big stars such as Wayne, Taylor, and Cooper were too popular to be touched by any informal discrimination.[102] When their acting careers began to decline, Ronald Reagan and George Murphy found new opportunities in Republican politics.

---

[98] Ring Lardner Jr., "30 Years After the 'Hollywood 10,'" *New York Times*, March 18, 1978.

[99] Lester Cole to Ring Lardner, Jr., January 29, 1977, Ring Lardner Papers, Academy of Motion Picture Arts and Sciences, Folder 183.

[100] Lester Cole to Ring Lardner, Jr., April 16, 1979; also Cole to Lardner, March 31, 1979; and Lardner to Cole, April 11, 1978, Ring Lardner Papers, Academy of Motion Picture Arts and Sciences, Folder 183.

[101] A. J. MacDonald to MPA Members, July 24, 1961, in John Ford Papers, Box 3.

[102] Levy, *John Wayne: Prophet*, p. 287.

In this respect, the 1947 hearings proved only to be a sideshow for Reagan and Murphy; for them, the larger story was to be the ascent of the Republican Party in California. Even in 1947, in the midst of the turmoil created by the HUAC hearings, which produced little but personal tragedy for many, Hollywood Republicans were already looking at the upcoming presidential election as they rallied to Thomas Dewey, the very man who had tried to prevent the hearings in the first place.

For many in Hollywood, communism in the film industry remained inexplicable. Screenwriter and mystery novelist James M. Cain noted, "I knew these guys, most of them, and they made no sense to me. Why should they be Communists? You understand, all these guys were highly paid and successful."[103] Novelist and screenwriter Raymond Chandler opposed the blacklist, but could not understand the communist mentality. Chandler believed that the refusal of the unfriendlies to testify was a "singularly incompetent attempt" to use "the democratic system to undermine or sabotage the function of the system." He added that the studios could have laid off the Hollywood Ten "without fanfare and striking poses of virtue." Nonetheless, he wondered how "any decent man can become a communist is almost beyond understanding" after "the Katyn Forest and the Moscow Treason trials, the Ukraine famine, the Arctic prison camps, [and] the utterly abominable rape of Berlin by the Mongolian divisions." He believed becoming a communist was similar to a conversion to a religious system, an act of faith, not reason.[104]

[103] "James M. Cain," in McGilligan, *Backstory*, pp. 120–121.
[104] Raymond Chandler to James Sandoe, January 27, 1948; and Raymond Chandler to Carl Brandt, December 5, 1948, in Frank Mac Shane, ed., *Selected Letters of Raymond Chandler* (New York, 1981), pp. 106–107 and 138.

CHAPTER 4

Nixon Plays Hollywood

Arguably, the one person whose career benefited from the House Un-American Activities Committee (HUAC) hearings in 1947 was Richard Nixon, the first-term congressman from Southern California. Following the hearings, Hollywood became infatuated with Nixon. For the next fifteen years, a romance followed, until Nixon lost his race for the California governorship in 1962. The story of Nixon and Hollywood reveals a California Republican Party in factional turmoil, a situation that set the stage for Barry Goldwater's presidential race in 1964 and Ronald Reagan's ascendancy to the governorship in 1966. The drama of California Republican politics in this period presents a complicated tale of shifting alliances, personal animosity among the leading players, and the vicissitudes of political life.

Nixon loved Hollywood. His relationship with the studio heads and actors was based on more than just political opportunism: at each step in his political advancement, Nixon courted Hollywood studio heads and actors for their money and celebrity. It was a relationship built on glamour and power. Nixon, the poor boy from Whittier, took great pleasure in corresponding with the stars, exchanging photographs, and securing invitations to movie premieres and opening nights on Broadway. He welcomed the opportunity to vacation at Walt Disney's retreat, Smoke Tree Ranch, and play golf with Bob Hope, Bing Crosby, and Jackie Gleason. He kept up a steady correspondence with movie stars, studio executives, and Southern California businessmen as they attempted to rebuild the state Republican Party.

George Murphy served as a liaison, as did director-producer Cecil B. DeMille, to Hollywood studios and celebrities with Southern California money interests. Especially important was the Republican Associates, a big donor club to target money to Republican candidates. The Republican Associates, comprising about 2,600 members by 1958, held as its sole purpose raising money for candidates who supported free enterprise, limited constitutional government, and a bipartisan Cold War foreign policy. George C. S. Benson, president of Claremont Men's College, chaired the organization. Robert Finch, a Los Angeles attorney closely associated with Richard Nixon, served as executive secretary and did most of the day-to-day work. Major contributors to the group included hotel mogul A. B. Hilton; mining millionaire Harvey Mudd; Harrison Chandler, brother of Norman, *Los Angeles Times* publisher; founder of American Cement Corporation Garner Beckett; Justin Dart of Dart Industries; Walter Knott of Knott's Berry Farm; and Leonard Firestone, heir to the Firestone Tire Company fortune. In 1956, DeMille joined this powerful group after he was recommended by hotelier A. B. Hilton.[1]

The Republican Associates ranged politically from moderate to far-right Republicans. What tied the Republican Associates together was their commitment to the Republican Party. They were anticommunist, pro–free market, and California business boosters. As important as ideology was in bringing this group together, political calculation often dictated individual support for candidates. Members of the Republican Associates were not unanimous in their choices, especially in Republican primaries, thus suggesting that politics is sometimes actually about politics. Henry Salvatori, for example, refused to support Nixon when he ran for governor in 1962, instead aligning himself with Nixon's rival Joe Shell. Walter Knott was close to, although not a member of, the John Birch Society, a right-wing group formed by New England candy manufacturer Robert Welch in 1958. In 1964, Justin Dart and Leonard Firestone supported Nelson Rockefeller against Republican rival Barry Goldwater in the bitter California presidential primary.

NIXON ENTERS THE POLITICAL STAGE

Nixon's entrance into electoral politics began in 1946, when he challenged incumbent Democratic congressman Jerry Voorhis for the twelfth congressional district in Los Angeles County. Nixon's entry into California politics came at a time when the state was undergoing rapid population change, which increased worries among Republicans that the state was going to be lost forever to the Democrats. Both during and following the Second World War, California experienced an exponential population growth that transformed the Golden State. From 1945 to 1948, three million people moved to the state. By 1950, the state population surpassed 10.5 million people, up from 6.9 million in 1940. Much of this was due to shipbuilding, military bases, and aerospace. Most of the migrants were Democrats, including Jews, southern whites, and African Americans. Most of this incoming population flooded into urban areas, increasing Democratic majorities. As a result, Democrats outnumbered Republicans by more than a million registered voters. Republicans continued to win elections for

---

[1] For the workings of the Republican Associates, see Homer M. Preston to Cecil B. DeMille, July 23, 1956, Box 473; Justin Dart to Cecil B. DeMille, February 17, 1956, DeMille Papers, Box 145.

key offices, largely because of cross-filing and the rootless and individualistic nature of the population, but Republicans realized they were as vulnerable as a snowman in Los Angeles. They held some advantages, however. The California GOP maintained a distinct advantage in support from the state's major newspapers including the *Los Angeles Times*, owned by the Chandler family, the *San Francisco Chronicle* and the *San Diego Tribune*, and Joseph Knowland's *Oakland Tribune*. In addition, most of the 125 dailies were pro-Republican. This helped Republican candidates immeasurably in a state divided by agricultural interests in the central valley; liberal pro-union strength in San Francisco; and anti-union, small business, and Protestant voters in Southern California.[2]

Governor Earl Warren remained the dominant force in Republican politics throughout this period, having easily won election to the governor's mansion in 1942 and then reelection in 1946, winning an extraordinary 90 percent of the vote after gaining both party nominations in the primary under cross-filing. The problem with Warren was that he projected himself as a "nonpartisan" governor, refusing to make partisan appointments, endorse Republican candidates, or intervene in California state politics unless it suited his own interests. His one overt political act was to appoint conservative William Knowland to fill the senate seat left vacant by the death of progressive Hiram Johnson in 1945. Knowland was the son of Joseph Knowland, owner of the *Oakland Tribune*, a key backer throughout Warren's rise in California politics. William Knowland and Warren had helped organize the California Republican Assembly in 1936, to give greater coherence to state GOP politics. (This was when Warren expressed more interest in GOP organizational politics.)

Knowland won election to his senate seat in 1946 in his own right against Will Rogers, Jr., son of the famous vaudeville and movie star Will Rogers. Hollywood Democrats lined up behind Rogers, attracting some of the biggest stars in the movie industry, including Groucho and Harpo Marx, Edward G. Robinson, Gene Kelly, and Ronald Reagan.[3] The list of those in Hollywood who declared that they were voting Republican was no less impressive, including stars such as Bruce Cabot, Hoagy Carmichael, Gary Cooper, Charles Coburn, Irene Dunne, Raymond Massey, Robert Montgomery, Walter Pidgeon, and Randolph Scott.[4] One reason that Knowland won was the standing "tradition" that one senator had to come from Northern California.

---

[2] James Worthen, *The Young Nixon and His Rivals: Four California Republicans Eye the White House, 1946–1958* (Jefferson, NC, 2010), pp. 9–11.

[3] Others endorsing Rogers were Charles Bickford, Eddie Cantor, Melvyn Douglas, Paulette Goddard, Paul Henreid, James Wong Howe, Burgess Meredith, Orson Welles, Cornel Wilde, Jane Wyman, and Kennan Wynn. "Will Rogers for U.S. Senate," in Cecil B. DeMille Papers, Box 123.

[4] Others on the list of those declaring themselves Republican were Hollywood stalwarts such as George Murphy, Adolphe Menjou, Ray Milland, Ozzie Nelson, Dick Powell, Ginger Rogers, Ann Sothern, Barbara Stanwyck, and Robert Taylor. "We've Had Enough, We'll Vote Republican" (1946), Cecil B. DeMille Papers, Box 112.

Warren's low standing among conservatives within his party was encouraged by his lieutenant governor, Goodwin Knight, who had won election to this office in 1946 by 330,000 votes. Warren despised the outgoing and often theatrical "Goodie" Knight as a lightweight. Knight, in turn, let it be known that he had no respect for Warren. Knight waited impatiently for Warren to step down as governor so he could take his seat. Warren, for his part, ignored the growing right within the state GOP because he believed that he did not need conservative Republicans to win election. In the 1940s, California had many liberal Republicans dating back to Hiram Johnson and the Progressive period – perhaps more liberals than the Democrats, with their conservative white, Okie, and Irish base. In San Francisco, Jews were liberal Republicans who read the *San Francisco Chronicle*, whereas Irish Catholics were conservative Democrats who read Hearst's *San Francisco Examiner*. Warren reached to his left, perhaps out of principle, but clearly also out of calculation, arguing for universal health insurance and backing off a strong stance on domestic communism.

Warren's selection as Dewey's running mate in 1948 tempered, for a brief moment, criticisms of Warren's indifference to fellow Republicans, but there remained strong undercurrents of resentment toward the governor, especially among conservatives.[5] Telling in this regard was the gradual loss of enthusiasm for Warren by the *Los Angeles Times*' powerful political editor Kyle Palmer and its publisher Norman Chandler. California Republican politics remained factionalized – as did Democratic politics in the state – with the cross-filing system continuing to play havoc in trying to build strong partisan support within both parties. The Cold War and anticommunism interjected themselves into state and national politics, reshaping the contours of the political landscape. This meant that Republicans no longer needed to rail against Roosevelt or the New Deal; instead, they went on the attack, labeling their Democratic opponents as "soft on communism," weak on national defense (in which California was heavily invested), and not representative of state voters or state interests. Although new to politics, Nixon astutely understood Democratic vulnerabilities on these issues and effectively seized on them in his rapid political ascent.

Voorhis personified the Democratic left wing. As a son of a wealthy automobile executive, Voorhis was educated at Hotchkiss and Yale before moving to California in 1927 to found a boys' academy. He became a local activist, organizing farming cooperatives and supporting agricultural worker strikes. He was a declared socialist, but, in 1934, when he ran for the California State Assembly, he changed his registration to Democrat. He endorsed Upton Sinclair for governor that same year. In 1936, he won election to Congress from a conservative working-class district east of Los Angeles, where he established one of the most liberal voting records in his five terms in office. He was an easy target for Republicans in 1946, a year in which the GOP would take control of Congress for the first time in more than two decades. Nixon's challenge drew

---

[5] Kevin Starr, *Embattled Dreams: California in War and Peace, 1940–1950* (New York, 2002).

mostly local support from small business in Southern California, but the chance to defeat Voorhis drew some Hollywood support from regular Republican contributors such as Louis B. Mayer and Cecil B. DeMille. Voorhis's support for Sinclair's End Poverty in California socialist scheme was not easily forgotten, but the driving force for Hollywood Republicans, shared by party loyalists in general, was Voorhis's left-wing record. Nixon won, even though the working-class district was Democratic. He showed he could get Democratic votes.

Hollywood Republicans swung fully behind Nixon in 1948, when he sought reelection to Congress against a weak Democratic challenger.[6] Under cross-filing, Nixon won both party nominations. He had firmly established himself as an anticommunist and a man in Washington to promote Southern California business interests. Nixon trod a fine line on his anticommunist stance, and Nixon's supporters understood that he had drawn the unforgiving animus of the left for his role in the Alger Hiss case. Writing shortly after Nixon's election as vice president in 1952, George Murphy wrote that he was disturbed that Nixon had become the "chief target of our misguided Fifth Amendment boys" and wanted to "come up with a constructive program of counter propaganda to really set them back on their heels once and for all."[7] Nixon publicly supported the studio heads in ousting communists from the industry, and he spoke on the U.S. Senate floor in support of Howard Hughes, who, as head of RKO Pictures, had brought legal action against screenwriter Paul Jarrico who had refused to answer questions before HUAC. Nixon, who had received campaign funds from Hughes, declared that Hughes deserved the "approval of every man and woman who believes that forces of subversion must be wiped out."[8]

At the same time, Nixon kept a safe distance from extreme anticommunists such as Myron Fagan, head of the Cinema Educational Guild, which proclaimed itself as the leading antisubversion crusade in Hollywood. In response to a letter by Fagan in which he insisted that Nixon declare himself unambiguously against "world federalism," Nixon warned his secretary Rose Mary Woods in a handwritten note that Fagan was "a Fascist and will pop up again 6 years from now in a campaign."[9] Fagan continued to pop up again in Hollywood, but eventually migrated to the South, where he emerged as an anti-Semitic white nationalist. While dealing with the extreme right, Nixon also sought to distance himself, especially as vice president, from anticommunist senator Joseph McCarthy

[6] There is an extensive literature on Richard Nixon, but the best book on Nixon's early political career is Irwin F. Gellman, *The Contender: Richard Nixon The Congressional Years, 1946–1952* (New York, 1999).

[7] George Murphy to Richard Nixon, November 20, 1952, George Murphy folder, Richard M. Nixon Pre-Presidential Papers, Series 320, Box 540 (hereafter cited as Nixon Papers).

[8] Richard M. Nixon, "Extension of Remarks in the Senate of the United States," April 3, 1952; Press Release, March 17, 1952 and Press Release, March 27, 1952; and "Paul Jarrico Is Sued by RKO," *The Hollywood Reporter*, Howard Hughes folder, Nixon Papers, Series 320, Box 360.

[9] Myron C. Fagan to Richard M. Nixon, June 7, 1951, Myron Fagan folder, Nixon Papers, Series 320, Box 248.

(R-Wisconsin). Nixon had received advice in late 1954 from Kyle Palmer, the *Los Angeles Times* chief political correspondent and Republican Party insider, that McCarthy and his investigation into alleged subversion in the U.S. Army was "doing no good for the party or the country."[10] Nixon played a key behind-the-scenes role in the Eisenhower administration in isolating McCarthy in the U.S. Senate, eventually leading to what was in effect his censure in that body in 1954. Nixon kept his role secret from McCarthy's avid supporters in Hollywood – people such as Hedda Hopper and Louis B. Mayer.

Nixon kept in close contact with what was happening in Hollywood and in Southern California politics through George Murphy, who emerged as a critical liaison in the growing alliance among studio heads, Southern California business interests, and Hollywood celebrities. Now and then, Murphy called upon Nixon to throw his support behind various business developments in California, such as the expansion of the Los Angeles Airport and defense contracts. As a leading force in the Hollywood Republican Committee, Murphy arranged for motion picture celebrities sympathetic to the Republican Party to be sent out to local campaigns to rally voters and donors. While providing a constant stream of political intelligence to Nixon, Murphy also tapped Nixon as a fundraiser at events that brought together "the motion picture crowd" with aircraft and oil interests, newspapers, and movers and shakers within the Republican Party.[11]

Southern California Republicans saw in Nixon their long-sought entry into the White House, last seen in the days of Hoover. The midterm elections that brought Nixon to Congress in 1946 fueled hopes that Republicans could win the White House in 1948. In what many Republicans took as a referendum on the New Deal, Republicans won control of Congress for the first time since 1932. In the House, Republicans won fifty-five seats and gained twelve seats in the U.S. Senate. Incumbent president Harry Truman looked vulnerable. History favored this view: the White House had changed hands after the opposing party won Congress in the midterm elections in 1896, 1912, 1920, and 1932. Given that Dewey had seriously challenged Roosevelt in 1944, he expected the White House was his in 1948. Dewey offered Earl Warren the second slot on the ticket. Truman looked like he was out: with Henry Wallace running as a third-party candidate on the Progressive Party ticket, attacking Truman from the left on his anti-Soviet foreign policy and with Strom Thurmond leading the Dixiecrats in the South, it appeared to be a Republican year.

Hollywood mobilized energetically. When a rally was held for Dewey in the Hollywood Bowl, eighteen stars appeared on stage to endorse Dewey. Another twenty-nine stars participated in the Band Wagon Radio Show, a Republican-

---

[10] Kyle Palmer to Richard Nixon, May 18, 1954, and Palmer to Nixon, November 9, 1954, Palmer folder, Nixon Papers, Series 320, Box 577.

[11] For example, see George Murphy to Richard Nixon, November 5, 1951, Murphy folder, Nixon Papers, Series 320, Box 540.

sponsored program broadcast across the state.[12] Even with this star power, Dewey presented a lackluster campaign. Believing that he was headed toward easy victory over Truman, he decided to play it safe by not talking about controversial issues such as domestic communism. Dewey compounded the problem by naming his cabinet before the election, which enraged those Republicans who were left out and struck many voters as arrogant, as if the election were already over. Dewey sought to appear nonpartisan, and Warren's nonpolitical image contributed to this projection. After a bruising campaign against Roosevelt in 1944, Dewey projected a milquetoast image. The GOP right wing screamed for him to raise the communist issue. He refused. They pleaded with him to defend the Eightieth Congress, which had passed the Taft-Hartley Act that had so aroused organized labor. He refused. They implored him to do something other than appearing bland; he refused. The result was that Truman surprised pundits, the press, his party, and the Republicans by beating Dewey by nearly 4 percentage points in the general election. In California, the vote was even closer, with Truman edging Dewey by less than 18,000 votes. As for Henry Wallace, his loss was humiliating. Although Truman might have done better in California if it had not been for Henry Wallace's Progressive Party, which won 4.73 percent of the popular vote, Wallace's vote in California was much higher than what he received nationally, 2.37 percent.

Following the 1948 presidential race, Warren faced growing opposition from the GOP right over his support for a compulsory national health care system – part of Truman's platform – and his handling of an anticommunist loyalty oath for state employees. After the failure of the Dewey-Warren ticket, dissident conservatives formed a new organization, "Partisan Republicans," denouncing Warren as "wishy-washy and namby-pamby." Warren entered the 1950 election for governor under the cloud of a divided party. In the general election for the governorship in 1950, he shored up his Republican base by the threat that his opponent, James Roosevelt, a left-wing liberal and son of the late president, might be elected. Warren's opposition to pro-labor legislation and his defense of the state crime commission further bolstered his support among Republicans, enabling him to defeat Jimmy Roosevelt by more than a million votes.[13] Complaints against Warren continued to grow. Cecil B. DeMille's lawyer Neil S. McCarthy expressed this hostility toward Warren when he wrote to Senator Barry Goldwater (R-Arizona) following the 1952 presidential election, opposing Warren's possible appointment to the Supreme Court because he refused to support Republican candidates for office in California, including Nixon's

---

[12] "What Does the Hollywood Republican Committee Do?," April 21, 1950, Cecil B. DeMille Papers, Box 424.

[13] Kurt Schuparra, *Triumph of the Right: The Rise of the California Conservative Movement, 1945–1966* (Armonk, NY, 1998), pp. 13–15. The loyalty oath issue within the California university system is summarized by Kevin Starr, *Embattled Dreams: California in War and Peace, 1940–1950* (New York, 2002), pp. 325–329.

1950 campaign for U.S. Senate against Helen Gahagan Douglas. In McCarthy's words, Warren displayed consistent "selfishness and an attitude of being for himself without regard to party."[14] As George Murphy noted more bluntly, by 1952 most California Republican insiders were "sick of Governor Warren's bipartisan posture and were almost in open revolt against his leadership at that time."[15]

HOLLYWOOD APPLAUDS NIXON ON STAGE

The HUAC hearings and the outing of Alger Hiss as a Soviet spy catapulted Nixon onto the national stage. In the 1948 presidential election, Nixon had campaigned heavily for the Dewey-Warren ticket throughout the country, and in 1950, Nixon set out to defeat Helen Gahagan Douglas for the U.S. Senate seat in California. Douglas, who had been elected to Congress in 1944 to represent the Fourteenth District, brought to the campaign a divided Democratic Party and a more liberal voting record than most. A Hollywood film actress who was married to actor Melvyn Douglas before entering Congress, Douglas had established a reputation for activist left-wing politics. She earned appointment to various federal agencies and party organizations during the Roosevelt and Truman administrations, including the national advisory committee of the Work Progress Administration and the Democratic National Committee. Much against the advice of senior party members, Douglas decided to challenge incumbent Sheridan Downey for the nomination. Because she and Nixon were in Congress, both knew of Downey's poor health before any potential challengers in California were aware of the fact. Downey presented himself as a centrist and had strong ties with California oil interests. Early in the primary, Downey, claiming ill health, dropped out. He threw his support to *Los Angeles Daily News* publisher Manchester Boddy, a conservative Democrat who questioned Douglas's votes against HUAC funding and aid to Greece in confronting a communist takeover. He labeled Douglas "the pink lady," a theme picked up by the Nixon campaign in the general election after Douglas won the Democratic primary. In the general election, Boddy endorsed the Republican nominee, Nixon.[16]

Douglas entered the general election with clear disadvantages. Not only had she split the Democratic Party, but many within her own party saw her as too left-wing to win. Her one advantage remained that, of the total 4.5 million registered voters, most were Democrats, 58.4 percent to 37.1 percent Republican.[17] Her campaign was so disorganized that she failed to take any

---

[14] Neil S. McCarthy to Barry Goldwater, March 20, 1953, Cecil B. DeMille Papers, Box 1134.
[15] George Murphy to Waller Taylor, II, Nixon Papers, Series 320, Box 540.
[16] Gellman, *The Contender*, pp. 296–97; Worthen, *The Young Nixon and His Rivals*, p. 69.
[17] This discussion of the 1950 Douglas-Nixon race draws heavily on Gellman, *The Contender*, pp. 296–343.

advantage of this strength. She might have noted that although Democrats had a 900,000-plus plurality over Republicans in registration, more voters had gone with Nixon in the primaries by close to 170,000 votes. She also found herself handicapped by her poor fundraising abilities; this gave the advantage to Nixon, who outpaced her in fundraising, even getting a contribution from his friend Joseph Kennedy, John F. Kennedy's father, who saw Douglas as a "Communist."[18] Adding to her problems was her tendency to drone on and ramble in her speeches. Her decision to present herself as a New Deal and Fair Deal liberal seemed out of touch with an electorate shifting to the right, but even more perplexing was her strategy of trying to portray Nixon as soft on communism and an ally of New York ultra-liberal Vito Marcantonio, exactly the strategy her primary rival Manchester Boddy had used against her and a theme continued by Nixon under Murray M. Chotiner's guidance. As Chotiner later recalled, "she was defeated the minute she tried to do it, because she could not sell the people of California that she would be a better fighter against communism than Dick Nixon. She made the fatal mistake of attacking our strength instead of sticking to attacking our weakness."[19]

The outbreak of the Korean War in late June 1950 encouraged Nixon and Chotiner to hammer Douglas, which reinforced Nixon's reputation within the left as a "red-baiter." The Nixon campaign's use of a pink sheet attacking Douglas as "soft on Communism" was widely distributed, especially when it became one of the most requested pieces of literature in the campaign. Although the theme of the pink lady was carefully crafted, the selection of pink-toned paper was simply a matter of circumstance. In a confidential memo written to Nixon in 1960, Chotiner recalled that the campaign wanted to make up literature on Douglas's voting record on national security issues that paralleled Marcantonio's. At the printer, Chotiner remembered, the campaign asked for something different from just black and white, so the printer showed them "blue and green, brown, and black, and in the stock we found pieces of paper that had a pinkish tinge to it, and for some reason or other it just seemed to appeal to us for the movement and we printed this record on pink paper."[20] Fortune as much as design has a lot to do with political campaigns – but whether calculated or not, Nixon and Chotiner went after Douglas as soft on communism.

Both Douglas and Nixon drew support from Hollywood, but Douglas needed to proceed cautiously in tapping this source. She was under attack for being ultra-left and being a Hollywood actress out of touch with California voters. For this reason, she refused Ronald Reagan's offer to campaign for her because she believed Reagan had a reputation (at this time in his career) for being too far to the left. When her husband, actor Melvyn Douglas, came under attack for his

[18] Gellman, *The Contender*, pp. 306–307.
[19] Murray Chotiner, "Fundamentals of Campaign Organization," January 20, 1960, Nixon Papers, Series 320, Box 148.
[20] Ibid.

Jewish heritage, she called upon Humphrey Bogart to introduce her husband to a radio audience. Bogart had not intended to give a speech, but once at the mike he declared, "I am angry because of the tactics that have been used by her opponent and those who support him."[21]

Nixon had carefully cultivated Hollywood Republicans since his first days on HUAC. During the hearings, Nixon's delicately balanced position in the Hollywood HUAC hearings had won him the favor of hardliners such as Adolphe Menjou and Hedda Hopper, while his defense of the industry as not being naïve apologists for the Soviet Union earned him the respect of studio heads. Republican fears of Douglas stepping into the U.S. Senate seat ensured studio support. Typical of this was Louis B. Mayer, who wrote to a friend, "I have not been close to Nixon. I did what I could so that he could defeat Miss Gahagan [Douglas]."[22] More active among the studio heads was producer Cecil B. DeMille, who understood, as one associate told him, that the election was more than "merely trying to beat another candidate for Senate with a deep-dyed Red record. This has important long term implications." DeMille worked closely with corporate heads through his DeMille Foundation to rally support for Nixon to defeat what they saw as a Big Labor takeover of the Democratic Party. DeMille concluded that Nixon was needed in the Senate to help maintain support for the Taft-Hartley Act. At the same time, DeMille actively supported Congressman John Wood's losing race for the Senate in Georgia and Robert Taft's successful reelection bid for the Senate in Ohio.[23]

Republican stars went to the airways to support Nixon. Hedda Hopper served as the host for a statewide broadcast of Women for Nixon. Highlighting the show were Irene Dunne and the popular African-American actress Miss Louise Beavers.[24] In another radio address, actor-producer Dick Powell narrated excerpts from Ralph de Toledano's pro-Nixon *Seeds of Treason: The True Story of the Chambers-Hiss Tragedy*.[25] At a massive rally held for Nixon at the American Legion Stadium on the eve of the election, Republican stars turned out for the candidate. Powell, a confirmed Republican, served as master of ceremonies. Co-chaired by actress Irene Dunne and director Harold Lloyd, the program included Powell's wife June Allyson, cowboy star Randolph Scott, dancer-actress Jane Powell, and the ever-present Hedda Hopper. Behind the scenes, George Murphy's Hollywood Republican Committee worked to ensure the success of the rally.[26]

---

[21] Quoted in Gellman, *The Contender*, p. 332.

[22] Louis B. Mayer to Col. Louis Johnson, August 3, 1956, Nixon Papers, Series 320, Box 485.

[23] Quotation is found in William Ingles to Cecil DeMille, September 25, 1950; fundraising for other Republican candidates is found in Meeting March 1, 1950 (Chicago); and Donald Hayne to William Ingles, October 6, 1950, in Cecil B. DeMille Papers, Box 1164, folder 9.

[24] Radio Script (n.d. 1950), Hedda Hopper Papers, Nixon File.

[25] Gellman, *The Contender*, pp. 332–333.

[26] George Murphy to Hedda Hopper, May 19, 1950, Hopper Papers, George Murphy File.

Murphy's committee did not have the big stars associated with the Hollywood Left. Ginger Rogers was the best-known star and an officer for the Committee. Robert Montgomery, who served as the Committee's first vice president, was in his waning years as an actor, as was Adolphe Menjou. Morris Ryskind, another officer, was no longer writing movie scripts. Many Committee members worked behind the scenes as producers, directors, and scriptwriters – and quite a few of these people came from a Hollywood of a different era. For example, Lewis Allen Weiss had made his money producing action dramas such as the Columbia Pictures serial *Jungle Menace*. Weiss was now working in television, a sign of where the industry was headed. The most successful scriptwriter on the committee was Charles Brackett, III, who at the time was serving as president of the Academy of Motion Picture Arts and Sciences. Working with Billy Wilder, Brackett had scripted *The Lost Weekend* (1945), starring Ray Milland (a Republican), and *Sunset Boulevard* (1950), starring William Holden (another Republican). Walt Disney, who served as second vice president of the Committee, was a major donor.

During the 1950 election, the Hollywood Republican Committee sent stars across the state. Actors including Adolphe Menjou, George Murphy, Ginger Rogers, Irene Dunne, Dick Powell, and an array of others were sent to Fresno, La Jolla, San Diego, Redondo Beach, San Luis Obispo, Long Beach, San Bernardino, and Pomona to attend rallies and events for Earl Warren in his race for governor, Goodie Knight running for lieutenant governor, and Richard Nixon.[27] For all this activity, many Republican actors worried about the repercussions within an industry still dominated by liberals. As one Cecil B. DeMille associate observed in 1950, they had "too many chicken-hearted" Republican friends. "There are just too many Republicans, both men and women, who are too busy to really work in politics. They are making money and are going to just continue to make money and let the situation drift. Another four years of this and we will all be in the ash can."[28]

Especially active in the Nixon campaign was Leo Carrillo, a registered Democrat who spoke before Spanish-speaking voters. By 1950, Carrillo's film career had spanned nearly thirty years. He had campaigned for Merriam in 1934 and continuously for Earl Warren. Carrillo brought to his campaigning his movie star status and a projection of Old California that appealed to Mexican-American voters. His great-grandfather, Carlos Antonio Carrillo, was the first provisional governor of California in 1837, and his grandmother was Doña Josefa Bandini, the daughter of Don Juan Bandini, the owner of a vast ranch that became the city of Riverside. Carrillo's father was the first mayor of Santa Monica. Before Leo Carrillo entered the motion picture industry, he had earned a university degree, worked with a pick and shovel for the Southern Pacific

[27] Hollywood Republican Entertainment Committee Mailing, April 21, 1950, Cecil B. DeMille Papers, Box 424.
[28] W. M. Jeffers to Cecil B. DeMille, April 24, 1954, Cecil B. DeMille Papers, Box 1201.

Railroad, and served as a cartoonist for the *San Francisco Examiner*, before turning to the stage in San Francisco and New York. In Hollywood, he often portrayed stereotypical Mexican roles in movies such as *The Gay Desperado* (1938). Television revived Carrillo's career when, at the age of seventy, he began playing the sidekick in the immensely popular *Cisco Kid* television series. During the campaign, California Republicans used Carrillo in their televised broadcasts, often giving him the opportunity to make short speeches at the conclusion of the broadcasts, which were judged to be highly effective.[29] He was a workhorse for the Republican Party throughout the next decade. In 1957, there was much talk about running Carrillo for the state senate seat against Richard Richards, although Carrillo eventually declined.[30]

The final election results made Nixon a clear winner over Douglas. He beat Douglas by 680,947 votes, winning 59 percent of the popular vote – the largest senatorial victory that year. He swept Northern California, Central California, and Southern California.[31] The race confirmed Nixon's reputation on the left as "Tricky Dick." His overwhelming victory set the stage for his next big performance: vice president of the United States.

NIXON AUDITIONS FOR A STARRING ROLE

For the next ten years, as U.S. senator from California (1950–1953) and vice president (1953–1961), Richard Nixon kept close tabs on California politics while serving business and constituent interests. He used his influence where he could to promote California as an international business center. Especially important to him was the entertainment industry in Southern California. George Murphy worked on his behalf as chairman of the Entertainment Division for the United Republican Finance Committee for Southern California, and further assistance came from studio executives such Harry Warner, Cecil B. DeMille, and Darryl Zanuck, among others. Harry Warner, for example, served as chair of the Entertainment Division for the United Republican Finance Committee of Southern California in 1952, again in 1956, and for a final time when Nixon ran for president in 1960.[32] Nixon kept up a steady stream of correspondence with actors, studio directors, and others associated with the entertainment industry. They were important to the Republican Party as donors, campaigners, and media advisors.[33]

Hollywood Republicans entered the 1952 presidential elections divided on whether to support Robert Taft, the conservative from Ohio, or General Dwight

---

[29] Leo Carrillo to Nixon, December 27, 1950; and Richard Nixon to Leo Carrillo, January 17, 151, Nixon Papers, Series 320, Box 135.

[30] Memorandum, George Murphy Telephone Call, November 26, 1957, Richard Nixon Papers, Series 320, Box 540.

[31] Gellman, *The Contender*, p. 335.

[32] Harry Warner to Richard M. Nixon, June 4, 1959, Richard Nixon Papers, Series 320, Box 798.

[33] George Murphy to Richard M. Nixon, June 4, 1959; Richard Nixon Papers, Series 320, Box 540.

D. Eisenhower. A few hoped that perhaps General Douglas MacArthur, whom Truman fired as head of the United Nation's command in Korea in April 1951, would run for president. This division expressed the perennial dilemma for conservative Republicans of whether to go with a candidate who reflected their highest principles – in this case Taft – or the candidate most likely to win election, that was, Eisenhower. Conservatives understood that any political candidate was flawed. They were not going to nominate Jesus Christ, after all, but at least they might nominate a disciple, and they did not mean to have a Judas who would betray Republican principles. After the lackluster performance of Thomas Dewey in 1948, hardcore conservatives within the GOP, including those in Hollywood, had enough of what they saw as domination by the Eastern wing of the party, which had foisted Wendell Willkie on them in 1940 and Dewey on them twice. Sensing that Truman's low poll numbers meant that 1952 would be a big Republican year, this was the time for serious Republicans to take a stance by nominating Robert Taft to head the GOP ticket. Taft was nicknamed "Mr. Republican" for a reason.

George Creel, a former Progressive Democrat who had turned to the right, conveyed this anger toward the Eastern Establishment's attempt to force Eisenhower on the party. In a speech given at the San Francisco Bohemian Club and sent to Taft supporters throughout the state, Creel declared that the Eastern Republican Establishment had ignored the insurgent right-wing protest against the "statism" of the New Deal and Fair Deal while trying to outbid Democrats for pressure groups. Although Creel admitted that Senator Taft "has his lacks, but not in honor, honesty, courage and forthright Americanism," Eisenhower, he declared, represents the Lodges, Wayne Morse, the Whitneys, Winthrop Aldrich, and "other international bankers." He concluded that Eisenhower was the same old "pseudo Republican" as was Dewey. Since Dewey was Ike's major backer, conservatives saw the hand of the Eastern Republican Establishment at work.[34]

Producer Cecil B. DeMille stood out as one of Taft's strongest supporters in Hollywood. He was joined by John Ford, Hedda Hopper, Louis B. Mayer, and Morris Ryskind. DeMille's relationship with Taft went back to 1947, when DeMille threw his foundation's support behind the Taft-Hartley bill, but DeMille's role in the California Republican Party went beyond his support of Taft. He played a key role in bringing big Republican donors together with Hollywood studio heads and celebrities to revitalize the postwar Republican Party.

Son of parents who were professional playwrights and fundamentalist Christians, DeMille came to Hollywood in 1913 at the age of 38 to make his

---

[34] George Creel, "The Bohemian Club," June 27, 1952, sent to Cecil B. DeMille, DeMille Papers, Box 440, Creel's papers are located at the Library of Congress.

first feature-length movie.[35] His gamble in the early film industry paid off. His first movie, *The Squaw Man* (1914), was a hit and was followed by a succession of popular films including *The Ten Commandments* (1923), *Sign of the Cross* (1932), and *Samson and Delilah* (1949). By the 1930s, he had become an active Republican. The people DeMille encountered were anti–New Dealers intent in turning the GOP away from what they called "me-too" Republicanism that accepted big government, high taxes, and corporate regulation.

In 1945, DeMille undertook his most ambitious political involvement – establishing right-to-work labor laws on the national and state levels. He established the DeMille Foundation for Political Freedom, as it was initially called, to push for right-to-work legislation. Angered by having to pay a $1 political assessment to the American Federation of Radio Artists of which he was a member, DeMille refused to pay and was suspended by the union. Without his union card, DeMille could no longer host his popular radio program, "The Lux Radio Theater", which had been broadcast on CBS since 1936. The suspension cost DeMille $100,000 a year in income. He saw it as a matter of principle that as a citizen he should not have to pay for a political campaign, in this case an anti-right-to-work referendum that he opposed.[36] DeMille believed a small clique of communists within the leadership of the Federation of Radio Artists had targeted him because of his anti-Soviet positions. He was informed that party officials had ordered that DeMille be brought down.[37]

Such information reinforced DeMille's anticommunist views. In 1934, DeMille had traveled to the Soviet Union with his family, and the authoritarian nature of the system shocked him. His opposition to communism and big labor involvement in politics became intertwined, and he became an active member in the Motion Picture Alliance following the 1947 HUAC hearings.[38] Nobody doubted his anticommunism, but, to his credit, he hired Hollywood blacklisted actor Edward G. Robinson and composer Elmer Bernstein for the box office record–breaking *The Ten Commandments* (1956). Robinson observed that there was no one more opposed to communism in Hollywood than DeMille, but no man with a greater sense of decency and justice. "Cecil B. DeMille," a grateful Robinson noted, "restored my self-respect."[39]

In restoring Robinson's acting career, DeMille revealed a side that contrasted with other Hollywood anticommunists. DeMille was by no means "soft on

---

[35] This biographical sketch is derived from an extensive reading in the DeMille archives, as well as from Scott Eyman, *Empire of Dreams: The Epic Life of Cecil B. DeMille* (New York, 2010), which primarily focuses on DeMille's film career.

[36] Background for DeMille's suspension is contained in Box 1134 in his papers. Early backers of the DeMille Political Freedom Foundation are found in Gladys Rosson to Donald Hayne, January 30, 1946, Box 123.

[37] "Interview with Arthur (unknown)," 1957, DeMille Papers, Box 29.

[38] For some insight into DeMille's role in the MPA, see Cecil B. DeMille to Robert Arthur, March 27, 1952, and Notes for Motion Picture Alliance, June 3, 1953, DeMille Papers, Box 1146.

[39] Edward G. Robinson, *All My Yesterdays: An Autobiography* (New York, 1975).

communism"; he joined with studio mogul Louis B. Mayer and Hedda Hopper in supporting the reelection of Senator Joseph McCarthy in 1952. If DeMille could forgive, at least on occasion, others could not. Lou Costello of the comedy team, Abbott and Costello, was a fervid supporter of McCarthy who fired his longtime gag writer, John Grant, when he refused to sign an anticommunist loyalty oath. He volunteered to serve as master of ceremonies for testimonials on behalf of McCarthy, and when asked by journalists if he worried about losing fans because of his anticommunist views, Costello replied, "Since when is it more important to have good box office than to be a good American?"[40]

Through right-to-work legislation, DeMille hoped to break the political power of Big Labor and left-wing control of unions by allowing an employee of a unionized company not to join a representative union. DeMille brought to the campaign the fervor and organizational skills found in his movie productions, and he used his extensive contacts in corporate business to fund his foundation and its crusade for right-to-work legislation. Automobile and steel interests in the Midwest became the foundation's major contributors.[41] Backed by these corporate interests, as well as by thousands of small donations from across the country, the DeMille Foundation undertook a massive campaign to enact right-to-work legislation. Thousands of pamphlets and editorials were written and circulated. Two major documentary films were produced to show to average Americans and local businessmen. He worked closely with Congressman Fred Hartley (R-New Jersey) in supporting what became the Taft-Hartley Act in 1947. The Taft-Hartley Act prohibited jurisdictional strikes, solidarity or political strikes, and monetary donations by unions to federal political campaigns. Passed over President Truman's veto by a coalition of Republicans and conservative Southern Democrats, the act also required union officers to sign non-communist affidavits, and it allowed states to pass right-to-work acts.

Working closely with Washington lobbyist William Ingles, DeMille kept in close contact with key members of Congress, including Robert Taft, Joseph Ball (R-Minnesota), and Barry Goldwater (R-Arizona) in the Senate and Fred Hartley in the House. (Hartley later asked DeMille for a job working on right-to-work legislation).[42] Over the course of the next decade, the DeMille Foundation conducted multiple campaigns that passed right-to-work laws in twelve states.

[40] Quoted in Bob Thomas, *Bud and Lou: The Abbott & Costello Story* (Philadelphia, 1977), p. 177.

[41] Within the DeMille Papers there are extensive correspondence and financial records showing support given to the foundation by Midwest business interests. See DeMille to Victor Rossetti, Walter Geist, et al. (telegram), August 30, 1948; Walter Geist to Cecil B. DeMille, January 17, 1949, DeMille Papers, Box 140; Cecil B. DeMille to William W. Jeffers, December 27, 1949, Box 1202.

[42] DeMille's lobbying efforts are found in William Ingles to Cecil B. DeMille, November 8, 1949; Notes on Telephone Conversation with William Ingles, July 25, 1949; Cecil B. DeMille to William Ingles, February 16, 1950; William Ingles to DeMille, June 12, 1950, Cecil B. DeMille Papers, Box 1164.

In 1950, DeMille played a major role in raising money for Taft's reelection bid in Ohio. As 1952 approached, DeMille declared for Taft as the best candidate to beat the Democratic Party labor bosses, and he carried his support for Taft into the 1952 election. During the primaries, he went on the campaign trail for Taft, speaking on his behalf in Chicago, in Ames and Des Moines, Iowa, and in New York.[43] As the primary fight heated up between Eisenhower and Taft, DeMille came out swinging, telling the Los Angeles Chamber of Commerce that a group of Republicans seeking to control the party in Texas openly solicited Democrats to register Republican, just long enough to take part in the Republican caucuses. Furthermore, a whispering campaign was being conducted saying that Taft could not be elected, even though he won more votes in Ohio than his very popular opponent and revived a beaten and broken down national party to the threshold of victory. To say that Taft could not be elected to the White House was nothing more than "psychological germ warfare."[44] DeMille wrote Nixon prior to the Republican Chicago Convention: "From my conversations with other voters and my analysis of all the factors involved, I believe that ROBERT TAFT PLUS GENERAL MACARTHUR is the strongest candidate the Republicans could nominate for President" [emphasis in original].[45]

NIXON, CALIFORNIA, AND 1952

DeMille was not alone in his commitment to Taft. Director John Ford also enlisted in the Taft campaign. As a Pacific war veteran, Ford entertained hopes of a Taft-MacArthur ticket. When Eisenhower won the nomination, Ford was left stunned. He wrote Taft that like "a million other Americans, I am naturally bewildered and hurt by the outcome of the Republican Convention in Chicago."[46] Adolphe Menjou, who campaigned for Taft in Ohio in his reelection bid for the U.S. Senate in 1950, once again went on the campaign trail for him.[47] Hedda Hopper became equally enthusiastic about Taft, after initially preferring General Douglas MacArthur. Ida Koverman, Louis B. Mayer's key political advisor, persuaded Hopper to shift her "very anti-Eisenhower" sentiment toward Taft. She arranged for Hopper to meet with former President Herbert Hoover, a Taft supporter, to convince her of the strengths of his candidate.[48] By May 1952, Hopper had become a Taft supporter, and she took to the airwaves in her radio program to announce her support for Robert

[43] Cecil B. DeMille to Albert C. Wedemeyer, May 26, 1952, DeMille Papers, Box 440.

[44] Cecil B. DeMille, "Talk Before the Wilshire Chamber of Commerce," June 25, 1952, DeMille Papers, Box 1174.

[45] Cecil B. DeMille to Richard Nixon, June 23, 1952, DeMille Papers, Box 1170.

[46] John Ford to Robert Taft, July 22, 1952, John Ford Papers, Box 2, May–July 1952.

[47] Adolphe Menjou to Westbrook Pegler, October 27, 1951, Westbrook Pegler Papers, Communist Infiltration Files.

[48] Ida Koverman to Miss Miller, April 18, 1952, Herbert Hoover Post-Presidential Papers, Box 92.

Taft, assuring her audience that General MacArthur personally told her that if Taft won the nomination, he wanted to be on the ticket. Hopper worked with Morrie Ryskind and silent movie star Mary Pickford, who in the 1920s was one of Hollywood's most popular actors, to organize Creative Artists for Taft. They were joined by actress Constance Bennett, whose popularity had soared playing opposite Cary Grant in the comedy film series *Topper* (1937–39).[49] Bennett, who had invested wisely, brought glamour and money to the committee.

Hopper kept in close contact with leading Republicans throughout California. She remained in touch with Richard Nixon, who Hopper assumed was naturally a Taft supporter.[50] That Hopper thought Nixon was a Taft supporter reveals just how close to the vest Nixon played his cards in 1952 by not revealing to her he was supporting Eisenhower. Writing Hopper shortly before the convention, he advised her that he believed there was considerable justification for the strategy of California delegates pledged to support Warren as their favorite son to avoid announcing their second choice until they were at the convention. Nixon told Hopper that he was opposed to lobbying delegates before the convention, although both Taft and Eisenhower were pressuring delegates to declare their preferences. Later, while on a train headed to the convention, Nixon was accused of lobbying Warren delegates to switch their votes to Eisenhower. Further rumors circulated that a deal was made with Warren to withdraw his nomination in exchange for securing a later appointment to the Supreme Court.[51] Political rumor is a constant that often finds its way carelessly into history, but there is little doubt that, after the convention, Warren despised Nixon. Warren had done everything he could to ensure a deadlock between Eisenhower and Taft, so he could emerge as a compromise candidate. Prior to the convention, Nixon sent out a letter asking California delegates who their second and third choice for president might be if Warren failed on the first ballot. When Warren learned of the telegram, he flew into a fury and insisted that Nixon withdraw the letter immediately, threatening to destroy Nixon politically.[52]

Dwight D. Eisenhower drew less support from Hollywood conservatives than did Taft, at least initially, but he was not without his early supporters. Actors Robert Montgomery and Irene Dunne endorsed him early. Montgomery, widely known to the general public, campaigned more for Eisenhower that did any other actor.[53] When Eisenhower won the nomination and selected Nixon as his running mate, most Hollywood Republicans dropped their doubts about Eisenhower and swung their support behind him.

[49] James P. Selvage to George Creel, May 22, 1952, in Hedda Hopper Papers, Robert Taft file.

[50] Hedda Hopper to Richard Nixon, June 6, 1952; Richard Nixon to Hedda Hopper, May 29, 1952; Hedda Hopper to Richard Nixon, June 13, 1951, Richard Nixon Papers, Box 354.

[51] This alleged deal and Nixon's lobbying of Warren supporters on the train headed to Chicago is challenged by Irwin Gellman, *The Age of Eisenhower* (in a forthcoming book on Eisenhower and Nixon, Yale University Press).

[52] George Murphy to Waller Taylor, II, May 11, 1962, Nixon Papers, Series 320, Box 540.

[53] Craig Allen, *Eisenhower and the Mass Media* (Chapel Hill, NC, 1993), pp. 27–35.

Eisenhower's opponent, Adlai Stevenson, attracted more support in Hollywood, but California Republicans understood the importance of having a native son as vice president. Hollywood Republicans, for their part, offered time and money to the Eisenhower campaign, as well as what they knew best – media advice. Robert Montgomery stands out in this regard, earning the respect of the Eisenhower campaign for the time and effort he put into advising Eisenhower how to present himself to the media and the general public. For his effort, after the election, Montgomery received an appointment to the Eisenhower White House as a media advisor. There, he continued to coach Eisenhower on timing, on using his ingratiating smile, and on camera position, the little things that made televised appearances by the president successful. For example, in Eisenhower's State of Union address in 1954, Montgomery raised the lectern to ensure that cameras focused on the president's face and not the top of his bald head. Eisenhower welcomed Montgomery's advice and allowed him to set up the first White House camera room.

Montgomery was only part of a larger Hollywood Right effort to support the Eisenhower-Nixon ticket. Working closely with the campaign, George Murphy organized the Hollywood Republican Club to mobilize speaking events and campaign rallies. Paralleling Murphy's efforts, studio heads Jack Warner, Darryl Zanuck, and Sam Goldwyn established the Entertainment Industry Joint Committee for Eisenhower-Nixon. Earlier, these powerful studio heads had come out for Eisenhower in the primary, so, on having gained the nomination for their man, they went all out in the general campaign. Although Murphy's Republican Club and the Entertainment Committee remained separate organizations, they kept adjacent offices and worked closely together.[54] Republican studio heads were especially irate about what they saw as Democratic Party attacks on the film industry during the tough economic times caused by global competition and a declining movie audience who preferred staying at home to watch television. Their efforts to win California for the Eisenhower-Nixon ticket focused primarily on their home base of Southern California. Zanuck helped organize a Nixon "whistle-stop" tour across the state, one joined by Hollywood celebrities. Murphy and the Entertainment Committee planted articles in key newspapers and developed radio and television spots for the campaign. In addition, Warner offered advice to the New York Eisenhower campaign on developing television commercials.

Zanuck assisted the Eisenhower campaign with organizing media and campaign events. In late July, in the midst of the general campaign, Zanuck became extremely upset when the campaign failed to build attendance for a speech Eisenhower gave at the Los Angeles Coliseum. Local newspapers had a field

[54] This discussion of Hollywood's involvement in the Eisenhower-Nixon campaign relies much on Kathryn Cramer Brownell, "The Entertainment Estate: Hollywood in American Politics, 1932–1972," Ph.D. dissertation, Boston University, 2011, pp. 219–226, which was graciously provided to the author by Ms. Brownell.

day with how poorly attended the event was – suggesting that Eisenhower was not terribly popular. Reporters noted that when Wendell Willkie spoke at the Coliseum in 1940, he had filled it to capacity. Prior to Eisenhower's appearance, Zanuck wrote the Eisenhower campaign to note that the Veterans of Foreign Wars, which were handling the event, were amateurs and were not building the crowd as had been done when Willkie spoke along with twenty Hollywood celebrities who rode in a parade to the bowl. After the poorly attended Eisenhower speech, Zanuck berated the Eisenhower staff in a personal letter he directly handed to Richard Nixon for ignoring his "desperate telegram" warning of the impending PR disaster. He concluded that Eisenhower had "splendid advisors but he suffers from the lack of expert advice ... in the field of public relations and 'showmanship.'"[55] Zanuck's message got through. The Southern California Eisenhower-Nixon campaign invited Zanuck and his staff to prepare ads used throughout the state. Prepared by the Hollywood Entertainment Industry Joint Committee under the label "Democrats for Eisenhower," the ads included ostensible Democrats such as actors Ronald Reagan and Leo Carrillo.[56] Zanuck also took it upon himself to write speeches for Eisenhower.

Hollywood drew a different conclusion about Nixon. He seemed media-savvy. When allegations appeared in September that Nixon had a secret slush fund as senator, one that had been set up by wealthy donors, pressure was placed on Eisenhower to drop him from the ticket. In one of the great political stratagems in American politics, Nixon took to television in what became known as the "Checkers speech." In his denial of the charges, Nixon launched into a disquisition on how his two daughters had received a little cocker spaniel by the name of Checkers, sent to him from a supporter in Texas. Nixon was not going to return this gift, nor did his wife Pat receive a mink coat to replace her good Republican cloth coat. Behind the scenes, Nixon called for his Hollywood supporters to come to his aid. He reminded them of his role in the 1947 hearings and "the good fight in the dark years." He urged Murphy to launch a "counter propaganda" campaign against "the smear attacks which were made on me."[57] In the end, Nixon kept Checkers, and Eisenhower kept Nixon.

Hollywood's embrace of Nixon and his skillful use of the new medium enthralled his California supporters. Right after Nixon's televised address of September 23, 1952, Harry Warner wrote Eisenhower that although he had met Nixon only once, the same night he had met Eisenhower, who was addressing the Veterans of Foreign Wars in Los Angeles, he saw in Nixon a man to whom he could entrust the future of his children: "That man is a fighter and in the years to

[55] Richard Nixon to Darryl F. Zanuck, December 8, 1952; Darryl F. Zanuck, August 7, 1952, Nixon Papers, Series 320, Box 841.

[56] Paul L. Johnson to Elwood J. Robinson, November 26, 1952; Richard Nixon to Darryl Zanuck, December 8, 1952, Nixon Papers, Series 320, Box 841.

[57] Richard Nixon to George Murphy, November 2, 1952, Nixon Papers, Series 320, Box 540.

come when you are the president of the United States, as I am sure you will be after November 4th, you are going to need a fighter, a man with the honesty and integrity of Senator Nixon by your side!" Warner concluded that "the Lord took my only son from me – and last night I wished that Richard Nixon was my son."[58] The "slush fund" attack on Nixon rallied his supporters, but also inflamed anti-Warren sentiment. Rumors spread that Nixon confidant representative Pat Hillings had received a phone call from Elliott Bell, Dewey's economic advisor and later editor of *Business Week*, stating that Governor Warren wanted Nixon to withdraw from the nomination. Their plan was to put Warren on the ticket as Nixon's replacement.[59]

Nixon's Checkers speech rallied Hollywood Republicans. Conditions in California right-wing politics were far from tranquil: extremism continued to ripple across the state, spilling over into Republican politics. Soon after the Checkers speech, Republicans in California confronted what they perceived as a crisis caused by Gerald L. K. Smith, a notorious anti-Semitic right-winger who had moved to California, and Jack Tenney, who had lost his state senate race in 1948. Through the Christian Nationalist Party and the Constitutional Party, Smith and Tenney urged write-ins for General Douglas MacArthur. The general feeling was that Smith and Tenney were trying to pressure the Republican Party to pay MacArthur cash to withdraw from the race. Given the perceived strength of the far right in California, establishment Republicans including George Murphy and Cecil B. DeMille took the threat seriously. Eisenhower was advised to say something nice about MacArthur to persuade him to denounce this write-in effort, while Herbert Hoover called on MacArthur to endorse Eisenhower.[60] In the end, the right-wing threat proved to be a tempest in a teapot – but the havoc played by the far right in California politics was just beginning.

In 1952, Republican worries about a third-party effort distracting voters proved unfounded. The Eisenhower-Nixon ticket carried the state with 56.8 percent of the votes to the Democrats' 42.2 percent, garnering nearly 3 million votes to Stevenson's 2.2 million. This was well above the national average in a landslide election: the Eisenhower-Nixon ticket took 55.1 percent of the popular vote (34 million total) to Stevenson's 44.3 percent (27 million total). California had gone Republican, and it was going to stay that way in presidential elections until 1964.

Republicans celebrated the election of Eisenhower-Nixon to the White House. That is, most Republicans celebrated. Ronald Reagan, who remained a registered Democrat, was an Eisenhower supporter who distanced himself from

[58] Harry M. Warner to Dwight D. Eisenhower, September 24, 1952, Nixon Papers, Series 320, Box 798.
[59] Donald Hayne to Cecil DeMille, September 27, 1952, Cecil B. DeMille Papers, Box 440.
[60] Telephone Conversation with Tom Coleman, October 16, 1952; Telephone Conversation with Joseph N. Pew, October 15, 1952, Cecil B. DeMille Papers, Box 440; and George Murphy to Herbert Hoover, October 2, 1952, Herbert Hoover, Post-Presidential Papers, Box 160.

Nixon. In 1952, he believed that Nixon was corrupt and backed by California oil interests. He grew friendlier with Nixon over time, although their relationship, cordial on the surface, became one of political rivals. Each man found the other strange.

Although Reagan might not have been excited about Nixon's being one heartbeat from the White House, others in California were ecstatic, including Hollywood moguls and Southern California business interests. Critical in the rebuilding of the Republican Party in California were the Republican Associates. Robert Finch, as executive secretary of this group, became acquainted with Nixon while serving as a congressional aide to Norris Poulson, who won a second term to Congress in 1946, the year Nixon won his seat. Poulson, Nixon, and Finch shared two interests: anticommunism and promoting Southern California business interests. (In 1952, Poulson left Congress to run for mayor of Los Angeles. He won the election by campaigning against "socialistic" public housing.) Finch and Nixon formed a formidable team and a mutual admiration society. Finch helped manage Nixon's 1960 presidential campaign and then won election in 1966 as California lieutenant governor under Ronald Reagan, before he became secretary of Health, Education, and Welfare under Richard Nixon.

In addition to Finch, Justin Dart played a major role in the Republican Associates as a fundraiser and Republican Party insider, bringing his entrepreneurial and organizational skills to the rebuilding of the California Republican Party. As a businessman, Dart reshaped the postwar drugstore industry. After graduating from Northwestern University, he married Ruth Walgreen, whose father founded the Walgreens drugstore chain. As an executive in the company, Dart conceived the idea of placing the pharmacy counter at the back of the drugstore, leading patrons to pass shelves of other goods for sale. Profits for the company escalated. After his divorce, Dart assumed control of United Drug Company and then consolidated its drugstores under the name Rexall. By the time Dart retired in 1978, he had a wide variety of major investments in leading national and Southern California businesses.

Corresponding frequently with Vice President Richard Nixon, Dart emerged as a major fundraiser and strategist within the party. He tapped into his business connections and Hollywood money, which often wanted to give more than Dart asked for. Dart liked to tell the story of how he asked actor Jimmy Stewart for a $5,000 contribution to the state Republican Party. After Dart made his pitch, Stewart replied in his slow, well-modulated voice, a voice familiar to millions of fans in such films as *Mr. Smith Goes to Washington* (1939) and *It's a Wonderful Life* (1946), and in a number of Alfred Hitchcock postwar films including *Rear Window* (1954) and *Vertigo* (1958): "Well," Stewart said, "this sounds like it is important for me, the country, and my family. Could I offer you $10,000?"[61]

---

[61] Justin Dart, Telephone Conversation with Vice President Nixon, October 8, 1957, Nixon Papers, Series 320, Box 202.

Stewart was not the only actor signing on to Dart's fundraising efforts. Dart drew on a fairly large pool of wealthy movie actors eager to support the rebuilding of the Republican Party nationally and in California, and this donor base became inseparable from Nixon's political operation. Especially important were actors known for their roles as cowboys. John Wayne stood out in this regard, but he was joined by western stars Randolph Scott and John Payne, a major movie star who made the transition to television. Other television western stars also enlisted in the Republican cause, including character actor Walter Brennan; Dale Robertson, star of *Tales of Wells Fargo*; and Chuck Connors of *Rifleman*. Television personalities Art Linkletter (*People Are Funny*) and Robert Cummings (*I Love Bob*) were committed Republicans as well. Older stars such as Robert Young, Helen Hayes, Ethel Merman, Douglas Fairbanks, Zasu Pitts, and Nelson Eddy placed themselves in the Republican column. They were a diverse lot ideologically. Some, such as John Wayne and Walter Brennan, became members of the John Birch Society, a right-wing anti-communist organization, when it was formed in 1959, although Wayne's stay in the group was short-lived. Randolph Scott and Zasu Pitts were staunch conservatives, whereas others, such as Robert Young and Bob Cummings, voted Republican and gave money to the party.

Nixon's proclivity to gossip about the stars revealed his obsession with politics, his own political ambitions, and the fascination of a poor boy from Whittier with movie stars themselves. He loved to gossip, as seen in his letters to George Murphy, whom he affectionately called "Murph." Writing in 1957, he told Murph that he was "very sorry" to hear of the separation of actors June Allyson and Dick Powell. He recalled June's appearance at the last rally of his 1950 campaign, when she was expecting: "She made one of the most persuasive and effective speeches I have ever heard in just five minutes!"

Hollywood Republicans provided celebrity and money to the party, while Republican strategists rebuilt party organization. Robert Finch played a key role in writing a handbook for precinct captains for the Los Angeles County Republican Party, and Richard Nixon wrote the introduction to the handbook, declaring "Your money – your property – your life – are invested in the biggest going concern on earth – AMERICA."[62] In the late 1950s, Finch quietly registered large numbers of Republicans, and these new voters enabled Nixon to win the state in 1960.

Partisanship and commercial interests drove an alliance between Southern California business and Hollywood. The two were intertwined. Businessmen such as Dart and his Republican Associates despised New Deal liberalism and saw the Republican Party as the friend of business. They did not find it contradictory that, while espousing free market ideology, they called on the Eisenhower-Nixon administration to exert influence on the federal government

---

[62] Los Angles County Republican Party, "Precinct Captain's Handbook" (1958), Nixon Papers, Series 320, Box 258.

to throw contracts their way. When Secretary of the Air Force Harold Talbott announced that he was not going to direct defense contracts to Southern California in 1955, there was an immediate and explosive protest in the state. George Murphy was directed to lobby the White House directly. In a three-page letter written to Wilton B. Persons, deputy assistant and later chief of staff to President Eisenhower, Murphy warned that Talbott's decision had caused a shift in feeling in favor of the Democrats. Murphy bluntly described Talbott as "stupid" and added that West Coast aircraft manufacturers had spent millions of dollars in developing plants and facilities that were now put in jeopardy. Los Angeles (Douglas and Lockheed) and San Diego (General Dynamics) employed tens of thousands of workers. Chambers of Commerce across Southern California called mass meetings to protest the decision. Murphy astutely added that local chambers of commerce were "very glad to get a popular incident such as this" so they could "align themselves with labor and management and the man on the street" because "so much of the economy of our State at the present time depends upon the aircraft business."[63] In the end, Talbott backed away from his decision and later resigned due to corruption charges. Defense contractors flourished in Southern California throughout the 1950s.

As the presidential election of 1956 approached, the Southern California Republican Party appeared to be on the mend. Although Democratic Party registration continued to increase, Republicans had begun to make serious strides in becoming a competitive party. The alliance among Southern California business, heads of movie studios, and Hollywood actors was firmly set. This informal alliance came together to sponsor a huge fund raising event, the "Salute to Eisenhower" dinner in early 1956. The event, chaired by Justin Dart, raised more than $250,000 at a time when the state party was $40,000 in debt. Half of the money raised at the dinner went to the Los Angeles Republican Party, and the rest went to the National Republican Committee. As Dart pointed out, it was easier to raise money for the president than to host an event for Richard Nixon. The targeted guest list of major donors included Leonard Firestone, Henry T. Mudd, Preston Hotchkiss, and twelve other movers and shakers in Southern California business. Hollywood men on this power list included Jack Warner, James Stewart, and Randolph Scott.[64]

Nixon kept in touch with the donors, personally writing to people such as Leonard Firestone that he appreciated all that Dart and Firestone were doing on behalf of the 1956 campaign.[65] Nixon wrote the same letter to Stewart, signed "Dick," with a personalized postscript telling him how much Pat and he had enjoyed the actor's movie *The Man from Laramie*. The same letter was also sent to Randolph Scott, with a personalized postscript reminding him of their first

[63] George Murphy to General Wilton B. Persons, May 23, 1955, Nixon Papers, Series 320, Box 540.
[64] Memorandum, Phone Call from Justin Dart, December 17, 1955, Nixon Papers, Series 320, Box 349.
[65] Richard Nixon to Leonard K. Firestone, January 3, 1956, Nixon Papers, Series 320, Box 260.

meeting in Whittier and having "a real satisfaction to have the best people in Hollywood on our side."[66] He wrote producer Darryl Zanuck to let him know that he was doing him a favor by recommending a friend to J. Edgar Hoover and that he appreciated meeting Zanuck to hear his views on domestic politics and international affairs.[67] He told actress Irene Dunne what a tremendous speech she gave at the Hawaii Lincoln Day Dinner meetings.[68]

Hollywood's mobilization for the Eisenhower-Nixon ticket in 1956 proved highly successful. Robert Montgomery and actor Wendell Corey actively participated in planning for the Republican National Convention in San Francisco to ensure that the televised proceedings entertained and held the audience's attention.[69] Once the general election campaign got under way, the Entertainment Committee, headed by Warner, Zanuck, Goldwyn, and Murphy, enlarged its involvement from 1952 to develop television and radio spots for Eisenhower's reelection. When Eisenhower campaigned in Los Angeles in October, he was greeted by dozens of stars. His televised address was preceded by an hour and a half of entertainment provided by Hollywood Republicans. Similarly, when Nixon campaigned in Southern California, he was accompanied by the Women's Brigade, an organization of Republican women volunteers led by Hedda Hopper. These women brought spirit to Nixon rallies and celebrities brought crowds.

The highlight of the campaign came on the eve of the election, with a televised gala, "Salute to Ike." The program featured a feature-length film, *Four Full Years*, produced with the cooperation of Spyros Skouras, president of 20th Century Fox, and a campaign documentary narrated by Gary Cooper.

The election was a foregone conclusion. Although Eisenhower won California by 1 percent less in the popular vote than he had in 1952, he received an impressive 55-plus percent of the popular vote compared to his rematch with Democratic nominee Adlai Stevenson. George Murphy was appointed to chair the inauguration gala in Washington, D.C.

Republicans now held the White House, the California state mansion under Goodwin (Goodie) Knight, and both senate seats with William Knowland and Thomas Kuchel. Nixon held the vice presidency, and Warren served as Chief Justice of the Supreme Court. Democratic registration, which had increased dramatically in the 1930s, continued to hold steady with about 60 percent of the electorate declaring themselves Democrats.[70] Restrictions in cross-filing in 1954, which required candidates to list their party affiliations, gave Democrats an added advantage. The party gained organizational muscle with the formation

[66] Richard Nixon to Randolph Scott, January 3, 1956, Nixon Papers, Series 320, Box 681.

[67] Richard Nixon to Darryl F. Zanuck, August 23, 1955, Series 320, Box 841.

[68] Richard Nixon to Irene Dunne, April 24, 1958, Nixon Papers, Series 320, Box 230.

[69] Details of the 1956 reelection campaign are found in Brownell, "The Entertainment Estate: Hollywood in American Politics, 1932–1972," Ph.D. dissertation, Boston University, 2011, pp. 226–237.

[70] Eugene C. Lee, *California Votes, 1928–1960* (Berkeley, CA, 1963), p. 28.

of the California Democratic Council, a voluntary organization comparable to the California Republican Assembly.[71] This placed California Republicans in a defensive position. Although Stevenson lost California to Eisenhower, he had increased the Democratic vote in California, and Democratic momentum was evident in other areas. In the 1956 elections, Democrats hosted a full slate of congressional candidates, ending for all general purposes the Republican advantage of cross-filing. Democrats ran dead even with Republicans in the state senate – twenty seats each – and the Republican majority in the Assembly fell from 45–35 seats to 42–38.[72]

CALIFORNIA REPUBLICANS FRACTURE

Behind these numbers lay an impending crisis that threw the Republican Party into complete disarray, from which it would not rebound until Ronald Reagan's election to the governor's mansion in 1966. Presidential ambition, sexual misbehavior, and hubris (often another word for stupidity) precipitated this disaster. The context for this crisis was set with Eisenhower's appointment of Earl Warren to the Supreme Court in late 1953. Warren's appointment left a huge political vacuum in the state party. Power abhors a vacuum, and this is especially the case when presidential ambition is involved. Vice President Richard Nixon, senior U.S. senator William Knowland, and Warren's replacement in the governor's mansion, Goodwin Knight – each having caught the presidential bug – feverishly rushed in to fill Warren's place. Knowland's long-held aspirations for the White House became more realistic – at least in his eyes – when he became Senate Majority Leader following the sudden death of Robert Taft in the summer of 1953. Knight's prospects for attaining the White House were less realistic, even though his ascent to the governorship of one of the largest states in the union allowed him to entertain a run for the presidency. Once in the governor's mansion Knight moved to the center, catering to organized labor.[73]

Meanwhile, Richard Nixon stood in the wings as heir apparent to Eisenhower. The three rivals – Nixon, Knowland, and Knight – understood that control of California was essential to their success.[74] Eisenhower's heart attack in September 1955 exacerbated tensions within the California Republican Party. While Eisenhower was recovering, Knight stepped forward to declare he was willing to carry the Republican banner in 1956, either as a presidential or vice presidential candidate. A presumptuous Knight gave

---

[71] For an account of the rise of the Democratic Party in California, see Jonathan Bell, *California Crucible: The Forging of Modern American Liberalism* (Philadelphia, 2012), pp. 83–123.

[72] Gladwin Hill, *Dancing Bear: An Inside Look at California Politics* (Cleveland, OH, 1968), p. 152.

[73] Hill, *Dancing Bear*, pp. 141–142.

[74] Worthen, *The Young Nixon and His Rivals*, pp. 139–167.

Eisenhower a March 1 deadline to declare he was up to a second term.[75] Then, in 1957, things took an even more bizarre turn when Senator Knowland announced he was not going to seek reelection for the U.S. Senate. This was stunning news, but matters took a further twist when he announced he was going to challenge Goodwin Knight in the Republican primaries for the governor's mansion in 1958. Knowland despised Knight and made the race personal.

Behind this political calculation lay a personal decision by Knowland and his wife Helen to leave Washington, D.C., where their lives had been thrown into turmoil by extramarital affairs involving both of them and another man and his wife. Helen Knowland had begun an affair with Arthur Blair Moody, a Detroit newspaperman and nephew of William Scripps. Blair was handsome, a Brown University graduate, and married to Ruth Moody. The two couples often socialized together. Not knowing of his wife's affair, Knowland began an affair with Ruth Moody. It was passionate, so much so that, at Ruth's insistence, Knowland underwent a painful circumcision to satisfy her. In July 1954, Blair Moody suddenly died of a heart attack. The heartbroken Helen tried to commit suicide. She had found out about her husband's continuing affair with Blair's wife and, after her recovery, she insisted that they return to their hometown of Oakland, California, where the Knowland family owned and operated the *Oakland Tribune*. A return to California made political and personal sense for Knowland. It could save his marriage – a divorce would ruin any chance of his becoming president – and as governor, he might have a clear shot at the presidency.[76]

Knowland believed that his popularity in California would be easily translated into a run for governor. He had won reelection to the Senate by a seven-to-one margin. He decided to focus his campaign on his support for the right-to-work referendum, Proposition 18, that had been placed on the California ballot for 1958. Advisors warned Knowland that the right-to-work referendum was going to mobilize organized labor and help the Democrats in electing Democratic candidate Attorney General Pat Brown. Knowland, typically, was obstinate in ignoring this advice. Knight openly denounced Knowland's position on right-to-work, but after polls showed him losing to Knowland in the primary. Under pressure from the *Los Angeles Times* and lacking popularity and donor support, Knight withdrew from the Republican gubinatorial primary to declare that he would run for Knowland's Senate seat.

---

[75] A full discussion of Republican infighting in this period is found in Irwin F. Gellman's forthcoming book on the Eisenhower-Nixon years, especially chapters 21 and 22, which the author graciously shared with me.

[76] The Knowland story is recounted in Gayle B. Montgomery and James W. Johnson, *One Step from the White House: The Rise and Fall of Senator William F. Knowland* (Berkeley, CA, 1998), pp. 220–266.

Nixon encouraged Knight to make what became known as the "Big Switch." The appearance of a deal offended California voters.

While trying to avoid direct involvement in the Knowland-Knight fight, Nixon kept a watchful eye on California politics through Finch, Murphy, and Dart. Prior to Knight's announcement that he would not seek reelection, Finch warned Nixon not to commit to either man. Finch said that his opinion was shared by Henry Mudd, George Murphy, and other Nixon supporters in California.[77] The Knowland-Knight fight spilled over into a struggle to control party positions in the state Republican Party. Finch astutely noted that the Nixon people had deciding votes in these fights.[78] Warfare between Knowland and Knight supporters allowed Nixon to take the high ground. He came across as the great reconciler in the party, a strategic position Nixon frequently sought to occupy throughout his political career.[79]

The governor's race in 1958 pitted Knowland, a wealthy, arch-conservative, Protestant millionaire against Edmund "Pat" Brown a former Republican, one-time San Francisco district attorney, generally liberal, and Roman Catholic convert.[80] Knowland's chances of winning the general election were slim at best, but his insistence on supporting the right-to-work referendum and a poorly organized campaign assured failure.[81] His wife, an almost fanatical right-winger, did not help matters when she sent out a pamphlet, "Meet the Man Who Plans to Rule America," an attack on Walter Reuther, president of the United Auto Workers Union. Joseph Kamp, an alleged anti-Semite, wrote the pamphlet, and Helen Knowland's distribution of this pamphlet became national news when the *New York Times* reported that Donald Brown, former vice chairman of General Motors; Pierre S. DuPont, II; and Charles M. White, chairman of the board of Republic Steel Corporation, financed it. This revelation created an opportunity for Pat Brown to declare that right-to-work was a well-orchestrated corporate attack on organized labor.[82]

California business was, in fact, divided on the issue of right-to-work.[83] Many in the business community feared Prop 18 and felt it was bad for labor

[77] Richard Nixon, Memo, August 20, 1957; and Telephone Call from Robert Finch, April 26, 1957, Richard Nixon Papers, Box 259.
[78] Richard Nixon, Telephone Call from Bob Finch, March 18, 1958, Nixon Papers, Box 259.
[79] Henry Salvatori to Richard Nixon, March 18, 1958, Richard Nixon Papers, Series 320, Box 669.
[80] Hill, *Dancing Bear*, p. 158.
[81] Morrie Ryskind provides an insightful perspective into Knowland's problems in "The Odds Against Knowland," *National Review*, August 30, 1958.
[82] Helen Knowland's passionate involvement in the campaign and her disgust with Knight is seen in Mrs. William F. Knowland to Bob Finch, October 29, 1958, Nixon Papers, Series 320, Box 259.
[83] Bell, *California Crucible*, p. 129. Also, for points of view arguing for greater business and conservative agreement on right-to-work legislation see Elizabeth Tandy Shermer, "'Is Freedom of the Individual Un-American?' Right-to-Work Campaigns and Anti-union Conservatism, 1943–1958"; Reuel Schiller, "Singing 'The Right-to-Work Blues': The Politics of Race in the Campaign for 'Voluntary Unionism' in Postwar California"; and Sophie Z. Lee, "Whose Rights? Litigating the Right-to-Work, 1940–1980," in *The Right and Labor in America: Politics, Ideology,*

relations. Cecil B. DeMille's Foundation for Freedom, however, supported the proposition. In 1957, through his chief aide Donald MacLean, the DeMille Foundation put together a master plan to place a right-to-work initiative on the ballot. By 1957, eighteen states had enacted right-to-work legislation, and momentum seemed to be on the side of right-to-work supporters. The first step, MacLean wrote, would be recruiting a handful of top men to underwrite initial organizational costs. "They must be assured of anonymity; telephone calls should be handled discreetly; nothing should be written down," he advised.[84] Leonard D. Keefer was appointed executive secretary for Citizens' Committee for Voluntary Unionism. Keefer reached out to Central Valley powerhouse L. E. Agnetti, the chairman of Carnation Ice Cream; H. F. Ellison, a food distributor; and Joseph Giannini of the Bank of America family; as well as to dairy owners, car dealers, and trucking companies. Generally, these were private businesses and not large corporate representatives. When Proposition 18 appeared on the ballot, DeMille took to the airwaves to declare, "I am Cecil B. DeMille, a suspended union member. For fourteen years my union has kept me from working in radio and in television because I refused to give a one dollar political assessment."[85] Given a national economic recession in 1958, DeMille's ploy of passing himself off as an unemployed worker appeared ridiculous.

Knowland's Democratic rival Pat Brown, joined by organized labor, continued to hammer Knowland on the issue, linking economic citizenship, labor rights, and civil rights. Brown warned that right-to-work expressed "a return to the ugly disruptive law of the economic jungle."[86] Brown's attack on right-to-work allowed California Democrats to paper over their ideological differences, especially on matters of foreign policy. In the end, pro–Proposition 18 groups spent less than a million dollars in their campaign, whereas organized labor and anti-right-to-work forces spent more than an estimated $2.5 million.[87]

Republicans across the state began to distance themselves from Knowland and the right-to-work issue. In Washington, Nixon stated that the Eisenhower administration refused to take a position because it was an issue to be decided by voters in the states. Nixon's neutral position did not sit well with many of his supporters and helped set the stage for his defeat in his 1962 run for governor. Longtime associate Murray M. Chotiner warned Nixon that many within the California Association of Manufacturers felt that if Nixon did not come out in public support of the right-to-work measure, they could not support him in

and Imagination, ed. Nelson Lichtenstein and Elizabeth Tandy Shermer (Philadelphia, 2012), pp. 114–136; 139–159; and 160–180, respectively.

[84] Donald MacLean, "Master Plan," (n.d. 1957?), Cecil B. DeMille Papers, Box 1191.

[85] Cecil B. DeMille, "Proposition 18" (1958), Cecil B. DeMille Papers, Box 212.

[86] Quoted in Bell, *California Crucible*, p. 139. Also, Ethan Rarick, *The Life and Times of Pat Brown: California Rising* (Berkley, CA, 2005).

[87] Cecil B. DeMille, "Proposition 18," October 27, 1958, Cecil B. DeMille Papers, Box 212. Also, Hill, *Dancing Bear*, p. 159.

1960.[88] Ignoring this lack of administration support, Knowland refused to back off, lashing back in a viciously negative campaign against Brown, which further alienated supporters and voters. Five days before the election, the *San Francisco Chronicle* withdrew its previous endorsement of Knowland, and Brown won the election by over one million votes. With the exception of longtime incumbent secretary of state Frank Jordan, the entire Republican ticket went down to defeat. Goodwin Knight lost his senate race to Representative Clair Engle, 2.9 million to 2.2 million votes. Democrats took control of the senate by twenty-eight seats to twelve and won control of the Assembly for the first time in decades, controlling forty-seven seats to the Republican's thirty-three. Democrats gained three congressional seats, including part of Nixon's former district. Prop 18 was defeated by a 60–40 percent margin.[89] After nearly a decade of trying to rebuild the Republican Party, the California GOP was left in shambles. Even before the final results of the election, an irate Justine Dart wrote Nixon, "California is a long, sad story. No organization, no unity, inadequate party leadership from the President and Vice President.... [W]e are not going to have any needed revival of the Republican Party."[90]

With Knowland's defeat, the path was cleared for Nixon's nomination for president.[91] Knowland continued to play a role in California politics while his personal life spun out of control. He became a compulsive gambler, incurring a huge debt rumored to be owed to organized crime interests. He divorced his wife to marry a woman he met in a Las Vegas casino. Heavily in debt, married to an alcoholic, spendthrift wife, Knowland committed suicide in 1974.[92]

Cecil B. DeMille's death came earlier. Shortly after the defeat of Proposition 18, DeMille died of heart failure, in January 1959. He had suffered an earlier heart attack while filming perhaps his greatest work, *The Ten Commandments*, starring Charleton Heston, who, within a few years, picked up the conservative flag. DeMille, the man who had helped create Hollywood and had spent the last twenty years of his life fighting communism and building the California Republican Party, left, in his final political act – Proposition 18 – the California GOP in tatters.

NIXON SEEKS THE ROLE OF A LIFETIME

When Nixon won the Republican presidential nomination to face John F. Kennedy in 1960, Hollywood Republicans were elated even though

---

[88] Nixon's position is outlined in Richard Nixon to Robert Finch, October 23, 1958, Nixon Papers, Series 320, Box 259. For a negative reaction from a Nixon supporter, George Shellberger to Richard Nixon, February 31, 1958, Nixon Papers, Series 320, Box 690. Chotiner's advice on right-to-work is found in Murray M. Chotiner to Richard M. Nixon, September 18, 1958, Nixon Papers, Series 320, Box 147.

[89] Bell, *California Crucible*, pp. 105 and 153. Also see Elizabeth Fones-Wolf, *Selling Free Enterprise: The Business Assault on Labor and Liberalism, 1945–60* (Urbana, IL, 1994).

[90] Memorandum, Telephone Call from Vic J., July 7, 1958, Nixon Papers, Series 320, Box 202.

[91] Quoted in Hill, *Dancing Bear*, p. 149.

[92] Montgomery and Johnson, *One Step from the White House*, especially pp. 228–254.

California Republicans were factionalized, and the right itself was divided.[93] Nixon's candidacy united the party briefly, but beneath the surface boiled a cauldron of tensions. The fallout from the Knowland-Knight disaster continued to have a poisonous afterlife. The Eisenhower administration's foreign policy, especially its apparent accommodation with the Soviet Union over nuclear testing and summit meetings, left many conservatives wary. The censuring of Joe McCarthy and the administration's stance against the anti-internationalist Connally Amendment reinforced their suspicions. As Loyd Wright, a Los Angeles attorney and Knowland man, told Nixon in late 1959, many true Republicans in California have "well nigh abandoned hope because of modern Republicanism and the crucifying of our real Republicans such as Joe McCarthy."[94]

California racial politics furthered divisions within the California Republican Party. A proposal to place an initiative on the ballot regarding a permanent state Fair Employment Practices Commission in 1960 promised a disastrous repeat of the right-to-work initiative in 1958. Writing on behalf of Nixon, Robert Finch told California assemblyman Joe C. Shell, a darling of the right wing, that such a measure could only "provide militant cohesion for the opposition and work towards bringing out an unfavorable vote."[95] If these problems were not enough, party organization in California had fallen apart as a result of the 1958 election.

Nixon relied heavily on California donors to finance his presidential campaign. Henry Salvatori, who had made a fortune in oil, became the state finance chairman for Nixon in California.[96] Major money backers such as Justin Dart and Walter Knott were elected as delegates to the Republican National Convention. Walter Knott opened his Knott's Berry Farm in heavily Republican Orange County for a huge Nixon rally, "Picnic with Dick."[97] Republican movie stars appeared at rallies such as this to bring out the crowds.

Democratic movie stars far outnumbered Republican stars. The Kennedy family, going back to John F. Kennedy's father, had strong ties in the film community, and the campaign tapped into the family's connections with these Hollywood celebrities for money and to add further glamour to Kennedy's image. The list of Democratic stars, reported by the *New York Times*, was spellbinding: Marilyn Monroe, Marlon Brando, Harry Belafonte, Frank Sinatra, Shirley MacLaine, Henry Fonda, Tony Curtis, Kirk Douglas, Gene Kelly, Sidney Poitier, Anthony Quinn, Robert Ryan, Sammy Davis, Jr., Peter Lawford, Shelley Winters, Nat King Cole, Eddie Albert, and Ralph Bellamy.

---

[93] Hill, *Dancing Bear*, p. 172.
[94] Loyd Wright to Richard Nixon, December 18, 1959, Nixon Papers, Series 320, Box 834.
[95] Robert Finch to Joseph C. Shell, June 1, 1959, Nixon Papers, Series 320, Box 259.
[96] Stanley E. McCaffrey to Henry Salvatori, November 29, 1960, Nixon Papers, Series 320, Box 669.
[97] Richard M. Nixon to Walter Knott, November 28, 1960, Nixon Papers, Series 320, Box 421.

They outraised Republican stars by huge amounts of money through a two-hour spectacular music and dancing show at the Democratic Convention. Murphy, who headed the entertainment committee for Nixon, lamely responded that "Republican entertainers are afraid they will be punished economically" if they declare themselves as party partisans. Allen Rivkin, Democratic chairman for the arts, had a different take: "Democrats just feel things more deeply." Both Murphy and Rivkin might have been right. The industry was liberal and becoming more liberal, so Republicans were beginning to keep their heads down. At the same time, Kennedy did draw more excitement from Hollywood in his campaign than did Nixon.[98]

What gave the Nixon campaign weight was not the stars' endorsements, but the informal network of California money interests (Dart, Salvatori, Firestone, Knott, Mudd, Chandler), Hollywood moguls (Selznick and Disney), and actors such as Stewart, Wayne, and others who provided both glamour and expertise to events. George Murphy, for example, served as a primary consultant in setting up a closed-circuit television program of Republican finance dinners carried in thirty-six major cities.[99] "Murph" proved to be a magical fundraiser. In April 1960, as the campaign was just getting under way, Murphy staged a fundraiser in Berkeley, California that featured dancer Jane Powell, ventriloquist Edgar Bergen, the comedy team of the Wiere Brothers, and Manny Harmon and his seventeen-piece orchestra. There were no political speeches. The event made $52,000.[100]

At the same time, Murphy and Adele Rogers provided names of speechwriters who could pen remarks for supporters, such as cowboy star Randolph Scott who campaigned for Nixon. Murphy also brought in younger Hollywood Republicans such as actor, composer, and arranger Buddy Bregman, who had arranged three music albums that went platinum, including two for one of America's greatest female jazz singers, Ella Fitzgerald.[101] Murphy formed the Celebrities for Nixon Committee in the summer of 1960, with a member list that was considerably more extensive than that reported by the *New York Times*.[102]

---

[98] Murray Schumach, "Democrats Lead G.O.P. in Filmland," *New York Times*, April 18, 1960. A highly readable account of movie stars during this time is Steven J. Ross, *Hollywood Left and Right: How Movie Stars Shaped American Politics* (New York, 2011), especially pp. 185–226.

[99] George L. Murphy to Richard M. Nixon, September 21, 1960, Nixon Papers, Series 320, Box 540.

[100] "Report on the "Centurama," April 26, 1960, Richard M. Nixon Papers, Box 540.

[101] George Murphy to Robert Finch, February 3, 1960, Richard M. Nixon Papers, Box 540.

[102] Charter members of the entertainment committee included John Wayne (movie star), Irene Dunne (movie star), Freeman (Andy) Gosden (comedian, "Amos and Andy"), Katherine Cornell (stage actress), Walter Pidgeon (movie actor), Jinx Falkenberg (supermodel), Barney Balaban (president of Paramount Studios), Faith Baldwin (romance author), Buddy Rogers (musician), Mary Pickford (silent film star), Dick Powell (actor-producer), Louise Beavers (African-American movie and television actor), William L. White (journalist), Cobina Wright (actor), Edward D. Stone (architect), Elizabeth Arden (movie and television star), Eddie (Rochester) Anderson (African-American actor), Dina Merrill (actor and socialite), Ted

Other stars proved useful as well. Television star Dale Robertson helped Nixon at a fundraiser in Texas. Actor Robert Young, enjoying his success in the television series *Father Knows Best*, joined a telethon with other stars on the eve of the election.[103] Dick Powell, who had become one of Hollywood's wealthiest actors through shrewd investments (a long road for a farm boy from Arkansas), was a featured speaker at the Nixon rally in the Pan Pacific auditorium.[104] Other actors, some from yesteryear including Douglas Fairbanks, Ethel Merman, and Helen Hayes, and other lesser-known actors such as comedian Zasu Pitts, gave their time and money to the Nixon campaign. So few actors were Republicans that television personality Art Linkletter made the news when he declared he was a conservative and a Republican – and a Nixon supporter.[105]

Action star John Wayne worked on the campaign trail, speaking at Republican dinners. His campaigning was less extensive than others' because he was busy making *The Alamo* – his own not so subtle contribution to the Nixon campaign. Wayne scheduled *The Alamo* premiere to coincide with the final stages of the 1960 election, seeing the film, a heroic story of Texan independence from Mexico, as an allegory for the Cold War. He was convinced that America was going soft in the Cold War struggle, and he despised the Kennedys for what he described as their "lace-curtain arrogance and unctuous liberalism." His production company spent $152,000 on a three-page red, white, and blue ad in *Life* magazine that read, "Very soon the two great political parties of the United States will nominate their candidates for President.... In this moment when eternity could be closer than ever before there is a statesman who for the sake of a vote is not all things to all men; a man who will put America back on the high road of security and accomplishment; without fear or favor or compromise; a man who wants to do the job that must be done and to hell with friend or foe who would have it done otherwise."[106] The ad concluded, "There are no ghostwriters at the Alamo. Only men." This was a dig at the recent announcement that Dalton Trumbo, who had ghostwritten Kirk Douglas's film, *Spartacus*, would receive credit for the film.

Support for Nixon among some movie stars was less than enthusiastic because they considered the Eisenhower-Nixon administration too moderate.

Williams (baseball player), Eleanor Steber (opera star), Ward Bond (movie and television actor), Jeanette MacDonald (singer and movie actor), Gene Raymond (television star), and Gordon McRae (actor and singer). Press Release, August 16, 1960, Nixon Papers, Series 320, Box 540.

[103] Stanley E. McCaffrey to Robert Young, November 30, 1960, Richard M. Nixon Papers, Box 840.

[104] Stanley E. McCaffrey to Dick Powell, November 30, 1960; Dick Powell to Richard M. Nixon, November 5, 1959; Dick Powell to Richard M. Nixon, August 1, 1960, Nixon Papers, Series 320, Box 607.

[105] "Nixon Favored for President by Linkletter: TV Star Here to Receive Degree," *San Diego Union*, June 15, 1960, Richard M. Nixon Papers, Box 454.

[106] Randy Roberts and James S. Olson, *John Wayne: American* (New York, 1995), pp. 471–473.

Nixon's calculated refusal to take a stand on the right-to-work initiative alienated some who were already leery of Eisenhower's foreign policy. This uneasiness became apparent when popular cowboy star Randolph Scott informed the Nixon campaign that he was not going to contribute to Nixon. Scott told Nixon that this decision was not easy because "my loyalty, support, and allegiance have been steadfast over the years."[107] Like other right-wingers in California, Scott expressed anger over the administration's decision to oppose the anti-internationalist Connally Amendment, a measure inserted into an early United Nations (UN) treaty that preserved American sovereignty over UN jurisdiction. It was largely a symbolic measure, but for right-wingers concerned about "one world government" and the UN, it was a matter of principle.

Scott's decision threw the Nixon campaign into a fit, with desperate internal messages exchanged trying to find "some way to encourage [him] to open up his money bags again." Scott was a big donor and a confirmed Republican, and the Nixon campaign could not afford to lose him. Scott had campaigned for Nixon against Helen Gahagan Douglas in the U.S. Senate race in 1950, having been a speaker at the American Legion auditorium rally for Nixon. As late as December 1959, he told Nixon that "I have that psychic feeling your political star will guide you to Pennsylvania Avenue."[108] In the end, after much smoothing of feathers, the Nixon campaign believed that they had finally gotten "Randy calmed down." Scott's reluctance should have presented Nixon with an omen of what was to come in 1962.[109]

In the general election, Nixon barely carried California, winning the popular vote in the state by less than 36,000 votes. This was slightly better than he did in the national vote: a narrow margin of 49.7 percent for Kennedy to 49.6 percent for Nixon. As a result of the election, Democrats controlled the White House, Congress, the governorship in California, and the California Assembly.

1962: NIXON LEAVES THE CALIFORNIA STAGE

Anticommunism remained a force within the Hollywood Right, but it was quickly losing momentum. The last great gasp of the Hollywood anticommunists came in 1961, in Fred Schwarz's huge anticommunist rally that filled the Hollywood Bowl and was televised across the state. Fred Schwarz, an Australian physician, had gained national notoriety for his well-organized School of Anti-Communism held throughout the country that drew hundreds of people who

[107] Randy Scott to Richard Nixon, September 19, 1960, Nixon Papers, Series 320, Box 682.
[108] Randy Scott to Richard Nixon, December 7, 1959, Nixon Papers, Series 320, Box 682.
[109] The archival record does not reveal whether Scott made further financial contributions to the Nixon campaign. He does not appear to have been a Nixon supporter in 1962, however. The exchanges over Scott's threat to withhold campaign donations can be followed in Randy Scott to Richard Nixon, August 23, 1960; Randy Scott to Richard Nixon, September 19, 1960; LLG to Russell Turner (n.d.); Russell Turner to Randolph Scott, October 1, 1960, Nixon Papers, Series 320, Box 682.

came to hear leading anticommunist speakers of the day. The Hollywood Bowl rally headlined more than forty major television stars aligned with the GOP and the conservative movement. Some of these actors already had established records for their anticommunist beliefs – Ronald Reagan, John Wayne, James Stewart, Walt Disney, and John Ford. Other celebrities thrilled the thousands who filled the Hollywood Bowl on that cool October evening of 1961, a year away from the governor's race. Lending their names to the anticommunist rally, headed by the chairman of Technicolor, Patrick J. Frawley, Jr., was actor Rock Hudson, an avowed Republican who would campaign for Barry Goldwater in 1964. Joining him were singers Nat King Cole and Pat Boone; television stars Ozzie and Harriet Nelson; the star of television's *The Untouchables*, Robert Stack; sex symbol Jane Russell, who became an evangelical Christian; and another movie star who made the transition to television, Donna Reed. Richard Nixon sent a congratulatory telegram proclaiming the cause of "pro-Americanism."[110]

The 1960s left the California GOP and the Hollywood Right once again divided, seemingly beyond repair, a fact that became all too apparent when Nixon decided to run for the California governorship in 1962, in order to resuscitate his political career and give him another shot at the presidency. Three months before Nixon announced he was running for governor, conservative assemblyman from Los Angeles Joseph Shell declared his candidacy for the governorship. Shell, a wealthy oilman and former Navy flier, brought to the campaign an established right-wing record. He had never voted in favor of a single state budget, then running at about $3 billion a year. He took to the campaign trail, delivering more than 300 speeches even before Nixon entered the race. He spoke in favor of right-to-work legislation and against what he called "nutty" welfare programs. He disavowed membership in the John Birch Society, but said he believed in many of the organization's precepts. He directly attacked Nixon, declaring that the "office of governor cannot be a place for retired political war horses nor can it be a stepping stone for future political office."[111] Shell won the financial support of A. C. Ruble, former chair of Union Oil, a sign of further discord within the party.

This was just the beginning of troubles for the Nixon campaign. When Nixon came out in favor of a resolution that banned John Birch Society members from

---

[110] The list of other celebrities who highlighted the rally included Edgar Bergen, Richard Breen, Walter Brennan, Linda Darnell, Dan DeFore, Andy Devine, Buddy Ebsen, Dale Evans, George J. Flaherty, Y. Frank Freeman, Johnny Grant, Connie Haynes, Jeanette MacDonald, Constance More, Loyd Nolan, Pat O'Brien, Maureen O'Hara, Tony Owen, Gigi Perreau, Mary Pickford, Vincent Price, Gene Raymond, Tex Ritter, Roy Rogers, Cesar Romero, Ann Sothern, Norman Tourog, Marshal Thompson, Jack Warner, and Van Williams. Telegram, Richard Nixon to George Murphy, October 16, 1961, Nixon Papers, Series 320, Box 540.

[111] Morrie Landsberg, "Shell Portrays Role of Giant Killer in Primary," *The Daily News* (Whittier), April 27, 1962. For the 1962 election, see Hill, *Dancing Bear*, pp. 163–178, and Jackson K. Putnam, *Modern California Politics* (San Francisco, 1984), pp. 45–58.

the Republican Assembly, the extensive right wing in California deserted his campaign. Nixon's attack on the Birchers as extremists alienated a powerful group in Southern California. As radio commentator Fulton Lewis noted in his national newsletter, "The Birchers in California are powerful, not only numeri cally but financially. Loss of their support, by itself can cost Nixon the election."[112] Walter Knott, a member of the Birch Society, endorsed Shell, putting his name on a mass mailing calling on conservatives to back Shell against Nixon. Divisions within the party were evident when Ronald Reagan, who had taken on the role of Loyd Wright's campaign manager in his race for the U.S. Senate, refused to endorse Nixon during the primary. Reagan deftly told the Nixon campaign that he could be more effective in the general campaign "leading his conservatives back after the primary."[113] Meanwhile, Nixon had alienated another Republican conservative, Howard Jarvis, by telling him that he was going to support moderate Republican Tom Kuchel for reelection.[114]

Nixon's nemesis, Goodwin Knight, also tested the primary waters. Knight told the press that Nixon had promised him in 1961 that he was not going to run for governor because he was only interested in "national and international" issues. Nixon broke this promise, Knight declared, and then promised to appoint him the Chief Justice of the California Supreme Court or "any job in California" if he would not run for governor. After hearing Knight's accusation, Nixon was livid. A bitter public exchange only reminded voters of Republican divisions and heightened perceptions of a conniving Richard Nixon. Poor health forced Knight to withdraw from the race, and this episode further damaged Nixon.

Nixon easily beat Shell in the 1962 gubernatorial primary, winning 1.2 million votes to Shell's modest 656,000. After some hesitancy, Shell endorsed Nixon. The GOP remained divided as it entered the general campaign against the fairly popular incumbent Governor Pat Brown, who would hammer Nixon as a carpetbagger more interested in the White House than Sacramento. Nixon mustered longtime financial supporters and a dwindling number of Hollywood stars to counter Brown's attacks, drawing on Justin Dart, Henry Salvatori, Leonard Firestone, and Alfred Bloomingdale for financial support, while relying on James Stewart and George Murphy to tap Hollywood support. Jack Warner, Samuel Goldwyn, Darryl Zanuck, David O. Selznick, and Walt Disney, members of the Southern California Finance Committee, contributed financial and political support for the campaign. Walter Knott came back on board the Nixon wagon. The list of other movie stars was impressive: Alan Ladd, Red Skelton, Clifton Webb, Spike Jones, Shirley Temple, Rhoda Fleming, John Payne, Jackie Gleason, Robert Young, Jimmy Durante, and Zasu Pitts endorsed Nixon and

[112] "Exclusive," *Exclusives*, April 4, 1962; and Victor Lasky to Fulton Lewis, Jr., April 10, 1962, Nixon Papers, Series 320, Box 449.

[113] Al Moscow, Memo on Ronald Reagan, April 18, 1962, Nixon Papers, Series 320, Box 621.

[114] Richard Nixon to Howard Jarvis, July 24, 1961; Memorandum: Murray Chotiner Telephone Call, April 17, 1962, Nixon Papers, Series 320, Box 381 and Box 147.

highlighted fundraisers and rallies during the campaign. Ronald Reagan broadcast a powerful television address on the eve of the election urging a vote for Nixon. Eloquent, full of historical allusions, and declaring that "You and I have a rendezvous with destiny," Reagan's speech introduced excitement into a dull race. He generated enthusiasm, while Nixon projected the image of a warhorse having seen too many battles.[115]

The election proved closer than might have been predicted. Brown won by 296,000 votes, garnering 51 percent of the popular vote to Nixon's 46 percent. Many in the Nixon camp blamed the Republican right for his defeat. This is doubtful. Registration showed 4,290,000 Democrats to 3,002,000 Republicans. Close to an 80 percent turnout gave Nixon virtually all of the Republican vote and about 400,000 Democratic votes.[116] Nixon carried most of Southern California, barely losing Los Angeles County. Brown's election was not a landslide, but it might as well have been for Nixon. His political career looked over, and his chiding remarks to reporters at his concession speech, to the effect that they would not have Richard Nixon to kick around anymore, seemed to confirm the end of his political career. A short time later, Richard Nixon and his wife Pat left California to move to New York City. Here were the financial and political power, restaurants, and Broadway theater they so enjoyed, and new career opportunities. The Golden State no longer glimmered for the Nixons. Richard and Pat left behind a deeply divided California Republican Party – which was to have deep implications for the 1964 presidential election.

Nixon appeared ready to leave the byzantine world of California politics behind him. The Hollywood Right's romance with Nixon appeared over as well. Jack Warner, who had seen many stars rise and fall in his long career in Hollywood, conveyed the sentiments of a hardened studio executive when he tersely wrote Nixon three days after the election, "I hope and trust that fate will be kinder to you in the future than it has been in the last few years. Our best to Pat."[117]

A week after *The Alamo* appeared in the theaters, in 1960, John Wayne's sidekick and fellow anticommunist Ward Bond died of a massive heart attack. Bond's career after the HUAC hearings had fallen on hard times until he got a starring role in the television series *Wagon Train* in 1957. Bond was just beginning to enjoy his celebrity when his high-living lifestyle caught up with him. Earlier that April, Gary Cooper underwent surgery for prostate cancer that was discovered to have spread to his colon and later his lungs. Cooper, well known in Hollywood for his womanizing, returned home to die. His earlier conversion to Catholicism brought him peace. Hedda Hopper reported that "after embracing

---

[115] Correspondence with financial supporters, movie moguls, and Hollywood celebrities can be found under their names in the Richard M. Nixon Pre-Presidential Papers, Series 320.

[116] Hill, *Dancing Bear*, p. 178.

[117] Jack Warner to Richard M. Nixon, November 9, 1961, Nixon Papers, Series 320, Box 798.

the Catholic faith he's never experienced such joy or happiness."[118] Just a few years earlier, in 1957, Louis B. Mayer died. This was the same year that the Warner Brothers Studio was sold. The big studio system that characterized the golden years of Hollywood was ending.

The deaths of DeMille, Mayer, Bond, and Cooper coincided with the end of the Red Scare in Hollywood. Anticommunism was no longer the issue in Hollywood. The studios accommodated themselves to unions and quietly archived the blacklist. Hollywood political culture returned to being liberal – a place in which it had always felt more comfortable. Although dwindling in numbers, the Hollywood Right was by no means dead. Indeed, its greatest political successes were to come, but not easily. The Hollywood Right remained steadfast in its support of the Cold War, but over the next decade their focus shifted to economic issues and reflected a backlash against the cultural left and Johnson's Great Society welfare state. They found a new political hero in Barry Goldwater in 1964, and, when he lost his bid for the presidency, they turned back to Richard Nixon in 1968. Yet, in this search for heroes, factionalism within the California Republican Party prevailed. In the end, the party was united by one of Hollywood's own, Ronald Reagan, an actor who had emerged from the factional wars in Hollywood and the divisive presidential campaign of 1964.

[118] Interview with Rocky Cooper, May 1961, Hedda Hopper Papers, Cooper File.

PHOTO 8 Actor Ronald Reagan and Nancy Davis before they married. Nancy convinced Reagan to become a Republican and was a key advisor in his rise to the presidency in 1980. *Academy of Motion Picture Arts and Sciences Library* (date unknown).

PHOTO 9 Sidekick of John Wayne, Ward Bond was a hardcore anticommunist Republican who gained a national following in his television series *Wagon Train*. *Academy of Motion Picture Arts and Sciences Library* (date unknown).

PHOTO 10 Legendary movie star John Wayne, who became a symbol of rugged, independent American and Hollywood conservatism. *Academy of Motion Picture Arts and Sciences Library* (date unknown).

PHOTO 11 Actor Gary Cooper, with his stunning good looks, remained one of Hollywood's most popular leading men. He was an outspoken critic of Roosevelt's New Deal. *Academy of Motion Picture Arts and Sciences Library* (date unknown).

PHOTO 12 Popular actor Jimmy Stewart and producer Cecile B. DeMille shake hands. Both were gung-ho Republicans. *Academy of Motion Picture Arts and Sciences Library* (date unknown).

PHOTO 13 Pictured here are three Republican women. Hollywood columnist Hedda Hopper (center), actors Mary Martin (left), and Helen Hayes (right). *Academy of Motion Picture Arts and Sciences Library* (date unknown).

George murphy   Gen. Doolittle   Mr. Mayer   Kenneth Thompson

PHOTO 14 Actor George Murphy meets with other conservatives, General James Doolittle and Hollywood mogul Louis B. Mayer. *Academy of Motion Picture Arts and Sciences Library* (date unknown).

PHOTO 15 Spanish-speaker and long time Californian Leo Carrillo became a frequent speaker at Republican rallies. Here is a young Carrillo before he became a television star in the 1950s television series *The Cisco Kid*. *Academy of Motion Picture Arts and Sciences Library* (date unknown).

PHOTO 16 Television star of *The Rifleman*, Chuck Connors became one of Hollywood's most articulate Republicans in the 1960s. *Academy of Motion Picture Arts and Sciences Library* (date unknown).

CHAPTER 5

The Hollywood Right Goes for Goldwater and Finds Reagan

In 1964, California Republicans and the Hollywood Right found themselves once again in a familiar pattern: disarray. Democrats held the governor's mansion, with Pat Brown's victory in 1962 over Nixon, and Democrats controlled both houses in the state legislature. As a result, the Democrats were able to push through a progressive social agenda. Nixon's loss left Republicans split into factions, divisions that were deepened in the following two years by the rapid rise of the hard line right led by the John Birch Society. Formed in 1958 by New England candy manufacturer Robert Welch, the Society attracted considerable support in Southern California. Birchers, as members of the Society were called, continued to believe that domestic communism was a real threat in the United States, going so far as to proclaim that communists controlled 80 to 90 percent of the federal government. This kept the communist issue alive in California politics at a time when most Americans, including most conservatives, wanted to move on to other issues. For mainstream conservative Republicans, the Soviet threat remained real, but looking for domestic communism was unnecessary and dead-end politics that only played into the caricature of the paranoid right portrayed in hundreds of newspaper articles, editorials, and even pop songs like the Beach Boys "The Little Old Lady from Pasadena."

The aggressive strategy of the hard right to purge the Republican Party of moderates following the 1962 election irritated Nixon supporters in California. When Nixon's nemesis Joe Shell, who had challenged him in the governor's primary, was appointed to an important position in the 1964 Goldwater presidential campaign in California, key Republicans such as Justin Dart and Leonard Firestone threw their support to Nelson Rockefeller in the California presidential primary.

Goldwater's campaign drew enthusiasm from the Hollywood Right, and Republican celebrities, such as John Wayne, Ronald Reagan (who had recently switched parties), Raymond Massey, and Rock Hudson, brought star power to his campaign. The celebrity gap between Republicans and Democrats, however, was evident to everyone. Many of the Hollywood stars in the Republican arsenal were aging and being superseded by younger, more iconoclastic stars such as Marlon Brando, Paul Newman, and Jane Fonda. By the 1960s, the studio system no longer existed, and Hollywood culture turned further to the left, alienated by Johnson's Vietnam War and inspired by the black civil rights movement. By the late 1960s, star after star declared themselves radicals. Marlon Brando announced he was for Native American liberation, Jane Fonda became an antiwar militant, Dennis Hopper and Candice Bergen (daughter of right-wing ventriloquist Edgar Bergen) actively supported the Black Panthers. If the studio system was dead and the Golden Age of movies was over, movie moguls such as Louis B. Mayer, Sam Goldwyn, the Warner Brothers, Howard Hughes, and David O. Selznick had the last laugh when George Murphy won his race for the U.S. Senate in 1964. Conservatives needed good news after Goldwater's whopping defeat to incumbent president Lyndon B. Johnson.

DEMOCRATS TRIUMPHANT; REPUBLICANS DIVIDED

In 1964, California Democrats under Governor Edmund "Pat" Brown felt that they had everything going for them. Brown had won election twice to the governor's mansion by defeating two Republican heavyweights, William Knowland and Richard Nixon, both of whom had eyed the presidency before being toppled by Brown. In 1958, Brown won by over a million votes and, although Nixon cut this margin in 1962 by about 600,000 votes, Brown proved once again his strength in the state. Democrats, for the first time since 1878, controlled both houses of the state legislature. Brown and his Democratic allies in the legislature pushed a liberal agenda, increasing welfare benefits, expanding funding for mental health facilities and hospitals, and undertaking massive building projects for new freeways, rail systems, and schools. New campuses were created within the University of California and Cal State systems. Brown's political maneuvering was not flawless, however, and he continued to face criticism from the left wing of his own party. Any left-wing complaints against Brown dissipated when Nixon entered the governor's race in 1962.[1]

Brown's triumph in 1962 over Nixon left Democrats euphoric. Brown called for a further expansion of a bold legislative program. Nothing, it seemed, stood in his way politically. But appearances in politics can be as deceptive as a roulette table to a compulsive gambler. The downfall of gamblers and politicians,

---

[1] For the state of California politics in 1964, see Matthew Dallek, *The Right Moment: Ronald Reagan's First Victory and the Decisive Turning Point in American Politics* (New York, 2000), especially pp. 1–80. Also, Kurt Schuparra, *Triumph of the Right: The Rise of the California Conservative Movement, 1945–1966* (Armonk, NY, 1998); Gladwin Hill, *Dancing Bear: An Inside Look at California Politics* (Cleveland, OH, 1968); pp. 150–191; Joel Kotkin and Paul Grabowicz, *California, Inc.* (New York, 1982), pp. 50–89. For Brown's political career, see Ethan Rarick, *California Rising: The Life and Times of Pat Brown* (Berkeley, CA, 2006).

especially when they are winning, is often brought about by a shared trait: hubris. Unlike the gambler, Brown had a social conscience, and this led him to push fair housing legislation through the state legislature against the advice of his closest advisors. His executive secretary Richard Kline had warned him as early as 1960 that "Housing is such an explosive social subject. . . . The question is not what has to be done in this field, but what can be done from a politically realistic standpoint."[2]

After pressure from civil rights groups and other lobbies, Brown announced on St. Valentine's Day, 1963, that he was in favor of fair housing legislation through the Rumford Fair Housing Act. The act banned discrimination in the sale or rental of private dwellings, with a few exceptions. The legislation had been floating around the state legislature for a while, bottled up in committee by a group of powerful conservative Democrats representing rural districts. Rallying liberal groups to his side, Brown pushed through the measure by the slim margin of twenty-two state senators in favor and eighteen against. Real estate interests in the state reacted immediately by placing Proposition 14 on the 1964 ballot to repeal the Fair Housing Act. Brown came out immediately against Proposition 14, attending rallies where he denounced right-wing extremism and racism in California. The anti–Prop 14 campaign labeled the proposition the "the segregation amendment" and attacked opponents as right-wing extremists. For political powerhouses such as Speaker of the Assembly Jesse Unruh, Proposition 14 was a powder keg worth staying away from.

By the fall of 1964, polls showed overwhelming support for Proposition 14. For many Californians, it was a matter of property rights over civil rights. If there was underlying racism on the part of voters supporting Proposition 14, it was not apparent in the surveys. Actually, surveys and later voter analysis revealed that proponents of Proposition 14 were more liberal on racial issues and civil rights than were voters in other states.[3] Brown's vituperative language alienated voters who did not like being accused of racism or of being the pawns of extremist right-wing forces. In October, the *Los Angeles Times* admonished Brown for provoking racial violence. This was hyperbolic. A leading historian later declared that the Proposition 14 campaign was "steeped not in the dark world of rightwing racism but in the murkier realm of California real-estate."[4] Real estate interests spent a fortune on television ads promoting the protection of a man's castle; when housing was portrayed that way, Proposition 14 could not lose. Brown placed himself on the line, against the better counsel of advisors and liberal politicians such as Unruh. He was left burned.

---

[2] Quoted in Dallek, *The Right Moment*, p. 45.
[3] Raymond E. Wolfinger and Fred I. Greenstein, "The Repeal of Fair Housing in California: An Analysis of Referendum Voting," *The American Political Science Review*, 62:3 (September 1968), pp. 753–769.
[4] Dallek, *The Right Moment*, p. 59.

Whatever political worries Brown felt within the Democratic Party were eased by disharmony within the Republican Party. After the 1962 Republican disaster, Richard Kline, Brown's key advisor, captured the general liberal sentiment that their Republican opponents were on the canvas, perhaps out for the count, when he wrote his boss, "The Republican Party is, at the moment, without leadership or direction. Its chances of reemerging as a major force in California depend largely on how well you succeed or fail in the next four years."[5] Joseph Shell's challenge to Nixon in the Republican primary in 1962 revealed the growing insurgence of the hard right within the California Republican Party. Nixon supporters such as Justin Dart and Leonard Firestone believed that, after the bitter primary contest, Shell's tepid endorsement of Nixon after losing the primary had cost Nixon the election. Conservative L.A. attorney Loyd Wright's challenge to oust moderate incumbent U.S. senator Thomas Kuchel brought further divisions within the party. Ronald Reagan served as Wright's campaign chairman, which left many within the party suspicious of Reagan. Following Wright's thumping in the primary, Reagan sought to distance himself from the campaign by declaring he was only an "honorary" chairman and was not actively involved in the campaign.

Factional divisions worsened following the 1962 election, when Joe Shell and his campaign manager Russ Walton formed the United Republicans of California (UROC) to take control of the state Republican Party by throwing moderates out of leadership positions. UROC aimed to challenge the authority of the moderate-controlled and formerly powerful California Assembly, a leading party organization. "Operation Takeover," as they called their strategy, proved remarkably successful. The formation of UROC was an early indication of the movement to win the Republican presidential nomination for Barry Goldwater. Declaring United Republicans a grassroots movement out to overthrow the Republican Establishment to ensure "the freedom of each individual citizen," Shell placed party leaders on the defensive.[6] By 1964, UROC had grown to around 20,000 members. Shell and his supporters were aided in these efforts by the recently formed John Birch Society, which found a natural home in Southern California among right-wingers concerned with communist infiltration into government. Shell was not a Bircher himself, but through the combined forces of unaligned conservative activists and Birch Society members, the right exerted unprecedented influence in the California Republican Party in the early 1960s, as key party organizations fell to right-wing control.

---

[5] Quoted in Dallek, *The Right Moment*, p. 45.
[6] Quoted in Schuparra, *Triumph of the Right*, p. 81. Also, Totten J. Anderson and Eugene C. Lee, "The 1964 Election in California," *Western Political Quarterly*, 18:2 (June 1965), pp. 452–474, especially pp. 458–459; and Kurt Schuparra, "Barry Goldwater and Southern California Conservatism: Ideology, Image and Myth in the 1964 California Republican Presidential Primary," *Southern California Quarterly*, 74:2 (1992), pp. 277–298.

In 1963, the right was able to elect Robert Gaston to the presidency of the California Young Republicans. In his campaign, Gaston received financial support from Shell and UROC to travel around the state. Opponents of the right publicly accused the John Birch Society of infiltrating the California Young Republicans.[7] Gaston's election shocked Republican moderates such as Caspar Weinberger, chairman of the state party. Weinberger was from San Francisco, where the party remained in moderate hands, including those of Mayor George Christopher. The clash between moderates and conservatives followed North-South fault lines, with Birchers concentrated in the South, especially in fast-growing Orange County.

Moderates and the insurgent right clashed again when the California Republican Assembly (CRA) convened for its annual meeting in 1963. The CRA had been controlled by moderates going back to the days of Earl Warren. At the meeting, the right put up for leadership retired Navy commander Harry Waddell, who openly courted Bircher support. Moderates fell behind a San Francisco labor official, William Nelligan. Waddell was defeated by the moderates, but the election fight left the two factions embittered. Near-violence erupted at the outset of the convention over the accreditation of delegates, leading the president of the CRA, Fred Hall, to denounce the conservative faction and its allies, the Birchers, as being fascist and un-American.[8] Any truce between the two sides for the sake of party unity appeared impossible. As Hall declared, the Nelligan election was "the turning point against the conspiracy of the John Birch Society and its supporters to capture control of the Republican Party."[9] The fight proved a prelude to the 1964 Republican presidential primary that pitted conservative Barry Goldwater against liberal Nelson Rockefeller.

The fight within the CRA was by no means over, however. In 1964, the right surged back at the annual convention and outmaneuvered moderates through parliamentary tactics. Under its conservative leadership, the CRA joined the California Young Republicans in endorsing Barry Goldwater for president. The CRA's endorsement of Goldwater came after a long and acrimonious floor debate that lasted into the night. Founding member of the Assembly colonel Ed Shattuck led the pro-Rockefeller faction. These pro-Rockefeller Republicans were party regulars and not wild-eyed liberals. They were upset by the political challenge coming from the right and the involvement of the Birch Society in Republican politics. The Rockefeller faction had tried to stave off an endorsement of Goldwater by calling for a no-endorsement policy for the organization. When the CRA endorsed Goldwater, it was a clear victory for the right. Now on

---

[7] Barbara Shell Stone, *The John Birch Society of California*, Ph.D. dissertation, University of Southern California, 1968, p. 34.

[8] Stone, *The John Birch Society of California*, p. 33.

[9] Quoted in Schuparra, *Triumph of the Right*, p. 86. This discussion of factional politics in California relies heavily on Schuparra's informative study.

his way out of the presidency, Nelligan bitterly warned that "fanatics of the Birch variety have fastened their fangs on the Republican Party's flanks and are hanging on like grim death."[10] Moderates formed within the CRA what they called the FAB Society – "Fuck a Bircher." The fight within the CRA was a prelude to a hotly contested Republican primary in the state.

With the hard right in control of the Young Republicans and the CRA, conservatives moved to secure the endorsement of Goldwater from these organizations. The Young Republicans, the CRA, and Shell's United Republicans of California endorsed Goldwater in 1964. The Young Republicans refused to support three incumbent assemblymen and two incumbent congressmen in Southern California. The United Republicans of California refused to endorse fourteen of twenty-eight Republican incumbent state assemblymen because they were deemed to be too liberal. The endorsements entailed financial support and precinct workers. These efforts were further supported by the formation of Citizens Committee of California that claimed 35,000 members and a campaign fund of $500,000 for ensuring that conservative candidates won elections.

The number of Birchers nationally or in California is unclear. Robert Welch, the founder of the John Birch Society, claimed 100,000 members. More accurate figures placed membership at considerably less. The Birch Society brought a fervid message that communists dominated the American government and that international communism was an immediate and advancing threat. Members of the Society swore that they would battle against communism until the last American patriot died with a sword in hand. Welch and the Society viewed all domestic and foreign policy through the lens of an intense anticommunism not seen since the early days of the Cold War and perhaps not even then.

The Birch Society gained particular strength in California, especially in Orange County. The greatest growth for the California Birch Society was between the years 1961 and 1964. A semblance of political respectability was imparted to the Society in California when Congressmen John Rousselot and Edward Hiestand announced that they were members of the group in 1962, although both were defeated for reelection that year. That same year, Bill Richardson, another Birch member, was defeated in his initial bid for election to Congress. Richardson later resigned from the Birch Society and was elected to the state senate, where he often joined forces with another state senator, John Schmitz, an Orange County Bircher. The Society in California was large enough to be divided into two districts, Northern California and Southern California. Following his defeat for Congress, Rousselot became the Western District Governor of the John Birch Society, later becoming National Director of Public Relations for the Society. His public relations and organizing skills enabled the Society to grow in membership in California and in many other Western states. The typical member of the California Birch Society was well-educated, affluent, and generally older. Most were professionals. The Birch

[10] Quoted in Schuparra, *Triumph of the Right*, p. 87.

Society was primarily an educational organization, but individual members became involved in state Republican politics, networking with other Birchers. Many of the Birchers were conspiracy minded. They believed that behind the communist conspiracy lay a larger conspiracy of the Bavarian Illuminati, a secret Masonic group. In 1964, the great majority of California Birchers were registered Republicans, although another 20 percent joined George Wallace's third party, the American Independent Party, in 1968. Surveys showed no members declaring themselves Democratic. As Republicans, Birchers were more active within the party than were average voters.[11]

The Birch Society attracted a few Hollywood conservatives. Its most notable member was John Wayne, who joined the Society in 1960, drawn to its conservative, anticommunist program. Now at the height of his movie career, Wayne could afford his association with this far right-wing organization, and his enthusiasm for the organization grew when the John Birch Society threw its support behind Goldwater in 1964.

After the election, Wayne broke with the organization over a series of issues. Welch's charge that Eisenhower was a conscious communist agent offended him. As he told one interviewer, "Ike was not my favorite politician, but he sure as hell was not a communist." Recovering from lung cancer, Wayne was extremely put off by the Bircher's conspiratorial views of medicine and health. He thought the Society's campaign against the fluoridation of public water, attributing the push for fluoridation to a communist plot, was downright silly. The final straw for Wayne came when the Birch Society launched a campaign against the American medical establishment claiming that doctors, drug companies, and the federal government were part of a communist conspiracy to keep cancer cures off the market. When a Bircher friend warned him that the Scripps Institute and Good Samaritan Hospital were part of this plot, Wayne responded in his typically blunt manner, "Jesus Christ, you people are getting scary!"[12]

Wayne's association with the Birchers was the most visible of such links in Hollywood, which in itself was interesting because Wayne had written Goldwater in 1959 that "I don't mind getting mixed up in the affairs of our country, but I don't think it's good for me to be active in politics." He clearly had changed his mind a year later.[13] Wayne was not the only film star to be attracted to the Society. Character actor and television star Walter Brennan also joined the Birchers and became an outspoken Goldwater Republican. He took time off from his career to "fight religiously" on the anticommunist front.[14] (Unlike

---

[11] Stone, *The John Birch Society of California*, pp. 161–162.
[12] Quoted in Randy Roberts and James S. Olson, *John Wayne: American* (Lincoln, NE, 1995), p. 569. This fine biography of Wayne discusses his involvement in the John Birch Society, pp. 568–569.
[13] John Wayne to Barry Goldwater, June 15, 1959, Barry Goldwater Papers, Alpha Files, John Wayne.
[14] Pat McDermott to Hedda Hopper, March 6, 1962, Hedda Hopper Papers, Walter Brennan file.

Wayne, who deserted the Birchers – and later broke with the right in the 1970s over key issues – Brennan stayed on, supporting the American Independent Party presidential candidate George Wallace in 1968 because he felt Richard Nixon was too liberal.) Lesser-known comic actress Zasu Pitts was also a member of the Society.

The emergence of the Birch Society within Republican politics exacerbated factionalism within the California GOP and presented a serious challenge to Barry Goldwater as he began to consider a run for the party's nomination. Goldwater did not want to alienate potential voters who might be Birchers, but he was concerned, and rightfully so, with being tagged with extremism. In early 1964, William Baroody, head of the American Enterprise Institute, called an extraordinary meeting with William F. Buckley, Jr., conservative author Russell Kirk, Barry Goldwater, and himself. They met in Palm Beach, Florida, where Goldwater was visiting his sister-in-law incognito to avoid reporters. The gathering began with a general discussion of the state of politics, then turned to what the meeting was truly about – what to do with the John Birch Society. Everyone at the meeting agreed that the Society should be denounced by Goldwater and everyone else. The problem, Goldwater said, is that "Every other person in Phoenix is a member of the John Birch Society.... I'm not talking about Commie-haunted apple pickers or cactus drunks. I'm talking about the highest caste of men of affairs. Any of you know who Frank Cullen Brophy is?" (Brophy was a leading Phoenix businessman and one of Goldwater's key backers.) After more discussion, it was agreed that Buckley's *National Review* would denounce Welch and expose his thinking to "scorn and derision." In the next issue of the *National Review*, Buckley published a 5,000-word excoriation of Welch that became known in conservative circles as Buckley's excommunication of Welch from the conservative movement. In response to Buckley's piece, Goldwater wrote praising average Birch members as "sincere conservatives," but he believed "the best thing Mr. Welch could do to serve the cause of anti-Communism in the United States would be to resign" as head of the Birch Society. Buckley's attack on Welch created a backlash from Birchers, who continued to despise him until his death in 2008.[15] For Goldwater, the ploy did not work. Despite it, he was tagged with the extremist label anyway in his presidential bid – and he entered the California GOP primary in June 1964 faced with a divided state party. Many Republicans who might have been his natural supporters, faced with an insurgent and militant right – one that thought Nixon too liberal – endorsed Rockefeller.

[15] William F. Buckley, Jr., "Goldwater, the John Birch Society, and Me," *Commentary*, March 2008, pp. 52–54; William F. Buckley, Jr. *Flying High: Remembering Barry Goldwater* (New York, 2008), pp. 65–70.

GOLDWATER AND THE QUAGMIRE OF CALIFORNIA PRESIDENTIAL POLITICS

Goldwater's bid for the GOP presidential nomination in 1964 elicited wild enthusiasm among conservatives nationally and the Hollywood Right in particular. His decision to run for the presidency came after long and agonizing contemplation, and, once the decision was made, Goldwater still remained reticent about the race. Goldwater had great doubts about whether he was presidential timber, and any enthusiasm he might have felt toward a presidential bid dissipated with the assassination of John F. Kennedy in November 1963. Goldwater believed that a race between Kennedy and himself would give a clear choice to the American people about the course of America's future. He had become friends with Kennedy when they served together in the Senate. As both men looked toward the 1964 election, there was serious discussion of the two of them staging a series of presidential debates across the United States, much in the same way that Stephen Douglas and Abraham Lincoln had done during the Illinois senatorial race in 1858, when the two men engaged in seven notable debates. Kennedy's assassination changed all of this. His death ensured, as much as politics is certain, that Lyndon Baines Johnson was a shoo-in to keep the White House in 1964.[16]

Whatever Goldwater lacked in enthusiasm was made up for by his devoted followers. Conservatives had waited for such a candidate since 1952, when Robert Taft lost the GOP nomination to Eisenhower. They found in Goldwater their perfect man. He was rugged, spoke his mind, and was a true conservative who believed in small government and a strong national defense – and he was anticommunist. His *Conscience of a Conservative*, ghostwritten by William F. Buckley's brother-in-law Brent Bozell, was a concise, eloquent statement on behalf of conservatism. As a native of Arizona, Goldwater represented the independence of the West. Whatever flaws Goldwater might have as a candidate – a senator from a lightly populated state, too quick to ad-lib, blunt in his language, and one of the few GOP senators to vote against the historic Civil Rights Act, he was not the one thing that conservatives in the party most despised – part of the Republican Eastern Establishment. That role fell to Nelson Rockefeller, the governor of New York, who wanted the nomination for himself.

The battle between Goldwater and Rockefeller for the nomination is often depicted as an ideological struggle, and there is much to be said for this

---

[16] There are a number of excellent biographies of Goldwater and studies of the 1964 election. The best biography to begin with is Robert Alan Goldberg, *Barry Goldwater* (New Haven, CT, 1997). Readable is Rick Perlstein, *Before the Storm: Barry Goldwater and the Unmaking of the American Censuses* (New York, 2006). An engaging account of Barry Goldwater and the 1964 election is found in John William Middendorf, *A Glorious Disaster: Barry Goldwater's Presidential Campaign and the Origins of the Conservative Movement* (New York, 2006).

characterization, but it does not tell the whole story. First, although Rockefeller was mostly liberal and was the governor of New York, he was a hawk on foreign policy, defense spending, and the Cold War. Rockefeller and Goldwater clashed over the civil rights plank in the 1964 GOP national platform hearings, but the differences in wording were more symbolic than substantive. Rockefeller wanted a plank that called for the support of sit-ins. Both men called for ending segregation in the South. Once Goldwater won the party's nomination, his campaign tried to move to the center, downplaying much of his earlier rhetoric about privatizing Social Security and the Tennessee Valley Authority and ending subsidies for farmers.

Those state Republican leaders who lined up for Rockefeller or Goldwater in the California primary did not fall always or easily into set ideological niches. Senator Thomas Kuchel, who headed the Rockefeller campaign in California, was a moderate, but other Rockefeller endorsers were less clearly defined.[17] The rise of the hard right in California created a maelstrom that shaped the course of the primary struggle between Goldwater and Rockefeller. The race for the GOP nomination came down to the winner-take-all June California primary after Goldwater and Rockefeller had stalemated one another in earlier state primaries. Both Goldwater's and Rockefeller's presidential bids got off to a bad start when Henry Cabot Lodge, Jr., the former Massachusetts senator, pulled a surprise victory in the first primary in New Hampshire as a write-in candidate. Lodge won in Massachusetts and New Jersey before he withdrew from the race. Goldwater won Illinois, Texas, and Indiana with little organized opposition. Rockefeller won West Virginia and a number of other state caucuses in the Northeast. William Scranton, the governor of Pennsylvania, won his own state. Rockefeller's chances improved immensely when he won a decisive victory in the May 15 primary in Oregon, receiving nearly double the number of votes that Goldwater received. At this point, all eyes turned to the California primary to be held on June 2.

On the surface, California looked like natural Goldwater country, but California Republicans were divided, with Northern California tending more liberal, whereas Southern California remained a hotbed of conservatism. For all of Goldwater's grassroots support in Southern California, many of the Republican big-wigs there threw their support to Rockefeller. Their problem was that Joe Shell, the man who had refused to endorse Nixon in 1962 and who had orchestrated the takeover of the Young Republicans and the Republican Assembly, was given a prominent place in the Goldwater campaign in California. For moderates such as state party chairman Caspar Weinberger, Joe Shell and his right-wing cronies represented the forces of both extremism and divisiveness. Justin Dart and Leonard Firestone, important figures in the effort to revive the Republican Party in Southern California, threw their support

[17] Goldwater was infuriated by Kuchel's support of Rockefeller. See Memo for the Week Ending January 26, 1964, Goldwater Papers, Series II, Box 120.

to Rockefeller. The issue was not ideological: Dart and, to a lesser extent, Firestone, were conservatives; both had spent exorbitant amounts of money and energy rebuilding the party in the state, and they were not about to have their efforts destroyed by what they saw as right-wing yahoos.

There were other reasons as well for Dart and Firestone to support Rockefeller over Goldwater. Rockefeller was not the knee-jerk liberal that his opponents described. He was tough on crime and had imposed harsh sentences for drugs. He had also rejected gimmicks and balanced New York's budget every year. Rockefeller was an excellent campaigner who connected well with voters. Goldwater proved undisciplined on the campaign trail and not a terribly exciting speaker, except to the devout who loved his message of limited government and strong national defense. There were personal reasons as well for Dart and Firestone to support Rocky. In his work on rebuilding the California Republican Party, Justin Dart had kept in close contact with Nelson Rockefeller by sending him speeches and United Republican material on fundraising techniques and state party-building materials. At the start of the 1960 campaign, Dart sent Rockefeller a box of candy to help him through the "hurly-burly of political life."[18]

Leonard Firestone, heir to the Firestone Tire fortune, enjoyed an even closer personal relationship with Nelson Rockefeller. They came from the same class – America's wealthiest. Both the Rockefellers and the Firestones were art collectors and philanthropists to the arts. They gave one another personal gifts, invited one another to their homes when they were in town, and exchanged condolences upon the death of family members. Firestone arranged for Rockefeller to speak in California before declaring he was running for the nomination. Given their close relations and Firestone's importance in Republican money circles, Rockefeller invited Firestone to be the Southern California finance chairman of his campaign.[19] Given Firestone's support for Nixon throughout his political career, Shell's costly attack on Nixon in 1962, and the right's attack on moderates, Dart and Firestone endorsed Rockefeller in the California primary. What is perhaps more surprising is that the *Los Angeles Times* endorsed Rockefeller over Goldwater in the primary as well.

Dart's and Firestone's endorsement of Rockefeller in this heated primary split the Southern California money interests that had hung together throughout the 1950s. Much of the division could be traced to the right-to-work fight in 1958.

---

[18] Justin Dart to Nelson A. Rockefeller, March 29, 1957; Francis A. Jamieson to Nelson A. Rockefeller, April 10, 1957; Nelson A. Rockefeller to Justin Dart, April 10, 1957; Nelson A. Rockefeller to Justin Dart, April 11, 1957; Francis A. Jamieson to Nelson A. Rockefeller, April 11, 1957; Nelson A. Rockefeller to Justin Dart, April 12, 1957, in Nelson A. Rockefeller Personal Papers, RG 04; and Nelson A. Rockefeller to Justin Dart, January 6, 1960, Rockefeller Personal Papers, Ann C. Whitman Series, Box 4, "D-General," in Rockefeller Family Archives.

[19] Full correspondence between Firestone and Rockefeller is found in Rockefeller Personal Papers, Ann C. Whitman, Box 005, F-General, RG 04, Rockefeller Family Archives.

William Knowland, who had been defeated for governor in 1958, chaired the Goldwater campaign in California. One consequence of this factional fight was that the United Republicans, the major fundraising group in Southern California, were divided over which candidate to support in the 1964 California primary. Goldwater's advisory committee included Henry Salvatori; Pat Frawley, chairman of the board of U.S. National Bank; C. Arnholt Smith; television station owner Helen Alvarez Hill; and oilman A. C. Rubel (Frawley and Rubel were close to the John Birch Society). Also on the advisory committee was Joseph Shell. Goldwater and his staff had no illusions about Shell. They understood that Shell had become a powerhouse in the state legislature, with a "wild-eyed following among all the rabid conservative elements" in the state.[20]

Opponents accused Rockefeller of representing "the Kingmakers," Eastern financial interests that had refused to back Taft over Dewey in 1948 or Eisenhower in 1952. In fact, Rockefeller *was* one of the Kingmakers: the Rockefeller family had given more money to the party than anyone else. Conservatives targeted Rockefeller as an enemy, ideologically and politically. The Hollywood Right generally kept out of the primary battle, with some notable exceptions such as John Wayne, Ronald Reagan, and Hedda Hopper, who came out early for Goldwater. Once Goldwater won the nomination, there was great enthusiasm on the part of the right. As early as 1963, Hopper had already been on the road for Goldwater, giving three speeches for him in the Midwest.[21] During the primary, Reagan appeared in a TV ad for Goldwater defending the senator's vote against the Civil Rights Act.[22]

Goldwater's rise in Arizona politics had been shaped by defeating Democrats allied with organized labor. In 1957, Cecil B. DeMille had arranged for Goldwater to speak at the Freedom Club in Los Angeles on right-to-work legislation. The Freedom Club had been organized in 1950 by a local Congregational minister to promote conservative speakers and, prior to Goldwater's appearance, such well-known conservatives as newspaper columnist George Sokolsky, *National Review* editor William F. Buckley, Jr., and radio commentator Clarence Manion had spoken there. Goldwater's speech at the First Congregational Church drew a large and enthusiastic audience, and the Committee for Voluntary Unionism, a DeMille organization, filmed the event. Women attending the speech were encouraged to wear slacks, and men were told to wear work clothes, overalls, and slacks to project the image of a working-class audience. The film of Goldwater's speech was widely distributed across the country and, while in Los Angeles, DeMille arranged for Goldwater to meet

---

[20] William F. Knowland to Dennison Kitchell, January 7, 1964, Barry Goldwater Papers, Series II, Box 120.

[21] Hedda Hopper to Morrie Ryskind, October 28, 1963, Hedda Hopper Papers, Ryskind File; and Roberts and Olson, *John Wayne: American*, p. 20.

[22] Joseph Lewis, *What Makes Reagan Run: A Political Profile* (New York, 1968), p. 78.

prominent Republicans.[23] Goldwater's right-to-work stance did not appeal to all Republicans, however. With his eyes on the presidency, Nixon did not endorse right-to-work, a position reinforced by Justin Dart, George Murphy, Harvey Mudd, and *Los Angeles Times* political editor Kyle Palmer. They saw right-to-work legislation as a dead-end issue for the Republican Party.[24] So did Ray Bliss, party chair in Ohio, who tried and failed to stop conservatives from putting a right-to-work initiative on the state ballot. The initiative lost, and Republicans were wiped out.

Given the stakes and the ideological divide, the California presidential primary proved to be especially nasty. While projecting a "middle of the road" image, Rockefeller assailed Goldwater as part of the "extreme right." To counter this, the Goldwater campaign drew on celebrities to project a nonthreatening, popular image. Ronald Reagan was used at many events as a superb stump speaker who did not come across as a "wacko" right-winger. Television star Efrem Zimbalist, Jr. introduced Goldwater at a 700-person fundraiser dinner in Long Beach.[25]

Basking in starlight was not enough to save Goldwater from himself. His statement that he favored delegating authority over the use of tactical atomic weapons to NATO was taken as evidence that Goldwater was "trigger happy." Rockefeller's campaign had done extensive research on the John Birch Society, which they now used to paint Goldwater as a candidate of the Birchers. The Goldwater campaign officially sought to downplay conflict with Rockefeller so as not to alienate moderates, but behind the scenes was a hard-hitting campaign that characterized Rockefeller as a home-breaker (he had divorced his first wife in order to marry Happy, a mother of four children), a liberal internationalist, and a representative of the Eastern financial wing of the party that was Republican in Name Only (RINO). Conservative author Phyllis Schlafly's *A Choice Not an Echo* (1964), a self-published polemic lauding the candidacy of Goldwater as a true conservative and denouncing Rockefeller as part of the internationalist Eastern Republican Establishment, was distributed in the hundreds of thousands throughout California. Both campaigns drew blood. A Harris poll taken five days before the election showed that 50 percent of Republican voters supported neither Rockefeller nor Goldwater. More than 35 percent of Republicans objected to Rockefeller's divorce and remarriage,

[23] L. A. Alesen to Barry Goldwater, November 27, 1957; L.A. Alesen to Barry Goldwater, October 12, 1957; Donald MacLean to Dorothy E. White, September 12, 1956, in Cecil B. DeMille Papers, Box 1192, Folder 5.

[24] Bob Finch, Memo, August 29, 1957; and Kyle Palmer Call, September 5, 1958, Richard M. Nixon Papers, Series 320, Box 258 and Box 577.

[25] "Goldwater Banquet, Rally Rickets on Sale," *Independent Press Telegram* (Long Beach), April 10, 1964, p. 16.

whereas 40 percent were disturbed by Goldwater's perceived association with extremists. Similar divisions prevailed among Republican county chairmen.[26]

In June, a record number of voters, more than 70 percent of those registered, turned out to vote in the primary. Nearly 80 percent of all Republicans voted, and 70 percent of Democrats voted in their primary. Both primaries were limited to party registrants. Many pundits expected Rockefeller to win, given his earlier victory in Oregon and his lead in the state polls during the last five days of the campaign. The election broke, as expected, along regional lines. Goldwater carried only fourteen of the state's fifty-eight counties – and all were in the southern part of the state. He won heavily in Orange County and swept Los Angeles County with a 60 percent margin. Rockefeller's margin of victory in San Francisco, where he won two-thirds of Republican voters, was not large enough to compensate for his thumping in Southern California, especially in Los Angeles County, where two-fifths of Republicans lived and voted. Goldwater won narrowly, by over 68,000 votes (1,120,403 to Rockefeller's 1,052,053). With the California victory, Goldwater's presidential nomination was assured, but the primary had inflicted damage. Rockefeller's attack on Goldwater's extremism was taken up in the general campaign by incumbent President Lyndon Johnson. And the primary reinforced divisions in the California Republican Party as well. Justin Dart and Leonard Firestone, as well as most other Rockefeller supporters, endorsed Goldwater after the primary, but hard feelings remained.

While California Republicans were wracked with factional division, these fissures were not evident when actor George Murphy swept the Republican U.S. Senate primary over his two opponents, Leland Kaiser, a San Francisco executive, and Fred Hall, a moderate Republican who had served as president of the CRA and, in the late fifties, as governor of Kansas. Kaiser was seen as too liberal for many Republican voters, and Hall, even though he was a University of Southern California graduate, was seen as both too liberal and a carpetbagger. Murphy, running as a former union president and a moderate, easily swept the California primary, winning 1.1 million votes, which translated into 54 percent of the vote. Kaiser won close to 700,000 votes, providing him with 33 percent of the vote. Hall, who had denounced "extremists" within the state Republican Party, received only 261,000 votes, a pathetic 12.6 percent of the vote. After endorsing Goldwater following his victory over Rockefeller, Murphy quickly distanced himself from the party's presidential nominee for fear he might be painted as an extremist by his Democratic opponent, in this case Pierre Salinger, press secretary to Kennedy and Johnson.

Salinger's candidacy revealed that divisions within the California Democrats had by no means mended. By 1964, Jesse Unruh, the powerful speaker of the state Assembly, wanted Governor Pat Brown's job. This helped set the stage for the Democratic primary for the U.S. Senate that occurred when incumbent

---

[26] Totton J. Anderson and Eugene C. Lee, "The 1964 Election in California," *Western Political Quarterly*, 16:2 (June 1965), pp. 460–462.

senator Clair Engle, a bipartisan favorite, underwent a brain tumor operation. Engle's illness pitted the Brown wing of the party against the Unruh faction. Democrats hoped that Engle might remain in the job, but the party organization decided that the nomination would be open to all comers, including Engle, who quickly dropped out. The liberal California Democratic Council endorsed Alan Cranston – forcing Representative James Roosevelt out of the race. Attorney General Stanley Mosk, Unruh's choice, withdrew under pressure from Brown. At this point, Mosk and Unruh, anxiously casting for an anti-Cranston candidate, approached Pierre Salinger, Johnson's press secretary and a former *San Francisco Chronicle* reporter, to declare himself a candidate. Salinger filed the day before the deadline.

The fight between Salinger and Cranston was nasty by any standard. Both were liberals, so the attacks were necessarily personal. Cranston unsuccessfully challenged Salinger's residency in the courts, and he lost the primary as well. Salinger's victory was narrow – 1,177,000 to Cranston's 1,037,000 votes. Although Engle had been forced to drop out, he received 119,000 sentimental votes. The campaign was the most expensive senate primary in California up to this time. When Engle died in July, Brown appointed Salinger to hold his seat until the November election.

THE HOLLYWOOD RIGHT RALLIES FOR GOLDWATER

Goldwater came to the Republican National Convention in San Francisco already a tarnished candidate. Shortly before the convention, William Scranton, governor of Pennsylvania, went on national television to declare that this was "an hour of crisis for the Republican party and for our nation."[27] Scranton pointed out specifically that Goldwater's vote against the Civil Rights Act of 1964 was akin to supporting racial segregation. Actually, Goldwater had a solid record on integration, having forced the integration of the Air National Guard in Arizona and his family's department store, and he was a member of the local National Association for the Advancement of Colored People (NAACP) in Phoenix. Goldwater had voted for the Civil Rights Act of 1957, but had broken ranks with the Republican senate leadership and his party in voting against the 1964 civil rights law because it expanded federal regulatory powers in public accommodations and employment. Scranton's goal, however, was not to set the record straight, but to prevent Goldwater from securing the nomination. Working behind the scenes was a coalition of anti-Goldwater Republicans that included Nelson Rockefeller and George Romney.

The media reinforced these perceptions of extremism. CBS reporter Daniel Schorr reported from Munich that Goldwater planned after the convention to

[27] Quoted in John H. Kessell, *The Goldwater Coalition: Republican Strategies in 1964* (New York, 1968), pp. 103–104. Also see Robert Alan Goldberg, *Barry Goldwater*, pp. 202–204; and Rick Perlstein, *Before the Storm*, especially pp. 366–375.

meet with German "right-wing elements." *Life* magazine portrayed the Republican Party as overtaken by the "unyielding right wing" and a tide of zealotry. Pat Brown told the press that, with Goldwater, "The stench of fascism is in the air." Senator William Fulbright (D-Arkansas) described Goldwater as the "closest thing in American politics to an equivalent to Russian Stalinism." *Time* magazine quoted a Munich banker as warning that "Goldwater was only a couple of steps away from Americans putting on brown shirts."[28]

Matters worsened when the Rockefeller-Scranton-Romney axis made a last-ditch effort by waging a floor fight on July 14 at the convention to insert planks repudiating the John Birch Society, supporting nuclear arms control, and strengthening the civil rights plank by supporting sit-in demonstrations. Goldwater supporters fought back against these planks. Emotions on both sides were already running high when Rockefeller came to the podium to address the convention. After a short plea to have the platform amended, he began talking about "goon squads, bomb threats ... and Nazi methods." On the floor, Goldwater supporters tried to drown Rockefeller out with chants of "We want Barry." At this point, Rockefeller turned directly to the television camera and declared, "This is still a free country, ladies and gentlemen."[29] Rockefeller had successfully baited the Goldwater delegates into looking like extremists.

Goldwater, with his inner campaign circle in his suite at the Mark Hopkins Hotel, became increasingly incensed by these attacks. He understood much of the hostile liberal media to be "sensation-seeking columnists and commentators," but what he could not fathom were Republicans who were joining in painting a portrait of him as an extremist. Many of these people had known him for years. He had worked with them. Now, they appeared irresponsible and did not give a damn about the "good of our party."[30] At this point, Goldwater decided to make what William F. Buckley, Jr. fittingly described as a "scorching comeback" by instructing the team writing his nomination speech to take on the issue of extremism. As a result, there were two lines in his acceptance speech that lit a firestorm of criticism from both within the party and from his critics, made an indelible impression on the minds of many supporters, and played right into the hands of his opponent, Lyndon Baines Johnson. Goldwater declared, "I would remind you that extremism in the defense of liberty is no vice. And let me remind you also that moderation in the pursuit of justice is no virtue." Such sentiments in themselves might have been acceptable. Under attack for being an extremist, Goldwater made a serious miscalculation in attempting to defend

---

[28] Brown, Fulbright, and *Time* quotations are found in Buckley, Jr., *Flying High*, pp. 150–152; and Perlstein, *Before the Storm*, p. 366.

[29] Quoted in Goldberg, *Barry Goldwater*, p. 204.

[30] Quoted in Buckley, Jr., *Flying High*, p. 151. Also, Robert E. Thompson, "Angry Goldwater Skips GOP Harmony Party; Senator Described as 'Boiling Mad' Over Letter from Scranton," *Los Angeles Times*, July 13, 1964.

extremism. Goldwater spent weeks after the convention talking to leading Republicans, trying to extinguish the brush fire he had ignited. The entire strategy of trying to disassociate Goldwater from the Birchers, as laid out a year earlier in Palm Beach, had collapsed in five seconds during his speech.

Goldwater was not going to win the election in 1964 in any case following the assassination of John F. Kennedy. Campaign manager William Baroody tried to salvage the campaign by trying to moderate Goldwater's message. Goldwater was instructed to stay away from issues such as Social Security, Vietnam, and civil rights. His opponent, incumbent president Lyndon Baines Johnson, must have felt like jumping for joy when Goldwater informed him in a private meeting in the White House at the start of the campaign that he had decided, for the good of the country and national security, that he was not going to talk about Vietnam or racial rioting (during the summer of 1964, racial riots exploded in Harlem, Brooklyn, and Rochester, New York; Jersey City, Paterson, and Elizabeth, New Jersey; Toledo, Ohio; and Philadelphia, Pennsylvania).

Even after Goldwater won the nomination, there were indications that not all was well in California – including in Hollywood. The first sign of trouble came at the Republican State Central Committee meeting shortly after the GOP convention. When the Committee met in early August, the Goldwater forces tried to seat Vernon J. Cristina, a Goldwater-pledged delegate backed by Joe Shell and Goldwater's primary campaign chairman William F. Knowland. Cristina challenged Gaylord B. Parkinson, a 45-year-old obstetrician who refused to take sides in the primary. When the final votes were counted, Parkinson defeated Cristina 518 to 374 votes, a major defeat for the Goldwater forces in the state. Attending the meeting, George Murphy, the GOP nominee for the Senate, tried to quell tempers by urging delegates to "let the struggle of the spirited primary be buried in the past."[31]

Further signs of disunity became apparent when the Goldwater campaign formed an executive committee of businessmen for Goldwater. Seventy-seven of the 450-member group came from California, most from Southern California, including the vice chairman of the committee, Patrick J. Frawley, chairman of the Schick Safety Razor Company and owner of Technicolor Corporation. Hollywood money was conspicuously lacking. The only others coming out the movie industry – even somewhat tangentially – were Riley Jackson, president of Parade Pictures, and Robert Riley, vice president of Technicolor. A clear sign of division was evident in Jack Warner's public comment that "only he and God knows how he would be voting this year." Warner had been one of the Republicans' largest financial contributors in past presidential elections, and now he was standing on the sidelines. Standing with him was Melvin Leroy, a producer-director who had traveled with the Eisenhower and later Nixon campaigns. He declared, "I'm not in politics this year."[32]

[31] Carl Greenberg, "Goldwater Forces Lose State Fight," *Los Angeles Times*, August 3, 1964, p. 1.
[32] "Film Stars Divided Over LBJ, Barry," *Long Beach Telegram*, September 16, 1964, p. 17.

Ronald Reagan, who had campaigned heavily for Goldwater in the primaries, was appointed co-chair of Citizens for Goldwater, along with Beverly Hills businessman M. Philip Davis. When asked by the press which actors were supporting Goldwater, Reagan listed twenty-six prominent Hollywood celebrities pledged to campaign for Goldwater, including Roy Rogers, Dale Evans, singer Pat Boone, Donna Reed, Efrem Zimbalist, Jr., Raymond Massey, Gene Raymond, and Robert Stack. Others named were out of Hollywood history, such as Jeanette MacDonald.[33] Cowboy stars such as John Wayne and Randolph Scott were still headliners, and Goldwater attracted an array of television stars, some of whom made the transition from film to weekly televised programs – Raymond Massey (*Dr. Kildare*), Gale Storm (*My Little Margie*), Walter Brennan (*The Real McCoys*), and baseball star turned TV actor Chuck Connors (*The Rifleman*). Ronald Reagan made the transition to television in the series *Death Valley Days* in 1964. After Reagan left in 1965, the series became a last stop for other Republican actors who hosted the show into syndication, including Robert Taylor, who became gravely ill in 1969 and was replaced by Dale Robertson, and then followed by Ray Milland, Rory Calhoun, and John Payne.

Republican celebrities could not equal the number of Democratic actors who rallied to Johnson's campaign. Lew Wasserman, head of MCA-Universal, the leading talent agency and media conglomerate in Hollywood, headed Johnson's entertainment committee. He drew upon stars such as Marlon Brando, Paul Newman and his wife Joanne Woodward, Kirk Douglas, Burt Lancaster, Janet Leigh, Angie Dickinson, Natalie Wood, and Steve McQueen, to name a few. These actors were at the height of their careers in the movie industry and had little to do with television.[34]

Goldwater's campaign in California leaned heavily on Hollywood celebrities to draw crowds to his speeches.[35] Irene Dunne and television host Art Linkletter

---

[33] Others listed by Reagan included western TV star Clint Walker; actress Coleen Gray, who had testified before Congress in favor of school prayer; Cesar Romero; Robert Taylor; James Stewart; June Allyson; James Drury; John Payne; Irene Dunne; director Norman Taurog; Hedda Hopper; bandleader Tony Martin; dancer Cyd Charisse; actor Marshall Thompson; and Walt Disney. See "Film Stars Divided Over LBJ, Barry," *Press Telegram*, September 16, 1964, p. 18.

[34] Democratic stars included Tony Curtis, Robert Vaughn, Frank Sinatra, Peter Lawford, Sammy Davis, Jr., singer Nat King Cole, comedian Milton Berle, singer–civil rights activist Harry Belafonte, singer Eddie Fisher, Shelley Winters, George Jessel, Henry Fonda, comedian Danny Thomas, actress-singer Connie Stevens, comedian Steve Allen, and actor Barry Sullivan. See "Film Stars Divided Over LBJ, Barry," *Press Telegram*, September 16, 1964, p. 18.

[35] The Goldwater campaign compiled an impressive list of stars supporting Goldwater (asterisk denotes those willing to travel on his behalf): *John Agar, June Allyson, Leon Ames, *Richard Arlen, Robert Arthur, Lita Baron, Constance Bennett, John Beradino, Ray Bolger, Charles Brackett, *Walter Brennan, Dean Burch, David Butler, Mrs. Harry Carey, *Rory Calhoun, Judy Carne, Hoagie Carmichael, Otis Carney, *Ben Cooper, Merian C. Cooper, Wendell

were used at fundraising events even before Goldwater was declared the official GOP presidential nominee.[36] Television actress Gale Storm was sent to a Republican women's fundraiser in the small Los Angeles suburb of Arcadia.[37] At another Hollywood fundraiser, guest stars included John Wayne, Walter Brennan, Efrem Zimabalist, Jr., John Payne, and Robert Stack.[38] The official launch of the California campaign began with a rally at Dodger Stadium on September 8, and the assembly opened with Ronald Reagan greeting Goldwater as he arrived from a series of speeches in San Diego. As master of ceremonies, Reagan brought the crowd to its feet with his jabs at President Johnson. Serving on the honorary host committee were Randolph Scott, television actress Gale Storm, and actor Raymond Massey. Goldwater gave a rousing speech on wasteful government spending under Johnson.[39]

Two days later, cowboy stars Rory Calhoun, Randolph Scott, and John Wayne were joined by actress Corinne Griffith (considered the most beautiful actress of the silent film era) in opening the Goldwater for President headquarters in Southern California.[40] Two weeks later, Calhoun was on hand to open the Democrats for Goldwater campaign headquarters right next to Disneyland in Anaheim.[41] When Goldwater appeared at the Hollywood Palladium, the campaign turned out a full regiment of stars who vigorously applauded his full-throated attack on Johnson's defense policy. Included in the audience were Robert Stack, Wendell Cory, Don DeFore, Buddy Ebstein, Harry von Zell, Raymond Massey, Roy Rogers, Irene Dunne, and silent film director Francis

---

Corey, Charles Correll, Jeanne Crain, *Philip Crosby, Ken Curtis, Dennis Day, Frances Dee, Don DeFore, Andy Devine, Irene Dunne, Mrs. Jimmy Durante, *James Drury, Joan Dru, Buddy Ebsen, Tony Eisley, Dale Evans, Alice Fay, John Ford, Mrs. Clark Gable, William Gargan, Tay Garnett, Mrs. Cedric Gibbons, Colleen Gray, Kathryn Grayson, Virginia Grey, Corinne Griffith, Phil Harris, Hedda Hopper, Jeffrey Hunter, Irene Harvey Johnes, Stan Kenton, Jack Kramer, Jock Mahoney, Jeanette MacDonald, Leo McCarey, Joel McCrea, Mrs. Eddie Mannix, *Raymond Massey, Terry Moore, Andrew W. McLauglin, Ken Murray, Lloyd Nolan, Tommy Noonan, *Lucille Norman, John Payne, Hal Perry, Mary Pickford, LeRoy Prinz, Gene Raymond, Mr. and Mrs. Reagan, Burt Reynolds, *Buddy Rogers, Roy Rogers, Cesar Romero, Mrs. Morrie Ryskind, *Susan Seaforth (Hayes), *Randolph Scott, Robert Stack, James Stewart, *Gloria Swanson, Robert Taylor, *Martha Tilton, Mr. and Mrs. Dimitri Tionkin, Marshall Thompson, Harry von Zell, *Clint Walker, *Pat Wayne, John Wayne, Bill Wellman, Cobina Wright, and *Efrem Zimbalist, Jr., "Stars for Barry," Goldwater Papers, Series II, Box 120, Folder 20. Not included in the list were other notable Hollywood Republicans such as television actor Troy Donahue and comedian Jerry Lewis.

36 "On the Goldwater Team," *Independent Press Telegram* (Long Beach), July 13, 1964, p. A3; "35000 at GOP Buffet," *Oakland Tribune*, July 13, 1964, p. D23.

37 "Celebrities to Attend GOP Anniversary Tea," *Arcadia Tribune*, June 10, 1968.

38 Walter Winchell, "Bobby Kennedy Miffed with Story," *Humbolt Standard*, July 27, 1964, p. 4.

39 Carl Greenberg, "Goldwater to Speak in L.A. Tonight," *Los Angeles Times*, September 8, 1964, p. 1; "Goldwater Blasts Democrats' Fiscal Policy," *The News* (Van Nuys), September 10, 1964, p. A10.

40 "Film Stars to Open Goldwater Office," *Los Angeles Times*, September 10, 1964, p. 13.

41 "Democrats Will Open Goldwater Headquarters," *Los Angeles Times*, September 25, 1964, p. F9.

X. Bushman.[42] Late in the campaign, more stars turned out for a televised "Captive Nations Rally" including movie stars John Agar and Don Haggerty, television actor James Drury (*The Virginian*), Buddy Ebsen, character actor Tris Coffin, Ronald Reagan, tough-guy Mike Muzurki, and Gloria Swanson.[43] In the waning days of the campaign, the Hollywood Right went full bore for Goldwater by joining him on a whirlwind tour that took them to Burbank, Sacramento, Woodland Hills, Santa Rosa, Livermore, Concord, Alturas, Susanville, Sonora, Patterson, and Stockton – hitting Northern and Central California.[44]

The use of these stars was by no means unique. Other presidential campaigns had used stars to draw crowds to campaign events and to impart a "star" quality to their candidate. In 1960, Kennedy had employed stars extensively in his campaign; in 1964, Johnson and Goldwater took the use of celebrities to new levels. Democrats had more stars to draw upon, but the Goldwater campaign drew from a hard core of Hollywood conservatives who were not afraid to back a candidate who was under national attack as a moss-back and an extremist.

Some on the Hollywood Right seemed to embrace an image of hard-core conservativism. Actor Raymond Massey presents a case in point. During the campaign, Massey agreed to narrate *Choice*, a documentary film produced by a Goldwater campaign group, Mothers for Moral America. The brainchild of political strategist Clif White, Mothers for Moral America sought to enhance Goldwater's grassroots credentials as a moral leader. Nancy Reagan and William F. Buckley's mother, Aloise Steiner Buckley, joined the organization. *Choice* sought to display in graphic detail that a Goldwater presidency meant the return of moral leadership to the White House. The film was made to be shown on NBC television, as well as on local stations and to women's clubs across the country. Directed by Raymond Morgan, producer of the immensely popular television program *Queen for a Day*, and political operative Rus Walton, the twenty-eight-minute documentary depicted Johnson's America in moral decay as urban rioters battled police and college students went wild on spring breaks. In the voiceover, Massey warned, "Now there are two Americas."

Ads appeared in local newspapers declaring that this was a documentary "every American must see.... A powerful, dramatic presentation of a troubled America."[45] When first shown to members of the Republican National Committee, it won unanimous praise. Then Drew Pearson, a liberal columnist

---

[42] "Barry Goldwater Campaigns," *Pasadena Independent*, October 10, 1964, p. 7; "Stars to Join Goldwater," *Hayward Daily Review*, October 8, 1964, p. 41; and "Barry's Stadium Rally Sparked by Celebrities," *Pasadena Independent*, October 9, 1964, p. 42.

[43] "A Golden Shower for Goldwater," *Oakland Tribune*, October 18, 1964, p. 24.

[44] Also in the tour were singing cowboy Stuart Hamblin; Ben Cooper, an actor who starred in dozens of television westerns and movies; glamour girl Linda Rogers; and Skip Ward, who appeared in many movies but never reached full stardom.

[45] Advertisement, *Los Angeles Times*, October 22, 1964, p. C15.

viewed a copy of the film that had been purchased by the Democratic Party. He denounced the film as "racist" and "vulgar." Following Pearson's attack, Clif White arranged for Goldwater to watch the film in his hotel room the next day. After seeing it, Goldwater told White, "I'm not going to be made out a racist. You can't show it." White defended the film, saying that Republicans who had watched it had not seen it as being "anti-Negro." Goldwater replied, "I don't care." The film was withdrawn.[46] Massey refused to apologize for narrating the film, and later historians and political commentaries have viewed the film as one of the greatest political blunders of the Goldwater campaign and the beginnings of Republican dirty campaigning. One historian compared the film to George H. W. Bush's "Willie Horton" ad, which focused on a black felon on a weekend prison release who brutally raped and tortured a white woman.[47]

The film depicted short clips of racial rioting as a sign of a "lack of moral leadership at the top." Most of the film showed white kids dancing, white campus protesters, partiers being arrested, school vandalism, and pornography. The message of the film was, as Massey narrated, that there were two Americas: the Old America founded on religious faith, industry, the Constitution, patriotism, and a pioneering spirit, and the New America, as depicted in the film, a hedonistic, don't give a damn about your neighbor, pleasure for pleasure's sake sort of place. The documentary featured a speeding Cadillac with beer cans being thrown out (a reference to Johnson on his Texas ranch). What is notable in the quick still portraits of Baker and Estes that flash across the screen is the absence of any photo of Walter Jenkins, a Johnson aide arrested for a lewd act in a YMCA and forced to resign. Goldwater was adamant that Jenkins not be brought up in the campaign, saying that Jenkins had a wife and children, and there was no need to further embarrass him. The concluding segments of the film had John Wayne urging voters to make the right choice in 1964. "Which America did they want?" he asked.

In actuality, how many people saw the film remains unclear, given the modest newspaper coverage of it and the Goldwater campaign's decision to pull it. Fifty years later, the film appears rather tame, not especially negative, and even quaint. Although the short scenes of racial rioting were disturbing and perhaps played to distorted racial stereotypes, seeing kids dancing the twist, billboards of topless dancers, kids arrested at spring break parties, and vandalized public schoolrooms would not arouse much ire today with American voters. After voting against the Civil Rights Act of 1964, Goldwater was particularly vulnerable on the race issue, and any depiction of blacks rioting, or any call for "law and order" to quell civil disturbances, allowed opponents to accuse the

---

[46] David B. Frisk, *If Not Us, Who? William Rusher, National Review and the Conservative Movement* (Wilmington, DE, 2012), pp. 123–124.

[47] Michael Flamm, *Law and Order: Street Crime, Civil Unrest, and the Crisis of Liberalism in the 1960s* (New York, 2005), p. 204; Michelle M. Nickerson, *Mothers of Conservatism: Women and the Postwar Right* (Princeton, NJ, 2012), pp. 164–166; and Perlstein, *Before the Storm*, p. 621.

Goldwater campaign of using "coded messages" to rally white voters, especially those in the South. But Goldwater was not going to be the last Republican presidential candidate to be charged with racism – however inadvertent.

Whatever the hoopla created by the film, a more important phenomenon was occurring, one overlooked by pundits at the time: what differentiated the Hollywood Right from the Hollywood Left is that film industry Republicans in 1964 produced politicians who would go on to win elected office. (A few progressives in Hollywood gave thought to running for election, including Robert Vaughn, star of the hit television series *Man from U.N.C.L.E.*, which premiered in September 1964.) Murphy and Reagan were actually elected, opening the door for other Hollywood Republicans in later years to run for higher office. Republicans in Hollywood appeared to make a successful transition into politics.

REAGAN AND GOLDWATER

Reagan emerged as the most charismatic speaker on behalf of Goldwater, appearing at campaign rallies, fundraisers, and myriad other events. Co-chairing the Citizens for Goldwater Committee in California, Reagan became a symbol of conservative Republicanism. His stock speech was so powerful that Henry Salvatori, finance chairman for the campaign in California, raised funds and arranged for it to be televised in the last month of the campaign. It set Reagan on his way to a political career that ended with his election as president in 1980, fulfilling the long-held dreams of the Hollywood Right.

Critics, then and later, said Reagan's entrance into politics came as a result of his decline as a movie actor. Actually, Reagan, even as an actor, was obsessed with politics. This showed in his involvement in politics first as a liberal Democrat, in his role in the Screen Actors Guild (SAG), and in his later emergence as a conservative spokesman for free market economics, anticommunism, and pro-American values. His transition from a liberal to a conservative presents a more complicated story. His move away from liberalism began with his fight against communists in the SAG and in the 1946 strike in Hollywood. This ideological shift was reinforced by two important factors – tax difficulties at a time when his acting career waned, and his marriage to Nancy Davis, the stepdaughter of a Chicago surgeon and outspoken conservative Loyal Davis. Nancy Davis's mother was an old college friend of Zasu Pitts, both hard line anticommunists. Nancy facilitated Reagan's shift to conservatism. Unlike his first wife, Jane Wyman, Davis loved politics and loved hearing Reagan talk about it. Reagan's shift to conservativism was reinforced by his close friends William Holden and his wife Arden, who had acted under the screen name of Brenda Marshall and had starred with Errol Flynn in *The Sea Hawk* (1940).[48]

---

[48] Axel Madsen, *Stanwyck* (New York, 1994), p. 285.

Holden exerted on Reagan a profound influence, politically and artistically. A confirmed Republican, Holden was too busy making movies as a leading man to become active in politics. He came from a wealthy family and had led a privileged life before he was discovered by Paramount agents as a student at Pasadena Community College. His rise to stardom came quickly when, at the age of twenty, he played a boxing hero in a movie version of Clifford Odet's *Golden Boy* (1939). Other successes followed: *Sunset Boulevard* (1950), *Stalag 17* (1953), *Love Is a Many Splendored Thing* (1955), and *Bridge on the River Kwai* (1957). Holden and Reagan shared much in common. Both had enlisted in the Armed Services during the Second World War, and they loved horses and wine. Most important was their involvement in the SAG. Holden became first vice president of the guild. He did not need to be convinced that communists were treacherous.

Reagan remained an anticommunist liberal well into 1947, but the Holdens, Nancy, and a few other friends in their social circle convinced him that he had become a Republican and was no longer a Democrat. In the early 1960s, Reagan finally switched his party registration to Republican.[49] His speeches as a spokesman for General Electric, his appearances before anticommunist rallies, and his support for Eisenhower and Nixon revealed he had already moved to the right. By 1962, he had published articles in *Human Events*, served on the national board of the conservative youth organization Young Americans for Freedom (founded by William F. Buckley Jr.) and he appeared regularly before conservative groups nationally and throughout California.[50]

Reagan's speaking skills were already known in California Republican circles. The more Goldwater supporters, grassroots activists, and the big money people heard him, the more they liked him. Reagan inspired enthusiasm, articulated conservative principles of government, passionately denounced communism, and enunciated the benefits of the free market better than any politician in the country. Reagan's stock speech during the Goldwater campaign was a variant of speeches he had been giving since the early 1950s as a spokesperson for General Electric. Typical of his speeches was an address he had given to the San Antonio Chamber of Commerce in San Antonio on February 21, 1962, in which he spoke in favor of the free market and denounced liberalism and socialism: "Well, let me, as one Conservative, say, I don't equate Liberalism with Socialism and Socialism with Communism, but this doesn't preclude my pointing out that they do have in common one characteristic – collectivism. All three of these philosophies seek to answer all human needs through more and more government."[51]

---

[49] Anne Edwards, *Early Reagan: The Rise to Power* (New York, 1987), pp. 420–421.
[50] Dallek, *The Right Moment*, p. 19.
[51] "An Address by Ronald Reagan before the San Antonio Chamber of Commerce and the Downtown Lions Club of San Antonio," February 21, 1962, in Bourke B. Hickenlooper Papers, Box 50, in Herbert Hoover Presidential Papers, Iowa City, Iowa. For background on Reagan's work for G.E. and the development of his conservatism, see Thomas W. Evans, *The*

But not everyone in the Goldwater camp was enamored with Reagan. Some saw him as a latecomer to the Republican cause, a sentiment expressed by Joseph Shell, who snubbed Reagan on the campaign trail. Even fellow actors James Stewart and Robert Taylor saw themselves as more Republican than Reagan. Stewart proclaimed, "He's [Reagan] just a Johnny-come-lately. He'll never get anywhere."[52] Many grassroots activists in Southern California expressed equal suspicion. At a mass meeting of the California Citizens for Goldwater-Miller in Orange County, California, in early August, two months after the primary and a month after the convention, Reagan came under attack. Goldwater activists expressed anger that Reagan had been appointed to head the citizens committee. Instead, they wanted Phil Davis, a right-wing businessman from Beverly Hills, appointed chair. Attending the meeting was Ronald Reagan, along with Clifton White, who had organized the grassroots movement that had won Goldwater his party's nomination. Both Reagan and White were seated in the vast hall when Davis launched into a full-scale attack on Reagan. Clif White started to rise in anger at the attack, when Reagan reached over, grabbed White by the arm, and whispered, "No Clif. This is my fight and I will handle it." Reagan came to the podium and began, "Folks, I'm the new boy on the block. I have not been involved in a campaign like this in the past. But I can see that there's trouble here and there ought not to be trouble here." Reagan then launched into his speech on behalf of Goldwater, ending by recommending that Phil Davis be elected co-chair of the committee. Reagan's years in Hollywood union politics and his natural political instincts paid off. He understood the art of compromise, and he proved this time and again throughout his political career.[53]

Reagan's oratorical skills attracted the attention of Henry Salvatori and Holmes Tuttle, who headed the Southern California finance committee for Goldwater. They had known Reagan on a personal level for over a decade. Certain of his fundraising skills, his affable manner, and his ability as a speaker, they invited Reagan to headline a $1,000-a-plate fundraiser for Goldwater. Reagan was in top form. He brought to his sharp conservative message warm anecdotes and telling statistics delivered as one-liners, for example, telling his listeners how the federal jobs training program under Johnson cost taxpayers 70 percent more than it would have cost to send each trainee to Harvard. After the dinner, Tuttle approached Reagan to ask if he would be willing to appear on television with his speech. Reagan, in his typically modest manner, replied, "Sure, if you think it would do any good."[54]

Education of Ronald Reagan: The General Electric Years and the Untold Story of His Conversion to Conservatism (New York, 2006).

[52] Quoted in Donald Dewey, *Stewart* (Atlanta, GA, 1997), p. 425.

[53] Clifton White, *Why Reagan Won: A Narrative History of the Conservative Movement, 1964–1981* (Chicago, 1981), pp. 14–16; Dallek, *The Right Moment*, p. 66.

[54] Dallek, *The Right Moment*, pp. 66–67.

However good this idea was, the Goldwater campaign people, including national campaign manager William Baroody, did not like it. Baroody's strategy for the general election was to move Goldwater to the center. After reading Reagan's speech, he nixed the idea. Baroody knew that in previous speeches Reagan had talked about privatizing Social Security, and he thought this would provide the final nail in Goldwater's coffin. Tuttle and Salvatori, now joined by Walter Knott, were livid. Knott threatened to cut off funding to the Goldwater campaign, even as grassroots activists clamored for Reagan to be put on the air. Marlan E. Bourns, founder of a global electronics firm in Southern California, telegrammed, "It is imperative that the nation's most eloquent and effective speaker [Reagan] be put on nation wide tv.... His appeal is miraculous and will be received and understood by all true freedom loving Americans regardless of party."[55] Reagan himself met with Goldwater to discuss the televised speech. Finally, Goldwater watched the speech, and, after viewing it, turned to an aide to say, "What the hell is wrong with that?"[56]

The Goldwater campaign agreed that Reagan's speech could be aired if outside money was raised to put it on national television. Tuttle, Salvatori, Knott, and others went to work. Behind the scenes, John Wayne tapped into his old fraternity buddies from Sigma Chi at the University of Southern California to contribute to the cause (Goldwater was a Sigma Chi as well). Reagan went on the air on October 27 to give his prerecorded "Rendezvous with Destiny" speech. The speech was 4,626 words. He began by declaring that for most of his life he had been a Democrat. He spoke now as a voter willing to cross party lines because of the issues facing the nation. He first turned to taxes, in a brief paragraph, before turning to foreign policy, the war in Vietnam, and the threat of Cuba. The speech addressed the rapid expansion of government under the Johnson administration, the failure of the "War on Poverty," and the threat to future generations. He warned of socialism and "a perversion" taking place in the meaning of liberty and freedom in America. "Our natural, inalienable rights are now considered to be a dispensation of government, and freedom has never been so fragile, so close to slipping from our grasp as it is at this moment." He warned of Soviet communism: "If you and I have the courage to tell our elected officials that we want our national policy based upon what we know in our hearts is morally right. We cannot buy our freedom or security from the threat of the bomb by committing an immorality so great as saying to a billion now in slavery behind the Iron Curtain, 'Give up your dreams of freedom because to save our own skin, we are willing to make a deal with your slave masters.'" He concluded, drawing from Franklin Roosevelt and Abraham Lincoln, without naming them, "You and I have a rendezvous with destiny. We will preserve for

---

[55] Marlan E. Bourns to Hedda Hopper (copy of telegram), October 2, 1964, Hedda Hopper Papers, Reagan file.
[56] Quoted in Dalleck, *The Right Moment*, p. 67.

our children this, the last best hope of man on Earth, or we will sentence them to take the last step into a thousand years of darkness."[57]

Within hours of the telecast, the Goldwater campaign headquarters was flooded with callers. Overall, Reagan generated an estimated $8 million. The Hollywood Right had encountered in this single speech its own rendezvous with destiny through Ronald Reagan.

AMERICANS MAKE A CHOICE (LBJ), REPUBLICANS FIND MORE THAN AN ECHO (REAGAN)

Reagan's eloquence, though, was not enough to save Goldwater or the Republican Party from a disastrous defeat in 1964. Although conservatives, who had spent years in the political wilderness, tried to take solace in the 27 million votes for Goldwater, Johnson received 43 million votes, for a margin of 16 million. This translated into 486 to 52 Electoral College votes. The Goldwater nomination and campaign was a political debacle, although it took on heroic qualities in conservative lore as the years passed. Although George Murphy won in California and conservative Roman Hruska won his senate race, liberal Republicans fared somewhat better. John Lindsay won a New York seat in the House, and George Romney won reelection as governor of Michigan. In the end, the 1964 election pushed conservatives back to the fringes of the GOP.

The Goldwater defeat in California was especially disheartening, if only because California had put Goldwater over the top in winning the primary back in June. On election day, California Republicans deserted Goldwater in droves. Nearly a quarter of Republican votes in California were cast for Johnson, although Goldwater did better among upper-income Southern Californians, the self-employed, and voters over 60 years of age. He lost low- and middle-income groups, especially in Northern California – the same groups who tended to favor Rockefeller in the primary.[58]

As disastrous as the Goldwater defeat was, two successes emerged from the 1964 campaign, both coming out of California: George Murphy's election to the U.S. Senate and Ronald Reagan's rise in politics, which would take him to the governor's mansion and eventually the White House. On election day, Murphy trounced Salinger, winning 3.6 million votes to Salinger's 3.4 million, and garnering close to 700,000 Democratic votes.[59] Murphy was able to run about 10 percentage points ahead of Goldwater in California. About 25 percent of Democrats voted Republican. Murphy's campaign against Salinger cast a "nice

---

[57] Ronald Reagan, "Address on Behalf of Senator Barry Goldwater: 'Rendezvous with Destiny,'" October 27, 1964, http://www.reaganfoundation.org/reagan/speeches/rendezvous.asp.

[58] Totten J. Anderson and Eugene C. Lee, "The 1964 Election in California," *Western Political Quarterly*, 18:2 (June 1965), pp. 463–465.

[59] Hill, *Dancing Bear*, pp. 188–189.

guy," cheerful, nonthreatening Republican candidate against a cigar-chomping, overweight, inside-the-beltway Democratic candidate. The courts ruled that Salinger could run, but he did not meet the residency requirement to register to vote. The carpetbagger issue was brilliantly exploited by Murphy in a radio ad that ended with "the only Senate candidate who lives and votes in California." The ad played nonstop. Murphy benefited also from the rapid growth of Southern California, whose voters tended to dislike San Francisco candidates.

Salinger made the same mistake that Knowland made in 1958 by campaigning in support of a state proposition. In Knowland's case, it was right-to-work; in Salinger's, it was the repeal of Rumford Fair Housing Act through Proposition 14. Both Brown and Salinger threw themselves fully into the campaign to defeat Proposition 14. Unruh, also a liberal, had the political smarts to stay away from the issue as much as possible, and he tried to warn Brown and Salinger that their campaign was a losing cause. Given popular opposition in California to open housing, and the anti–Prop 14 campaign denouncing proponents as bigots and racists akin to the Ku Klux Klan, Brown and Salinger placed themselves in an untenable place where self-righteous principle overcame pragmatic politics.

Murphy, for his part, perhaps because he had been an actor most of his life, understood the importance of appearance before an audience. He projected himself as a moderate. He refused to take a stand on Proposition 14, an issue he declared outside the scope of his campaign. He was able to distance himself from the Goldwater presidential campaign, knowing that his credentials as a Hollywood anticommunist were enough to win him conservative voters. Truth be told, Murphy's anticommunism, although genuine, had been to defend the movie industry from charges it was harboring communists. He had not joined the Motion Picture Alliance or taken a hard stance on keeping former party members from reentering the industry. He was a Nixon Republican, and Robert Finch, Nixon's man in California, served as the campaign manager for Murphy's Senate race. He crafted a well-conceived campaign that attacked Salinger as a carpetbagger, without appearing nasty. He was the first Hollywood actor to be elected to the U.S. Senate, opening a path for other actors to follow him into the political arena.

The exceptionally well-connected Murphy drew upon Hollywood Republicans to help his campaign. He employed celebrities in much the same way as the Goldwater campaign: for fundraising and attracting crowds. He asked Walt Disney to chair a fundraising dinner that drew regular Hollywood Republicans – John Wayne, Ronald Reagan, Irene Dunne, Leon Ames, Randoph Scott, Buddy Ebsen, and others. He added some new names that had not appeared at Goldwater events. Fred Astaire was there, as was actor John Galvin, who later was appointed as ambassador to Mexico under President Reagan.[60] But Murphy's list of stars did not come anywhere close to matching

---

[60] Bob Houser, "Goldwater Cruise to Catalina Slated," *Press Telegram* (Long Beach), May 1, 1964, p. 2.

those Hollywood stars who turned out for Pierre Salinger. In a single event, "Stars Rally Round Salinger," held at the Hollywood Palladium, more than one hundred Hollywood stars appeared, from Gene Kelly, Ida Lupino, Carl Reiner, James Garner, Marlo Thomas, and Robert Wagner, to Jumbo the Clown and the Flintstones.[61] With Fred and Wilma Flintstone in your camp, you might think the election is yours, but, in this case, star power did not carry the election for Salinger, thus showing its limits in any political campaign. In the end, campaigns come down to the candidate.

The strange nature of California politics was evident in the passage of Proposition 14 repealing the Rumford Fair Housing Act. Although Goldwater lost the state and Murphy won election, Proposition 14 won by a greater majority than any candidate on the ballot. (The Goldwater-Miller campaign also decided to stay away from the issue. Lyndon Johnson, on the other hand, spoke out against the proposition.) Proposition 14 was carried by over 60 percent of the vote. Although it proved to be a futile exercise when the U.S. Supreme Court held it to be unconstitutional, proponents of the initiative made the issue one of property rights, not civil rights. Opponents of the measure labeled it racist and backed by extremists. For most voters, it was a matter of protecting their homes. Later analysis of the election showed that Californians in both the northern and southern sections of the state voted in favor of the measure. The San Francisco Bay Area voted 48 percent "yes" whereas the Los Angeles area voted 68 percent "yes." The measure drew support from Democratic voters across the state, and income and educational levels for white voters appeared to make little difference on how people voted on the issue. The Catholic Church campaigned heavily against Proposition 14.

A later survey showed that only 42 percent of Catholics in Southern California supported the Rumford Act, whereas 49 percent of Catholics in Northern California supported it. Overall, about 61 percent of whites were hostile to the Rumford Act. What was most interesting in later analysis of the vote was that Californians were particularly liberal on racial attitudes, ahead of the rest of the country. Most California voters believed, however, that blacks were not discriminated against in California employment or housing opportunities; as a consequence, the attack by Brown, Salinger, and other opponents of Proposition 14 as a "racist" measure proved ineffective, whereas proponents who characterized the measure as supporting "property rights" struck a sympathetic chord with voters.[62]

The political importance of Proposition 14 went beyond just a housing issue. The vote in favor of Proposition 14 showed that simply attacking opponents as extremists and racists did not assure victory. Further damage was inflicted when

[61] "Meet 100 Stars and Celebrities" (advertisement), *Los Angeles Times*, October 16, 1964, p. D19.
[62] Raymond E. Wolfinger and Fred I. Greenstein, "The Repeal of Fair Housing in California: An Analysis of Referendum Voting," *The American Political Science Review*, 62:3 (September 1968), pp. 753–769.

student protesters at the University of California, Berkeley, became national news in the fall of 1964 and when a racial riot broke out in Watts, the black section of Los Angeles in August 1965. These events gave Republicans an opportunity to frame the 1966 governor's election as a referendum on "law and order" versus weak-kneed liberalism. Ronald Reagan proved to be the beneficiary. A week following the 1964 election, Reagan told a meeting of "wildly enthusiastic" Young Republicans who had gathered at the Ambassador Hotel in Los Angeles that "The conservative philosophy was not repudiated." He noted that 27 million voters had supported Goldwater and that "the eight or nine million voters who were led astray by the false image of our candidate" should not be allowed to regain control of the party. He called for conservatives to "stay together and keep working" within the Republican Party.[63] He spoke as a leader of the conservative movement and a new voice within the Republican Party. The Hollywood Right was about to achieve its greatest victory – Reagan's election to public office.

---

[63] Richard Bergholz, "Young GOP Reaffirms Support of Goldwater: Cheers Statement by Ronald Reagan That Party Won't be Turned Over to 'Traitors,'" *Los Angeles Times*, November 11, 1964, p. 20.

CHAPTER 6

Ronald Reagan

Triumph and Decline of the Hollywood Right

In 1966, Ronald Reagan won election to the California's governor's mansion. Fourteen years later, he became president of the United States. His rise to the highest elected office in America marked the final triumph of the Hollywood Right. The coterie of conservative Hollywood activists who had emerged in the late 1940s to combat communist influence in the film industry had no expectation that out of their group might emerge a future U.S. president. Nonetheless, the foundation for Reagan's success began with the anticommunist struggle in these early years. Reagan honed his political skills as president of the Screen Actors Guild (SAG), and his shift to conservatism was rooted in his battle against communist influence in Hollywood. One can conjecture that without the growth of the Communist Party in Hollywood, there would not have been a conservative Ronald Reagan. He was a committed liberal in the 1940s, and he might well have remained one if he had not entered into a fierce battle with this political faction within the SAG and the movie industry. After all, most within Hollywood did remain liberals.

One of the ironies of Reagan's advance in politics is that the Hollywood Right itself was in decline. Although Reagan drew upon Hollywood stars in his 1966 governor's race, in his race for the presidency in 1980 the Hollywood Right had become so small that the campaign did not even try to form an entertainment committee with named stars. Instead, it focused on fundraising from agents and studio executives. By the 1970s, Hollywood had become a bastion of liberalism and left-wing activism.

HOW REAGAN WON THE GOVERNORSHIP IN 1966

Reagan entered the race for governor faced with a divided state Republican Party anxious to unify; he faced a Democratic opponent, Edmund Brown, who headed an equally divided party determined, by all appearances, to maintain its divisions. Reagan, a Hollywood actor without professional political experience, proved to be a much abler politician than incumbent Governor Brown, who had spent most of his life in politics. Brown underestimated Reagan, dismissing him as simply an actor and wannabe politician, one given to and associated with extremism. So dismissive was Brown that, initially, he directed his campaign to conduct research and focus its energy on Reagan's primary rival, San Francisco Mayor George Christopher. Brown was convinced that Republican voters were going to reject Reagan as a lightweight in favor of Christopher. It proved to be a serious error on Brown's part, made worse during the general election campaign by Brown's strategy of attacking Reagan as an extremist. Charges of extremism seemed to many voters beside the point in the context of the upheaval on college campuses and the Watts riot in 1965. When the charge of extremism failed to gain traction with the voters, Brown switched to attacking Reagan as an actor. This too failed. Like later opponents, Brown underestimated Reagan.

When the riot broke out in the Watts section of Los Angeles in August 1965, Brown was on a family holiday cruise in the Mediterranean. The riot started with a minor incident when a white patrolman stopped a black youth driving drunk through the streets of South Central Los Angeles. When a crowd from the neighborhood gathered, the patrolman asked for backup; things got out of hand, and a riot ensued. As the rioting continued, Los Angeles Chief of Police William Parker called on Lieutenant Governor Glenn Anderson, acting on Brown's behalf while he was out of the state, to call out the National Guard. Anderson arrived in Los Angeles on the second day of rioting, only to conclude that the riot had been quelled. He was actually more anxious about campus protests in Berkeley. On Friday, full-scale rioting erupted in Watts, becoming the largest domestic disturbance in the twentieth century. Snipers were shooting firefighters and police, and a desperate Chief Parker pleaded with Anderson and Brown's executive secretary to call out the National Guard. Neither trusted Parker, known for his tough stance on law and order, and they refused his request. Brown was finally reached and informed of the situation. He cancelled his holiday in Europe to fly back to California. On his way back, he telephoned an order to call out the National Guard but, by this time, the riot was out of control. The five-day riot resulted in thirty-four deaths, more than 1,000 injuries, 3,400-plus arrests, and $40 million in damage. Liberals blamed the riot on poverty and a history of racism in the Los Angeles police force. Although not dismissing social conditions as the cause of the riot, California voters, white and black, supported police and National Guard intervention to restore order. For Brown, the political damage from the riot hung over him throughout the campaign.[1]

---

[1] Curt Gentry, *The Last Days of the Late, Great State of California* (New York, 1968), and Matthew Dallek, *The Right Moment: Ronald Reagan's First Victory and the Decisive Turning Point in American Politics* (New York, 2000), pp. 129–149.

Troubles at the University of California, Berkeley, ten months earlier had convinced many that Brown was a governor unable to control law breakers and left-wing extremists. In October 1964, student radicals launched a massive protest movement for free speech on campus when university officials, under public pressure, tried to ban political booths from campus. By December, the Free Speech Movement undertook a huge sit-in demonstration in which more than a thousand students took over the administration building at Sproul Hall. University president Clark Kerr made various attempts to negotiate with the students, even as they were becoming increasingly militant in their tactics. During the one-day takeover, Governor Brown arranged through his son Jerry to talk to Free Speech leader Mario Savio, a philosophy major, to try to calm things down. Savio refused Brown's offer to negotiate. In the process, he denounced liberals for banning political activity on campus and for their support for Johnson's war in Vietnam. Shocked by Savio's arrogance, Brown concluded after the telephone conversation that these radical students were out of control. He ordered the police to remove the students from Sproul Hall, and hundreds were arrested. Brown's actions alienated liberals, whereas conservatives saw Brown and Kerr as having encouraged student protests by not taking a firm stand at the outset of the protests. Even after the arrests, campus protests continued. A "Dirty Speech Movement" followed, along with "teach-ins" about the war in Vietnam. The image of indulged college students, getting one of the best and most inexpensive educations in the country, yet creating chaos on campus, made an indelible print in the minds of many California voters – one that Reagan discovered he could play on during the campaign.[2]

However damaged Brown might have been by these events, he felt assured going into 1966 that Reagan was a lightweight whose campaign would collapse once he came under attack. Reagan and his advisors understood that Brown's line of attack would be to label Reagan an extremist. Already, newspapers in the state were portraying Reagan as the darling of the extreme right, and the Reagan team decided to counter this ploy early. To the dismay of many conservatives, Reagan hired a major political consulting firm in California, Spencer-Roberts, to direct the campaign. Stu Spencer, a former director of parks and recreation in Alhambra, and Roberts, a former television salesperson, had quit their jobs in the late 1950s to form Spencer-Roberts. In the 1964 presidential primary in California, they worked for Nelson Rockefeller – the arch foe of conservatives and Goldwater's opponent. Many on the right despised the firm, seeing it as part of the moderate wing of the California GOP. After meeting with Reagan, who convinced them he could be a disciplined candidate who understood the need for pragmatic compromise, they agreed to take on his campaign. The firm had worked with Justin Dart and Leonard Firestone in the Rockefeller campaign, and they were assured by them of Reagan's qualities as a candidate. The support of Holmes Tuttle and Henry Salvatori, who had convinced Reagan to challenge

---

[2] W. J. Rorabaugh, *Berkeley at War: The 1960s* (New York, 1989).

Brown, meant that Reagan was going to have the financial resources for a successful campaign. Spencer-Roberts concluded that their toughest job with Reagan was "going to be proving that he isn't a right winger."[3]

These men understood that Reagan's dilemma was how to distance himself from the John Birch Society. At first, this task did not come easily to the Reagan campaign. In the early 1960s, Birchers had become state and national news after Governor Brown launched a public attack on them. Brown's attack was framed within a larger campaign against what was called the "radical right" in America. National newspapers and magazines, including the *New York Times* and *Time*, depicted the John Birch Society as an extremist, undemocratic organization conspiring to take over the Republican Party. Dozens of books appeared at this time painting the Birchers as far-right kooks.[4] Under attack, Birchers in California were on the lookout for any sign that Reagan was going to denounce the Society. Rumors were rampant among conservatives as early as 1965 that Reagan was about to abandon the right in favor of the moderate wing of the state Republican Party. His hiring of Spencer-Roberts excited such gossip.[5]

After a series of fits and starts, Reagan hit on a salable formula: members of the John Birch Society who voted for Reagan were supporting his program and not vice versa. In September 1965, Reagan issued a one-page press statement on the John Birch Society. In it, he labeled Robert Welch, the founder of the Birch Society, "utterly reprehensible" for smearing Eisenhower as a conscious agent of communism, but added that, in fairness to members of the Birch Society, the Federal Bureau of Investigation (FBI) and state government investigations had cleared the organization from subversive activity. Although some Birchers took issue with Reagan's statement, he managed to win over Birchers such as John Rousselot, a former congressman, and John Schmitz, a California State Assemblyman and member of the Society.

Reagan proved even more effective on the campaign trail in defusing this issue. He told Spencer and Roberts that instead of giving set speeches (although written by him), he wanted to give shorter talks and allow more time for questions and answers from the audience and press. At first, Spencer and Roberts were hesitant, but Reagan insisted. He told them that this format would help disarm attacks that he was just an actor giving speeches scripted by people behind the scenes. Reagan also understood that by answering questions from the press about his alleged "extremist" connections, he had a better

---

[3] Quoted from Dallek, *The Right Moment*, p. 131. This discussion of the 1966 election draws heavily from Totton, J. Anderson and Eugene C. Lee, "The 1966 Election in California," *Western Political Quarterly* 20:2 (June 1967), pp. 535–554, as well as from Kurt Schuparra, *Triumph of the Right: The Rise of the California Conservative Movement, 1945–1966* (Armonk, NY, 1998), pp. 123–144; and Gladwin Hill, *Dancing Bear: An Inside Look at California Politics* (Cleveland, OH, 1968), pp. 203–221.

[4] For a discussion of this campaign, Donald T. Critchlow, *Phyllis Schlafly and Grassroots Conservatism: A Woman's Crusade* (Princeton, NJ, 2005), p. 340.

[5] Quoted from Dallek, *The Right Moment*, pp. 108–109.

chance to move the press off this issue. It worked. When accusations or questions about his association with extremist groups came up, he used his stock line that he was not seeking support from bloc groups, but from individuals who endorsed his philosophy. After a while, the media stopped asking questions about Reagan's relationship to the John Birch Society, disarmed by his affable manner in dismissing these accusations. When the Brown campaign directed State Comptroller Alan Cranston to hound Reagan at his speaking events with a pamphlet compiled by Democratic operatives, "The John Birch Society: A Soiled Slip Is Showing," the ploy failed utterly. Catching up to Reagan at one campaign event, Cranston handed Reagan the pamphlet as news cameras looked on. Reagan shrugged off this ploy to use the media and told reporters that the Brown campaign was trying to distract voters.[6]

Reagan was helped also by a Republican Party anxious to heal its factional wounds. This effort was aided by Gaylord Parkinson, a San Diego physician who was chair of the Republican Central Committee. Prior to becoming head of the state GOP, Parkinson helped form the Republican Associates, which sought to bring order to the party through targeted support for GOP candidates in the form of fundraising, endorsements, and political consultation. To avoid the factionalism that had wracked the party in 1962 and 1964, Parkinson issued what became known as the Eleventh Commandment: Republican candidates should not say a bad word about other Republican candidates. This mandate served Reagan especially well in facing his major rival, George Christopher, in the primary. Christopher, who had served two terms as mayor of San Francisco, presented himself as a moderate who could best Brown in the general election. As a result, Reagan's biggest challenge in the primary came from the left, not the right. Holmes Tuttle had personally convinced Joe Shell, the candidate who had spoiled Nixon's campaign in 1962, not to run. Tuttle told Shell that Reagan was the choice of conservatives. While Reagan followed Parkinson's Eleventh Amendment, Christopher blasted Reagan as an extremist. Given the growing backlash against rising crime rates in California, the Watts riot, and Berkeley protesters, Christopher's charges did not gain traction among Republican voters.

Reagan brought flair and celebrity to his primary campaign, deftly using rising crime and Berkeley protesters as evidence that California was in a state of chaos. In early May 1965, Reagan made Berkeley into a major campaign theme at a rally held at the San Francisco Cow Palace, where Goldwater had given his famous "Extremism is no vice" acceptance speech. He was introduced by television actor Chuck Connors as "a man in a state that needs a man." Actor Buddy Ebsen, star of the wildly popular *Beverly Hillbillies*, added humor to the rally when he declared "better an actor than a clown in Sacramento." The crowd was already worked up when Reagan took the stage and asserted that "a small minority of beatniks, radicals and filthy speech advocates" brought "shame to a

[6] Dallek, *The Right Moment*, p. 231.

great university." These protesters were polluting higher education in the state, encouraged by a permissive leadership in Sacramento and a university administration unwilling to expel these misfits.[7] Reagan followed this speech with a major television address in January 1966, contending that disorder plagued the state. "Our city streets," he cried, "are jungle paths after dark, with more crimes of violence than New York, Pennsylvania, and Massachusetts combined." He claimed that university administrators confronted "neurotic vulgarities" from students with "vacillation and weakness." Californians needed leadership in Sacramento, he continued, not moral turpitude.[8]

Whatever chance Christopher might have had against Reagan came to a crashing halt when the Brown campaign arranged for columnist Drew Pearson to write a piece revealing that Christopher had been arrested and charged with the price-fixing of dairy products when he was in private business in the 1940s. This information had been used in the past against Christopher, so Brown decided to resuscitate the issue. The attack on Christopher was a complete miscalculation on Brown's part. First, the Brown campaign was convinced that Christopher was going to win the GOP nomination over Reagan – another indication of how Brown continued to underestimate the Reagan threat. In addition, this attack ensured that Christopher would never switch parties to endorse Brown in the general election. Finally, this kind of dirty trick campaigning helped cement Brown's image as an old-time politician willing to do anything to win election. When the primary votes were calculated, Reagan won 77 percent of the vote – 25 percent more than Goldwater had won in 1964.

In the general election campaign, Brown followed the same unsuccessful strategy that Christopher had pursued in the primary: attack Reagan as a right-wing extremist and a politically inexperienced actor. It did not work for Christopher in the primary, and it did not work for Brown in the general campaign. State Democratic Party Chairman Roger Kent explained the strategy simply, "Well he's just a damned actor. He's never run a business; he's never run a political office. And he's getting his money from these crooks!"[9] Such an attack was particularly weak given that actor George Murphy's election in 1964 should have settled this issue. Any voter with a political memory knew that the Democrats had elected actor Helen Gahagan Douglas to Congress and had put her up to run against Nixon for the U.S. Senate in 1950. Also, as a matter of political trivia, actors Lucile Gleason and Albert Dekker had been elected to the state Assembly in the 1940s, and, earlier, Will Rogers had been elected mayor of Beverly Hills.

In the new media age of television, being an actor brought its own assets. As political scientist Totton Anderson observed in 1966, rather obviously, "An actor had several distinct advantages over a non-professional in the use of the

[7] Quoted in Dallek, *The Right Moment*, pp. 103–104.
[8] Ibid., p. 195.
[9] Ibid., p. 229.

media, especially television." A more astute point, albeit an arguable one, was made at the time by psychologist Chayler Mason, who noted, "When people vote, they hope to vote for an idealized image of themselves. Voters want a political leader who is more capable, more intelligent, taller, more experienced – possibly more honorable – than they are. They also fear and distrust 'politicians.' So voters seek and hope for the rise of nonpolitical figures."[10] Reagan exemplified this projected image of the nonpolitician exactly.

Brown tried to beef up his general election campaign by bringing in long time political operative Fred Dutton, who, although a tough and dirty in-fighter, was neither terribly intelligent nor very familiar with California politics. Divisions within the Democratic Party did not help. Blacks were angry at Brown's handling of the Watts riot, and many Mexican Americans felt affronted when Brown refused to meet with Cesar Chavez, head of the United Farm Workers Union. Facing a backlash from the general electorate, Brown was in trouble by election day. As California pollster Don Machmore reported on the eve of the election, "This is the year of the mood of uneasiness – of uneasiness about Viet Nam, inflation, Negro riots, crime, everything."[11] Both Brown and Reagan sought to move to the middle. Reagan, without a legislative record, proved more successful by projecting an optimistic "citizen politician" embracing a new future for a broken state.

In the campaign, Reagan mustered the Hollywood Right to go full throttle for him. While Brown drew some support from the Hollywood Left, it did not equal the enthusiasm that Reagan drew from his troops. Brown's attacks on actors outraged Reagan's Hollywood supporters. In a campaign documentary, Brown was captured telling a group of young black female students, "You know I'm running against an actor. Remember this, you know who shot Abraham Lincoln, don't you. An actor shot Lincoln."[12] Actor Jack Palance, a Brown supporter, personally complained to Brown about the comment, and Ginger Rogers wrote a well-publicized letter to the editor to denounce the "smear" on her profession, especially on Ronald Reagan, who had "dedicated a third of his adult life to public and citizenship duties." She put in her own shot at Brown noting that Lincoln's assassin John Wilkes Booth was a "Democrat acting as a Democrat."[13] Reagan, for his part, told reporters that he had not heard about Brown's comment, and then added that he did not think it was true because Brown would never say anything like that.

The Hollywood Right rallied to one of their own as Reagan drew from his extensive contacts in the film industry to provide glamour to his campaign. This mobilization differed from Murphy's campaign for Senate in 1964, in which

[10] Quoted in Bob Thomas, "Actors in Politics – An Analysis," *The Daily Review* (Hayward), October 26, 1966, p. 44.
[11] Bruce Biossat, "Capital Letter," *Anderson Daily Bulletin* (Indiana), November 2, 1966, p. 4.
[12] Quoted in Dallek, *The Right Moment*, p. 235.
[13] Ginger Rogers, "Actress Deplores Brown's Smear," *The Daily Review*, November 1, 1966, p. 20.

stars were primarily used for fundraising events and a few appearances in television advertising and campaign rallies. Reagan in 1966 was unabashed in using movie and television stars at rallies, to open campaign offices, to participate in telethons, and in newspaper and television ads. He was not afraid of being identified with Hollywood. He took pride in his career as an actor and in his association with actors: these were his friends in the industry. His primary campaign opened with a prominent list of "Celebrities for Reagan," a committee headed by Mrs. Robert Arthur, wife of actor Robert Arthur, who later became a gay rights activist aligned with the Log Cabin Republican faction. The entertainment committee began with a short list of about thirty actors, but, by the end of the campaign, the list had grown to more than 200.[14]

For example, one campaign ad entitled "The People Who Work with Reagan Say ... ," placed in newspapers across the state, listed more than 160 actors, entertainers, musicians, and studio executives who endorsed Reagan for governor. The ad read, "As members of the industry in which Ronald Reagan first demonstrated his capacities for leadership, executive administration, and absolute integrity, we know that as Governor he can and will bring effective leadership to California." The ad cleverly wove in celebrity names who could speak directly to Reagan's administrative abilities as a union leader. Prominent among those signing the ad were popular celebrities such as Pat Boone, James Cagney, Chuck Connors, Bing Crosby, Yvonne DeCarlo, William Demarest, Buddy Ebsen, Dale Evans, John Ford, Joel McCrea, Walter Pidgeon, Dale Robertson, Roy Rogers, Fred MacMurray, Randolph Scott, Jack Warner, John Wayne, and Efrem Zimbalist, Jr. These men and women were white, with few exceptions (Eddie "Rochester" Anderson was a black comedian best known for his work with comedian Jack Benny). All had been major stars in their time. Unlike Democratic celebrities in the campaign, who continued to appear in movies, only a few of these Hollywood Republicans continued to appear in films, but many were known to a younger audience of television viewers.[15]

[14] The first enlistees to the Reagan campaign included the best-known stars, including John Wayne, Robert Taylor, Forrest Tucker, Cesar Romeo, Mary Pickford, Walter Pidgeon, Lucille Norman, Lloyd Nolan, Tony Martin, June MacMurray, Ken Murray, Mrs. Clark Gable, Andy Devine, Hoagy Carmichael, Eddie Anderson, and Nick Adams. They were quickly followed by John Agar, Leon Ames, Richard Arlen, Warner Anderson, Wendell Carey, George Chandler, Don Dubbins, Anthony Eisley, Nanette Fabray, Coleen Gray, William Golden, Virginia Grey, Stuart Hamblen, and Monte Montana. Others included Jock Mahoney, Hal Peary, Fess Parker, Don Penny, Buddy Rogers, Dale Robertson, Gene Raymond, Ginger Rogers, Lela Rogers, Gale Storm, Martha Tilton, Harry von Zell, Clint Walker, Patrick Wayne, Clinton Webb, Alan Young, and Skip Young. "Reagan Aided by Movieland Celebrities," *Valley News* (Van Nuys), May 8, 1966, p. 18.
[15] Prominent among the endorsers were also Nick Adams, John Agar, Leon Ames, Eddie Anderson, Rex Allen, Walter Brennan, Ray Bolger, Edgar Bergen, Joan Blondell, Ken Curtis, Merian Cooper, Ben Cooper, Rory Calhoun, George Chasin, Wendell Corey, Andy Devine, Don DeFore, Frederick DeCordova, James Drury, Joanne Dru, William Demarest, Nanette Fabray, Virginia Grey, Jeffrey Hunter, Harold Lloyd, Ken Murray, Tony Martin, Raymond Massey,

Reagan used a coterie of stars who traveled on his chartered plane as he hopped around the state conducting his question-and-answer sessions and political rallies. These actors gave speeches and sometimes joined in town meetings with voters. In his travels to Santa Barbara, Fresno, Sacramento, San Jose, San Diego, and Burbank, Reagan traveled with Irene Dunne, Chuck Connors, Pat Boone, Robert Taylor, Buddy Ebsen, Dale Robertson, George Chandler, Roy Rogers, and Dale Evans. Television actor Chuck Connors was an especially powerful speaker; singer Pat Boone brought charm; and Buddy Ebsen wit to the campaign trail. Roy Rogers and Dale Evans appealed to Christian groups.[16] Reagan's road show drew huge crowds. Tickets were sold out for an appearance at Oakland, California, which was used by the campaign as a half-hour fundraising telethon. A cast of western movie and television stars, including Walter Brennan, Andy Devine, Chuck Connors, Rex Allen, and dancer Ray Bolger (the scarecrow in the movie classic *Wizard of Oz*), drew in the audience. A short time later, a crowd of 2,400 packed the Hollywood Palladium for a $100-a-plate dinner honoring Reagan.[17] Celebrities brought glamour to the campaign, but they also added to the excitement of what had become a political juggernaut. Reagan embraced his Hollywood past, and it paid off, defusing Brown's limp attacks on him as an ill-informed, has-been actor.

On election day, Reagan won by almost a million more votes than Brown. He took fifty-five of California's fifty-eight counties, losing only in the Bay Area, in the largest turnout at that point in state history. Reagan won nearly 60 percent of the vote, and his coattails carried over to other state races. Republicans won six of the partisan statewide offices, losing only the attorney general's race. They picked up five new state senate seats, closing the gap after the 1964 race to 21–19. In the state Assembly, Republicans took seven new seats to become a 42–38 minority. In congressional races, Democrats lost three seats, narrowing their majority from 23–15 to 20–18. What Reagan's campaign accomplished was to make gains in Congress, the state senate, and the state Assembly through a combined Republican vote greater than the Democratic vote. This had not occurred since 1952, when the Eisenhower-Nixon ticket swept the state.[18]

Many of these gains came because of population growth in Southern California, which was generally more conservative than in the Northern part of the state. Reagan won heavily the white working-class vote, especially among

Constance Moore, Dennis Morgan, Virginia Mayo, Joel McCrea, Ray Milland, Lloyd Nolan, Fess Parker, Mary Pickford, LeRoy Prinz, Buddy Rogers, Cesar Romero, Dale Robertson, Gene Raymond, Ginger Rogers, Gale Storm, Susan Seaforth, Randolph Scott, Forrest Tucker, Robert Taylor, Claire Trevor, Norman Taurog, Harry von Zell, Rudy Vallee, King Vidor, Clint Walker, William Wellman, and Alan Young. "The People Who Work with Ronald Reagan Say ..." *Independent Press Telegram* (Long Beach), November 3, 1966, p. 2.

[16] Joseph A. St. Amant, "Reagan Hopping All Over California," *Redlands Daily News*, November 7, 1964, p. 9.

[17] "Brown 'Pressured' at UC, Says Reagan," *Oakland Tribune*, November 12, 1966, p. 2.

[18] The following discussion of the 1966 election relies on Totton J. Anderson and Eugene G. Lee, "The 1966 Election in California," *Western Political Quarterly*, 20:2 (June 1967), pp. 535–554.

union members. The campaign stressed that Reagan had been president of his union, the SAG. Divisions within the Democratic Party also benefited Reagan. After a bitter and personal Democratic primary between Brown and flamboyant conservative mayor of Los Angeles Samuel Yorty, many Democratic voters, who had switched party votes after Goldwater's 1964 presidential race, continued to vote Republican. The liberal California Democratic Council, which had helped elect Brown governor in 1958, was in sharp decline, torn apart by disputes over the Vietnam War, and by financial debt. Brown's misfortunes with his own party were mirrored in Reagan's success within the Republican Party. Reagan's campaign reunited Goldwater conservatives and Rockefeller moderates. He brought back to the conservative fold California business leaders such as Leonard Firestone and Justin Dart, who had played such instrumental roles in building the loose formation around Southern California commercial interests, movie moguls, and Hollywood celebrities. Reagan, the former actor associated with the Hollywood Right, had apparently restored the Republican Party in California.

In his eight years in office, Ronald Reagan accomplished much, including welfare reform that became a model for other states. He easily defeated Jesse Unruh for a second term as governor in 1970.[19] Celebrating his inauguration for the second term were stars such as John Wayne, as well as newcomers to the Republican cause, singers Frank Sinatra, Sammy Davis, Jr., and Dean Martin.

VIETNAM, CULTURAL WARS, AND THE DECLINE OF THE HOLLYWOOD RIGHT

By the 1970s, time had taken its toll on the Hollywood Right. Those closely associated with its formative years were no longer around to see the triumph of their cause. Adolphe Menjou died a year before Goldwater's nomination in 1964; Hedda Hopper passed away shortly before Reagan's nomination and victory for governor in 1966. Robert Taylor, who had been instrumental in the fight against communism in the film industry during the 1950s and a workhorse for the Hollywood Right, died of lung cancer in 1969. The most visible celebrity on the right remained John Wayne, who became a symbol for conservatism in Hollywood. Wayne, of course, was not the only Republican in Hollywood, but they were a dwindling breed. Bob Hope remained a steadfast Republican, although after public criticism for his support of the Vietnam War,

---

[19] Insight into Reagan's administration is found in Lou Cannon, *Governor Reagan: His Rise to Power* (New York, 2003); and Garin Burbank, "Governor Reagan and California Welfare Reform: The Grand Compromise of 1971," *California History*, 70:3 (Fall 1991), pp. 278–289; Garin Burbank, "Speaker Moretti, Governor Reagan, and the Search for Tax Reform in California, 1970–1972," *Pacific Historical Review* (May 1991), pp. 193–214; and Garin Burbank, "Governor Reagan's Only Defeat: The Proposition 1 Campaign in 1973," *California History*, 72:4 (Winter 1993/94), pp. 360–373.

he backtracked from the political limelight in order to maintain his career as America's favorite comedian. In the 1980s, Charleton Heston emerged as a proponent of a strong national defense and later became a spokesman for the National Rifle Association. Republicans picked up some recent converts to the cause, most notably singer/actor Frank Sinatra. Sinatra's association with Richard Nixon and Ronald Reagan appeared largely personal and not ideological. For those who followed Hollywood politics, Sinatra's switch to the Republican Party was seen as a result of what he took as a personal insult when President Kennedy sought to distance himself from Sinatra after the 1960 election.

The breakup of the studio system allowed independent film producers entry into the movie business, and films in the 1970s reflected an American culture seemingly more disposed to explicit violence and sex. Typical of the era were films directed by Sam Peckinpah, *The Wild Bunch* (1969) and *Straw Dogs* (1971), which depicted human nature as brutal, dark, and violent. Peckinpah considered himself a Republican but few inside or outside of Hollywood thought of him as political. However brilliant he was as a director, he suffered from severe substance abuse, and in this respect, he was similar to John Ford, also a masterful director whose Republican politics were less important to him than making movies.

Ford's alcoholism brought a tragic end to his film career. He died in 1973, a broken man, a personality out of step with his times, deploring what he saw as gratuitous violence and sex on the screen.[20] The box-office failures of his last films, the passing of war movies and western films, and his own conservative views made him nearly a pariah in the film industry. Although moving to the right politically in his later years, Ford's politics were never terribly clear because they were largely personal and had much to do with his pride as a Navy veteran of the Second World War and a reserve officer after the war. In 1947, he had orchestrated a petition drive in Hollywood against the blacklist, and he spoke against Cecil B. DeMille's attempt to impose a loyalty oath on the director's guild.[21] At the same time, he joined the Motion Picture Alliance, although he often defended those within the film industry accused of prior communist associations, including actor and war hero Audie Murphy and fellow director Frank Capra when he was refused a security clearance in 1951.[22] He wrote friends that he was "ashamed" by the inability of Hollywood to make "anti-commie" pictures.[23] He was disappointed that Taft did not win the Republican nomination in 1952, telling Taft that he, like millions of other Americans, was

[20] A comprehensive biography of Ford is Joseph McBride, *Searching for John Ford: A Life* (New York, 2000).

[21] "Statement, Republican and Democratic Joint Committee of Hollywood for the Preservation of Civil Liberties and the Defense of the People of the Motion Picture Industry," October 1947, John Ford Papers, August–October 1947 files.

[22] Frank Capra to John Ford, December 19, 1951, John Ford Papers, August–October 1947 files.

[23] John Ford to Donald Monteith, July 21, 1948, John Ford Papers, May–July 1948 files.

"bewildered and hurt at the outcome of the Republican convention in Chicago."[24] In 1960, he supported fellow Catholic and anticommunist John F. Kennedy for president, only to support Goldwater in 1964, although he claimed at various times not to have voted that year. In 1966, he supported Reagan in his governor's race and his reelection in 1970.[25] He supported Nixon in 1968 and 1972.[26]

Ford was, above all else, a film director, devoted to making dramatic, historically accurate western movies. He made more than westerns, but for him, "making western pictures" after the Second World War was a "crusade," adding that "I must say with thanksgiving a successful one because millions of people left in the country are still proud of their country, their flag, and their traditions."[27] He continued directing Hollywood films throughout the early 1960s, while at the same time working with the Department of Defense to make patriotic documentary films. In 1968, he consulted with the United States Information Agency in making a propaganda documentary, *Vietnam! Vietnam!* He traveled to Vietnam in order to advise on telling the "true story of Vietnam to the world." This documentary went out of its way to place antiwar protesters in a contemptible light. Ford's grandsons served in Vietnam, so the war took on a personal quality, as did most of Ford's politics. Privately, Ford confided to a friend, "What is the war all about? Damned if I know. I have not the slightest idea what we're doing there."[28]

In 1973, shortly before his death, the American Film Institute honored Ford with its first lifetime achievement award. The ceremony was attended by President Richard Nixon, who awarded the famed film director the Medal of Freedom. Also attending were Ford's troupe of stars including Maureen O'Hara, John Wayne, and James Stewart. Ronald Reagan and Barry Goldwater also attended the ceremony.[29] Ford rose to the occasion, declaring during the award ceremony that, "There are people in this world who don't think that we movie folk have any religion." When he was informed about the award and Richard Nixon's attendance, coinciding with the release of Vietnam POWs, he recalled, "I reached for my rosary and said a decade of the beads, ending with a fervent prayer. Not an original prayer, but one that is said in

---

[24] John Ford to Robert Taft, John Ford Papers, May–July 1952 files.
[25] John Ford to Ronald Reagan, January 7, 1967; Reagan to John Ford, June 18, 1967, John Ford Papers, 1967 file; and Ronald Reagan to John Ford, May 29, 1970, 1970 files.
[26] McBride, *Searching for John Ford*, p. 691.
[27] John Ford to Thomas B. Dawsen, November 7, 1949, John Ford Papers, November–December 1949 files.
[28] Bruce Herschensohn to John Ford, September 3, 1968; Bruce Herschensohn to Mrs. John Ford, December 6, 1968; and John Ford to Almah Johnston, May 21, 1969, John Ford Papers, 1968 and 1969 files.
[29] McBride, *Searching for John Ford*, pp. 706–714.

millions of families in the United States today. It is simply, 'God Bless Richard Nixon.'"[30]

He lamented what he saw as the change in Hollywood culture, in which directors made films in the belief that the way to make a fast buck is to fill the theaters with pornography.[31] In 1969, four years before his death, he was asked by a reporter if he had seen the Oscar winner for best picture, *Midnight Cowboy*, which was X-rated. Ford was blunt: "No! Especially not that! I don't like porn – these easy, liberal movies. A lot of junk. I don't know where they're going. They don't either."[32]

The old Hollywood that Ford knew from his start in silent films to his epic westerns had changed dramatically. The Vietnam War, civil rights protests, and the assassinations of Martin Luther King, Jr. and Robert Kennedy in 1968 pushed many in Hollywood to the left. For most in Hollywood, this shift was less a conscious ideological awareness than a cultural development in what author Tom Wolfe described as "radical chic." To be on the left became fashionable, so much so that it was assumed everyone in Hollywood was there. Politically active actors such as Jane Fonda; Shirley MacLaine; her younger brother, actor Warren Beatty; and Candice Bergen protested the war in Vietnam, attended Black Panther fundraisers, joined the fight to ratify the Equal Rights Amendment, and campaigned for Democrats such as George McGovern in 1972. They remained liberal Democrats who liked to see themselves as radicals. In reality, they were a far cry from those actors and screenwriters who had joined the Communist Party in the 1930s and 1940s. While being on the left in the Depression and during the Second World War was fashionable, there was a greater political consciousness and a deeper radicalism in this period than much of the faux radicalism of Hollywood in the 1960s and later. Conversely, by the 1970s, declarations of conservatism or affiliation with the Republican Party marked one as outside the accepted political culture, such as it was, in Hollywood.

Stars such as Wayne and comedian Bob Hope were seen as political dinosaurs in Hollywood. Their star power allowed them to prosper in Hollywood aside from their politics, and they continued to use their celebrity status to campaign for Republicans and to promote what they believed were traditional patriotic values. This meant supporting the war in Vietnam, even as Richard Nixon sought an "honorable" withdrawal from a war that had polarized the country.

Wayne became Hollywood's most vociferous supporter of the war in Vietnam. In 1967, Wayne narrated a Defense Department film defending the war in Vietnam, *A Nation Builds Under Fire*. Wayne had become increasingly irate with antiwar student protesters. A year before the release of the film, Wayne

---

[30] John Ford, Speech, American Film Institute Award, March 31, 1973; John Ford to Richard Nixon, May 4, 1973, John Ford Papers, 1973 files.
[31] Philip Dunne to John Ford, July 7, 1969, John Ford Papers, 1969 file.
[32] Quoted in McBride, *Searching for John Ford*, p. 679.

had attended an event with Bob Hope to raise money for a University of Southern California scholarship fund. Rehearsals for the event were disrupted by obscene catcalls and chanting from protesters in the crowd. As a result, Wayne decided to change his speech for the program. When he showed his changes to Hope, who had kept generally out of the political limelight, Hope was aghast. "You can't give a speech like that here, Duke," he declared, "unless you intend to turn those kids out there into a lynch mob howling for your blood." Wayne retorted, "I don't give a shit. . . . It's about time someone talked turkey to those kids. Let 'em lynch me!" On the night of the event, before an audience of ten thousand, Wayne declared, "We aren't going to sit by and let you destroy our schools and system. This is a great university. You owe it your best." He was given a standing ovation for his straight talk.[33]

Wayne's compulsion to rally the American people to the war in Vietnam – a war he saw as a continuation of the anticommunist crusade – led him to make *The Green Berets* (1968). Based on a best-selling novel of the same title, *The Green Berets* told the story of an antiwar journalist, played by David Janssen (another Hollywood Republican), who experiences the heroism and humanitarianism of a regiment of Green Berets stationed along the Cambodian and Laotian border. The plot of the film itself was preposterous. Green Berets parachute into Vietcong country to capture a Vietcong general who has been lured into a villa by a beautiful Vietnamese woman working for the Americans. The film had human waves of Vietcong attacking the Green Beret base camp and a Navy engineer, played by Wayne's son Patrick Wayne, driving a bulldozer against the enemy. The film had been cleared by the Pentagon, and the shooting occurred at Fort Benning, Georgia, where the army provided hardware including Huey helicopters. While the film was being shot, antiwar protests had escalated. In October 1967, more than 100,000 antiwar protesters marched in Washington, followed by a massive march on the Pentagon, where U.S. troops had to be called out for protection. The march became world news. Wayne responded, "I think they oughta shoot 'em if they're carrying the Vietcong flag. A lot of our boys are getting shot lookin' at that flag. As far as I am concerned, it wouldn't bother me one bit to pull the trigger on one of them myself."[34]

This set the stage for the hostile reception of the film by protesters and movie critics. The film premiered in Atlanta in June coinciding with the city's "Salute to America" celebration. The film's friendly reception in Atlanta proved misleading. In other cities – New York, Los Angeles, London, Paris, and Rome – protesters picketed, carrying signs denouncing Wayne and the film as fascist. Antiwar congressman Benjamin Rosenthal from New York publicly accused the Pentagon of wasting money in supplying helicopters, rifles, transportation

[33] Quoted in Randy Roberts and James S. Olson, *John Wayne: American* (Lincoln, NE, 1995 edition), p. 538.
[34] Quoted in Roberts and Olson, *John Wayne: American*, p. 545. Roberts and Olson provide a full account of the making of the film and its reception, pp. 537–553.

vehicles, and personnel to Wayne. Wayne replied that Rosenthal was an "asshole liberal politician trying to make news."[35] Movie critics from the *New York Times* and other major newspapers denounced the film as inane propaganda. Writing in *Glamour* magazine, critic Michael Korda described the film as "immoral." He wrote, "It is a simple-minded tract in praise of killing, brutality, and American superiority over Asians" in the best tradition of British novelist Rudyard Kipling.[36] The irony was that these protests and critical reviews offered free publicity for the film, which proved to be only a modest success. Domestic ticket sales after eighteen months stood at $20 million.

Two months before the film's release, however, all hell had broken loose in Vietnam when North Vietnam regulars and Vietcong launched a major offensive on January 31, 1968. Known as the Tet Offensive, the first wave of the planned attack set Americans back on their heels. The U.S. embassy in the capital of Saigon came under attack, and major cities such as Hue were initially captured by the Vietcong/North Vietnamese. After weeks of fighting, Americans turned back this offensive. Militarily, the Tet Offensive was a major setback for North Vietnam; more than 20,000 Vietcong and North Vietnamese regulars were killed. The Vietcong, the South Vietnamese rebel army controlled by North Vietnam, was annihilated as a combat force. For Americans watching the war on their television sets, however, the Tet Offensive belied President Johnson's and Pentagon claims that the war was being won.

The consequence of the Tet Offensive was President Lyndon Johnson's decision not to seek reelection in 1968, after Bobby Kennedy announced he was going to challenge him in the primaries. Antiwar Democrats had already rallied behind Senator Eugene McCarthy (D-Minnesota), who had done surprisingly well in the New Hampshire primary. Bobby Kennedy's assassination in June 1968 intensified a feeling on the part of many Americans, including many on the right, that the country was coming apart and the pieces were not going to be put back together again any time soon. Nixon played on this anxiety, making one of the great political comebacks when he won election to the White House in 1968. Wayne had stumped the country for Nixon in 1968, so he was overjoyed by his film's financial success and Nixon's victory.

1968: REAGAN, NIXON, AND A NATION IN TURMOIL

Goldwater's defeat in 1964 and the divisions within the Republican Party between its moderate/liberal and conservative wings set the stage for Richard Nixon's presidential nomination in 1968. At the same time, Ronald Reagan's election to the California governorship in 1966 caused many conservatives to hope that he might win the nomination instead of Nixon, the frontrunner within the GOP. Understanding Nixon's appeal as a party unifier, Reagan decided on

---

[35] Quoted in Roberts and Olson, *John Wayne: American*, p. 549.
[36] Ibid., p. 548.

the advice of political strategist Clif White to pursue a stealth campaign by not declaring himself a presidential contender. Reagan hoped that delegates to the GOP convention in Miami would become deadlocked between Nixon and Rockefeller, and then turn their eyes to Ronald Reagan. Rockefeller came into Miami with about 300 of the 667 delegates he needed to win the nomination. He hoped that his allies, George Romney of Michigan and Ohio governor James Rhodes, might swing their 182 delegates to him. Rockefeller instructed his operatives to join forces with Reagan in search of further delegates to prevent Nixon from winning on the first ballot. There was one simple flaw in Reagan's strategy in hoping to emerge as a compromise candidate at the convention: by 1968, a "non-candidate" such as Reagan could not round up enough delegates to win the nomination. Douglas MacArthur had tried this strategy in 1952 in the Eisenhower-Taft melee, and it had failed.

Choosing between Nixon and Reagan placed Hollywood conservatives and Southern California money men in a dilemma. They had backed Nixon through-out his political career, but his failure to win the governor's race and his subsequent move to New York following that defeat dampened their enthusiasm for him. Republicans such as Justin Dart and other members of Reagan's "kitchen cabinet" in Sacramento were eager for the GOP to win the White House. If winning was the bottom line, Nixon was their first choice. If they stood on ideological principle, then Reagan was their man. Most chose winning.

But not everyone. Reagan drew support from the grassroots right and hard-core ideological conservatives who distrusted Nixon. Typical was Betty Newman, a good friend of Barry Goldwater and a former model who had appeared in a couple of Hollywood films. She was a conservative who admired Reagan, writing Goldwater at the start of the Republican primaries that Nixon was "pathetic" in his desperation to win the nomination. "If he [Nixon] falters," she declared, "I cannot see anyone but Reagan."[37] Behind the scenes, Goldwater was supporting Nixon, providing advice and gossip on what he was picking up in Republican circles, even though Reagan and Goldwater were frequent corre-spondents. Reagan considered himself a Goldwater acolyte, carrying the banner of anticommunism and American values forward but, as early as 1966, Goldwater and Nixon were discussing how to head off a Reagan nomination in 1968. Nixon understood Reagan's media attraction and his ability to conflate image with reality. On June 8, 1966, even before Reagan had won the governor-ship in California, Nixon and Goldwater met in a hotel room to discuss how Nixon could win the presidential nomination. They agreed that the field was wide open to a Nixon, Rockefeller, Reagan, or even George Romney or Charles Percy nomination. Goldwater told Rockefeller that if Reagan won his race against Brown, he could see Clif White organizing a draft Reagan movement. The "great bulk of conservatives," he declared, "will cry for it [Reagan's

---

[37] Betty Newman to Barry Goldwater (n.d., 1966), Personal General Correspondence, Series II, Barry Goldwater Papers.

nomination]." Nixon and Goldwater agreed to stay in close touch while strategizing how to win the nomination for Nixon and prevent the "Eastern Establishment from regaining control of the Republican Party that now rests in the West."[38]

As it became clear by late 1967 that efforts were being made to organize a Reagan for President movement, Goldwater urged Nixon to meet with Reagan in the near future to make some accommodation with his rival. Goldwater told Nixon that there was strong evidence of a Reagan organization in Florida, a definite one in Texas, and he was sure there were others in various states. Reagan, he wrote, "tells me that he has no control over it" and "he can't help what his backers are trying to do." Goldwater told Nixon that he was "inclined to believe him, but at the same time we can wind up in a position where he, as an unannounced candidate," wins in New Hampshire and Wisconsin. In that event "his hand can be forced and he might become an announced candidate which could mean the two of you would be seeking votes from the same pocket." Reagan, he advised, should be placed second on the ticket. He added, but "for the love of everything we want to do for the good of our country, let us not allow Reagan to get into this" unless he understands what it might do to his chances and the Party's chances to win the White House. He told Nixon that a secret meeting should be held between Reagan and Nixon in which Nixon could "lay your cards on the table." The "overzealous" support for Reagan, Goldwater declared, presented a problem for Nixon and the Republican Party.[39] In the end, Reagan's strategy based on a convention deadlock failed. Nixon won the Republican nomination on the first ballot, and, in an extremely close general election, Nixon defeated the Democratic nominee, Hubert Humphrey.

Nixon won the support of old Republican campaigners including cowboy stars Randolph Scott, Hugh O'Brian, Chuck Connors, and Rory Calhoun. He was well represented by the musical entertainment community including actress Ginger Rogers: dancer Ray Bolger; singers Pat Boone, Rudy Vallee, and Tony Martin; and bandleader Lawrence Welk. Aging sex symbol Zsa Zsa Gabor was an enthusiastic Nixonite. But perhaps his biggest celebrity at the time came not from Hollywood but from the National Basketball Association, the legendary Wilt Chamberlain.[40] After Nixon won the nomination, Wayne went out on the campaign trail stumping for him, but Nixon's best use of celebrities came on the eve of the election, when his campaign held a national telethon introduced by the popular comedian Jackie Gleason, who gained national prominence in the 1950s playing New York bus driver Ralph Kramden in the television program *The Honeymooners*. In introducing Nixon to the audience, Gleason expressed

---

[38] Barry Goldwater, Memo, June 8, 1966, Alpha File, Box 15, Barry Goldwater Papers.

[39] Barry Goldwater to Richard Nixon, November 11, 1967; and Barry Goldwater to Richard Nixon, November 7, 1967, Alpha File, Box 15, Barry Goldwater Papers.

[40] Jerry Buck, "Primaries Offer 'Show Biz' Names," *Uniontown Morning Herald*, May 4, 1968; "Wilt Chamberlain for Nixon," *New York Times*, June 29, 1968, p. 9.

the sentiments of most Republicans, "this country needs Dick Nixon, and we need him now."[41] The camera then turned to Richard Nixon, who sat in a studio designed by Jack Rourke, who worked on the popular afternoon television talk program *The Merv Griffin Show*. (Griffin, who became a millionaire producing other television programs, was also a Republican, but kept his politics out of the public eye.) Nixon accepted studio audience questions that had been screened and scripted by Paul Keyes, the head writer and producer for the popular television show *Rowan & Martin's Laugh-In*. The telethon had been carefully staged by Nixon's media team, composed of Bill Gavin, Len Garment, Ray Price, Harry Trevelan, and Frank Shakespeare. Also joining the campaign was a newcomer to politics, Roger Ailes, who went on to head Fox News television. Nixon had met Ailes, a television producer, while preparing to go on the afternoon television program *The Mike Douglas Show* in 1967. Nixon was so impressed with Ailes's understanding of television as a way of reaching voters that he directed his staff to bring Ailes into the campaign. Borrowing from Kennedy's media-savvy 1960 campaign, Nixon's successful use of television during the 1968 campaign helped win the election for him.

If Hollywood's Right was a dwindling group, they remained steadfast in their support of Nixon after he won election, even though many expected a more conservative agenda once he took office. Under Nixon, the entitlement and regulatory state was expanded. His foreign policy included arms control agreements with the Soviet Union and, shortly before 1972, recognition of mainland China. On the other hand, Nixon reduced the top income tax rate for earned income from 70 to 50 percent. For Hollywood stars, this tax cut mattered, and many of them did not care that the top bracket at 70 percent remained for wealthy investors like Rockefeller and other representatives of the Eastern Establishment. The right stuck with Nixon, including Hollywood's most well-known politicians, Reagan and Murphy. Reagan won reelection as governor in 1970, but Murphy lost his bid for reelection that year to John Tunney. Shortly before the campaign, Murphy had his larynx removed because of throat cancer, leaving him unable to talk above a whisper. The good-looking, youthful Tunney made a sharp contrast to the aging actor. In many ways, Murphy typified the Hollywood Right – aged and unable to speak above a whisper.

Hollywood Republicans clung to Nixon for many reasons. Most remained loyal to Nixon because they were Republicans, and a Republican was in the White House. They despised the left as much as liberals hated Nixon. The more the press and fellow actors attacked Richard Nixon and his vice president Spiro Agnew, the more they rallied to the president. And, there was status in attending

---

[41] Quoted in Joe McGinniss, *The Selling of the President, 1968* (New York, 1969), p. 151. Also see Kathleen Hall Jamieson, *Packaging the Presidency: A History and Criticism of Presidential Campaign Advertising* (New York, 1984), especially pp. 221–275; and Kathryn Cramer Brownell, The Entertainment Estate: Hollywood in American Politics, 1932–1972, Ph.D. dissertation, Boston University, 2011, pp. 297–322.

White House dinners and receptions and playing golf with the president or vice president. Frank Sinatra became good friends with Vice President Agnew, inviting him frequently to Palm Springs to play golf. There was also the war in Vietnam. While Nixon pursued a policy of negotiated peace in Vietnam, Hollywood Republicans sought to rally the nation to support American troops fighting a war against communism. It was a matter of patriotism. Given the deep division over the war, Hollywood Hawks, those supporting the war, placed their careers in jeopardy. Their careers as entertainers were built on public popularity, and declarations for an unpopular war portended public backlash.[42]

Even one of America's most popular personalities, Bob Hope, discovered this when he became involved in National Unity Week in November 1969. Hope heard about the proposed rally from Richard Nixon, who asked him to help organize the event, first proposed by young Redlands, California, orthopedic surgeon Edmund Dembrowski. Hope decided to join the effort. He ordered his staff to organize a news conference at his Toluca Lake home to announce the event.[43]

After a series of movie flops in the 1960s, Hope's career had revived with his televised Christmas specials visiting troops in Vietnam. Since the Second World War, Hope had toured with the USO to entertain American troops stationed abroad. Hope took no pay for these tours; he could afford to do so because he had made a fortune in Los Angeles real estate. In 1965, he decided to take his tour to Vietnam, with actress Jill St. John, opera singer Anna Maria Allbeghetti, and Australian beauty Ann Sydney. After the televised show received high viewership, he convinced his sponsors at Chrysler that there should be a sequel program. For Hope, this was a mission to support the war in Vietnam, telling the press, "Listen, if the Commies ever thought we were not going to protect the South Vietnamese, there would be other Vietnams all over the world. . . . Like it or not, we've fallen heir to the job of Big Daddy in the free world."[44]

The January 1966 televised sequel attracted 55 percent of the total viewing audience. Hope, who voted Republican and gave money to the party, had throughout his career kept his politics out of the public arena. He had denounced McCarthyism in the 1950s and was bipartisan in making jokes at the expense of Republicans and Democrats alike. Antiwar protests and the youth counterculture moved Hope to take stronger positions. His anger at draft card burnings by antiwar protesters led him to write (with the aid of his staff) an article for *Family Life*, a Hearst-owned Sunday supplement. He angrily wrote, "Can you imagine returning from a combat patrol in a steaming, disease-infested jungle, tired, hungry, scared and sick, and be reminded that people in America are demonstrating against you being there. That people in America are burning draft cards

[42] For a contemporary view of Hollywood and Vietnam, see Julian Smith, *Looking Away: Hollywood and Vietnam* (New York, 1975).

[43] Quoted in William Robert Faith, *Bob Hope: A Life in Comedy* (New York, 2002), p. 330.

[44] Quoted in Faith, *Bob Hope*, p. 304.

to show their opposition, that some of them are actually rooting for your defeat."[45] As he grew more incensed with protesters, he began calling them traitors in the press. When Nixon suggested to Hope in 1969 that he get involved in Unity Week, Hope accepted the challenge. Joined by Young Americans for Freedom, a conservative activist youth organization, the National Unity Rally was a fiasco, drawing tens of thousands of supporters, but large numbers of counterdemonstrators as well, who disrupted the proceedings.

By the early and mid-1970s, Hope's politics had become fully visible. In 1970, he raised more than $350,000 at a luncheon in support of former Ohio governor Jim Rhodes, a vociferous critic of student protesters, in his unsuccessful bid for the U.S. Senate. Hope also publicly supported Lenore Romney, the wife of former Michigan governor George Romney and the mother of future Republican presidential candidate Mitt Romney, in her unsuccessful race for the U.S. Senate. He donated to Reagan's reelection in 1970 and actively raised money for Republican candidates throughout the state. He was a key supporter of Barry Goldwater, Jr., the son of Barry Goldwater, who won special election to Congress in 1969 to fill the seat vacated by Ed Reinecke, who won election as lieutenant governor that year. (Reinecke's own career in politics came to a crashing halt when he became caught up in the Watergate scandal.)[46] Hope joined John Wayne and Buddy Ebsen in heading up Goldwater Associates, providing the young Goldwater Jr., with a political fund. Beginning in 1969, Goldwater, Jr., won election to Congress for six consecutive terms, before losing his seat to redistricting in 1982. Backed by Hollywood conservatives, Goldwater Jr., made a strong bid for the Republican nomination for the U.S. Senate, raising over a million dollars in the primary campaign. He led in the polls until the last few weeks of the campaign, when he became ensnarled in a drug scandal. He came in third behind San Diego Mayor Pete Wilson, who went on to win the election.

Hope's own involvement in politics cost him public support and a media backlash. Although married to former singer Dolores DeFina, a devout Roman Catholic, Hope was known in Hollywood as a womanizer. Prior to the 1970s, the sexual life of stars (and politicians) was usually kept out of the press by studios, which carefully guarded the images of their moneymakers. The press, other than a few scandal sheets, generally went along with this self-imposed censorship because the sexual lives of entertainment and political celebrities were considered private. As a consequence, Gary Cooper's many known sexual conquests in Hollywood (and he liked to brag about them) were kept out of the public eye. Fellow Republican Rock Hudson, the heartthrob of many American women, was well known in Hollywood to be a homosexual, a fact that did not

[45] Ibid., p. 311.
[46] Leo Rennert, "The Downfall of Ed Reinecke," *California Journal* (September 1974), pp. 305–307.

come to the public's attention until the early 1980s, when Hudson was dying of AIDS.

Hollywood conservatives also did not concern themselves much with the sexual mores of fellow actors or others in the film industry. Most Hollywood Republicans were more concerned about the Soviet Union, free markets, and lowering income taxes than about personal sexual morality. Although, beginning in the 1960s, some on the Hollywood Right complained about excessive violence and sex on the screen, this had more to do with the artistic content of films than with the personal sexual morality of those making or starring in the films. After all, many on the Hollywood Right lived in glass houses themselves. Cooper, for example, had insisted that his mistress, actress Patricia Neal, have an abortion when she became pregnant with his child, but little thought was given at the time to the morality of abortion. Neal agreed to an abortion, a decision she later regretted, and one which led her to later become active in the prolife movement. There are further examples of tolerance on sexual issues. Republican Rock Hudson carried on a heated affair with a well-known football player while on location during the 1969 filming of John Wayne's *The Undefeated*. Wayne, who was personally repulsed by homosexual behavior, became good friends with Hudson on the set and did not comment on Hudson's affair. Making movies was a business (and an art), so Wayne was not going to let morals stand in the way.[47] Similarly, in Reagan's first term as governor, a public scandal was headed off when a clique of top staff in his administration was discovered to be engaged in homosexual group sex parties. At first Reagan, the old Hollywood hand, refused to tackle an issue that threatened a major scandal in his administration. Only under extreme political pressure did Reagan finally act by forcing resignations.

As a consequence, when suggestions of Hope's infidelity began to appear in the regular press, including *New York Times Magazine*, *Life*, and *Time* in 1969 and 1970, fearing that this was going to hurt his income, especially from the college lecture circuit, the millionaire Hope retreated from making more visible political pronouncements, although he continued to wear a POW bracelet, a right-wing cause suggesting that there were still American prisoners of war in Vietnam.[48]

The end of the Vietnam War was being negotiated when Nixon came up for reelection in 1972. The Democrats put up antiwar candidate George McGovern, the U.S. senator from South Dakota. The liberal McGovern proved to be an easy target for Nixon, who was able to paint his opponent as a peacenik who was soft on American defense, law and order, and spending. Once again, Nixon brought out celebrities who backed his reelection. As one unidentified Nixon campaign aide told the press, "If you appear by yourself, you'll perhaps get 10,000 people to hear you speak. If you are introduced by

---

[47] Roberts and Olson, *John Wayne: American*, pp. 371–372.
[48] Faith, *Bob Hope*, pp. 348–389.

John Wayne you can bet on 20,000. . . . It's amazing how many Americans who are normally bored stiff by politics will turn up to rallies when they know there's going to be a movie star there."[49] Some were surprises for the voters, including television star Mary Tyler Moore and comedians Dan Rowan and Dick Martin (hosts of the television hit *Laugh-In*), along with Republican stalwarts Jimmy Stewart and John Wayne. Added to the list of regulars were singer Glen Campbell; comedians Red Skelton, Jack Benny, and George Burns; actress Debbie Reynolds; and Merv Griffin. Frank Sinatra and Charleton Heston, golfing buddies with Vice President Spiro Agnew, also endorsed Nixon. Zsa Zsa Gabor, who had been born in Hungary and spoke with a strong accent, was used to attract the Eastern European immigrant vote.[50]

Nixon's resignation in 1974 in the midst of the Watergate scandal demoralized Republicans across the country, and California Republicans in particular. Hope remained friends with Nixon after he left the presidency, as did a few other old-time stars, including Ronald Reagan, but the setback for the GOP nationally and particularly in California was obvious as Republican after Republican lost elections. But, in less than six years, Republicans were on the rebound, led by Hollywood's most famous actor turned politician, Ronald Reagan.

HOW RONALD REAGAN WON THE WHITE HOUSE (WITHOUT HOLLYWOOD'S SUPPORT)

In 1974, the Republican Party was again in chaos. Fewer than 20 percent of the voters identified themselves as Republican after Nixon's disgrace. Nixon's successor, Gerald Ford, tried to reassure a nation traumatized by the lost war in Vietnam, the first resignation of a president in the country's history, and an economy experiencing the pincer of inflation and high unemployment. Ford pursued Nixon's program in domestic and foreign policy, although he was more aggressive in vetoing spending bills coming from a heavily Democratic Congress. His general equivocation on social issues such as abortion and the Equal Rights Amendment upset the ascendant grassroots right. What riled most hardcore conservatives was Ford's continuation of Nixon's foreign policy of arms control with the Soviet Union and negotiations with the military government of Panama to turn over the canal zone.

The Ford White House marginalized conservatives within the party, dismissing any threat posed by them to his nomination for the presidency. Ford's moderation – in style and substance – invited a primary challenge in 1976. It came from Ronald Reagan, who had been underestimated throughout his

---

[49] Quoted in Ross Madden, "Will Hollywood Pick the Next President?," *Kingston Gleaner*, October 15, 1972, p. 65.
[50] Stars supporting Nixon included also Ronald Reagan, Richard Crenna, Glen Ford, Eddie Fisher, Red Skelton, Clint Eastwood, Andy Devine, John Payne, Michael Landon, and Bob Hope. "Stars Turn Out for Nixon Party," *The Times* (San Mateo), August 28, 1972, p. 2.

political career. Ford and most of his staff remained contemptuous of Reagan, who was now sixty-five years old and had been out of the governor's office for two years. Even when conservatives began to coalesce around Reagan, the Ford staff continued to dismiss him as a lightweight extremist who would not attract many votes. Not having learned from history, Ford made the same mistake as did Brown and Unruh when running against Reagan in California.

Ford, a low-key personality, attracted considerable celebrity support, although the Hollywood Right was divided, with many supporting Reagan. Ford's own son Steven became a Hollywood actor, later appearing briefly in the romantic comedy *When Sally Met Harry* (1989). Ford's Hollywood supporters were a mix of older celebrities such as Fred Astaire, Cary Grant, Hugh O'Brien, Ella Fitzgerald, Jayne Meadows, and Zsa Zsa and Eva Gabor, and a few younger Republicans such as singer Sonny Bono, best known as the partner of singer Cher. After backing Humphrey in 1968, Bono cast himself as a tepid Ford supporter, obviously testing the Republican political waters. He was used by the Ford campaign at a number of fundraising events, including a $1,000-plate fundraiser in Palm Springs, and he later was master of ceremonies at Ford's primary victory party. He told the press, rather astutely, "I don't think a star can be a major influence on voting. An actor isn't a profound voice in the public mind."[51] What stars brought to a campaign was the celebrity draw for campaign events – and name recognition if they sought a political career of their own. Bono went on to have his own career in politics, winning election to mayor of Palm Springs in 1988, and then, after a failed attempt for the U.S. Senate, winning a congressional seat in 1994 representing the Forty-Fourth district.

Reagan's top celebrity supporters were mostly older, including stars of the 1950s and earlier, such as Yvonne De Carlo, Irene Dunne, Fred MacMurray, Robert Stack, Gilbert Roland, Merle Oberon, and Pat Boone. Efrem Zimbalist, Jr.'s hit television series *The F.B.I.* had ended a few years earlier. Jimmy Stewart and John Wayne continued to have careers on screen and to back their long time friend Ronald Reagan.[52]

Reagan zeroed in on Ford's détente policy with the Soviet Union, the decline of American military preparedness, and reports that the administration was negotiating the turnover of the Panama Canal back to Panama. He found crowds cheering when he mentioned his opposition to the proposed turnover of the Panama Canal, and he warned that giving the canal to a left-wing Panamanian regime headed by General Omar Torrijos threatened American

---

[51] Quoted in Vernon Scott, "'Icing on the Cake,' Sonny Bono to MC Ford Victory Bash," *Elyria Chronicle Telegram*, August 19, 1976, p. 3.

[52] Cleveland Amory, "Lucy, on the Record," *Denton Record*, October 29, 1976, p. 20; Vernon Scott, see full citation above Vernon Scott, "Celebrities Draw Big for Candidates," *Albuquerque Journal*, June 10, 1976, p. 22; Phil Kerby, "What's a Fan to Do If Star Backs Wrong Candidate," *Capitol Times*, August 16, 1976, p. 17; and Marilyn Beck, "Carter Camp Mum When Asked about Hollywood Stars Backing," *Star News*, July 21, 1976, p. 14.

national security by cutting off United States naval access between the Pacific and Atlantic Oceans. Crowds went wild with Reagan's line, "We built it, we paid for it, and it's ours, and we should tell Torrijos and company we are going to keep it." Reagan began attacking "Dr. Kissinger and Mr. Ford." Throughout the next two months, Ford and Reagan see-sawed back and forth in winning delegates. By the time of the Republican National Convention, the delegate count appeared too close to call.

Reagan's bid for the nomination created inevitable division within the Republican Party. Senator Barry Goldwater, loyal to the Republican Party, remained steadfast in his support of Gerald Ford, and the refusal of other conservatives to back Ford perplexed him. He saw a new conservative movement that was different from the one he had led in 1964, and he told actor Efrem Zimbalist, Jr., in no uncertain words that "I can appreciate the fact that there are strong feelings within the party though and I have been the target of the more emotional assaults, I can understand it. What is getting tougher to understand by the minute, however, is how we can finally come so close to achieving what we set out to achieve three elections ago and risk it all now over a hair-splitting debate within the party about which of two genuine and bona fide conservatives [Ford and Reagan] is more conservative."[53] Zimbalist, who had been a Goldwater delegate in 1964, replied bluntly, telling Goldwater that he was disappointed in Goldwater's inability to discern "any difference between the two candidates in question, in degree of quality, idealism or intention; who can with equanimity accept, on one hand, a Kissinger foreign policy and, on the other, the largest federal budget in our nation's history." He concluded even more severely, "I am, to be blunt, astounded that, as a Republican, you can see no difference, either with respect to the philosophy or the ability to implement it, between the two years of this appointed administration and the eight years of the Reagan mandate in California."[54]

At the same time, Reagan's hard line position on the Panama Canal alienated Hollywood conservatives such as John Wayne, who supported the turnover. Reagan's opposition to Panama won him support among other stars, however, including actor Charleton Heston. In early 1974, Heston wrote Goldwater that he was concerned by reports that he had been hearing that the State Department was negotiating with the Republic of Panama to turn over the canal. Surely, Heston warned Goldwater, this is a "strategically important area for the security of this hemisphere. This would seem to me to a grievous error, but not at all

---

[53] Barry Goldwater to Efrem Zimbalist, Jr., June 29, 1976, Ronald Reagan Series (unprocessed), Rosalind Kress Haley Collection, Eagle Forum Archives, Clayton, Missouri. Also, for an overview of the debate within the Republican Party in 1976, see Donald T. Critchlow, *The Conservative Ascendancy: How the Republican Right Rose to Power in Modern America* (Lawrence, KS, 2012), pp. 144–152.

[54] Efrem Zimbalist, Jr., to Barry Goldwater, July 15, 1976, Ronald Reagan Series, Rosalind Kress Haley Collection, Eagle Forum Archives.

inconsonant with the fashion of treaties these days."[55] Heston opposed SALT I
and the Helsinki Accords, and later opposed SALT II in 1979.

Goldwater's refusal to support Reagan in the 1976 primary caused a rift
between the two men although, prior to this, they had been personal friends.
Reagan looked to Goldwater as a kind of political mentor and, Goldwater, for
his part, offered Reagan political advice and helped raise money for his 1966 and
1970 campaigns.[56] The Reagan challenge to an incumbent Republican president
placed Goldwater in a bind. He agreed with Reagan on many issues, but he did
not want to divide the party. He wrote in a memo to himself in early spring 1975,
"I have to play this [primary] very cool. If I come out and oppose him [Reagan]
openly now we'll disturb about 20 percent of the Party; if I embrace him I'll
disturb about 80 percent of the Party."[57]

Reagan's rhetoric against the canal turnover forced Goldwater to take sides.
Goldwater called a press conference to warn Reagan that his rhetoric on Panama
was unproductive and based on inaccurate information. After talking to the
press, Goldwater explained to Wayne that Reagan was setting himself up to be
accused of being a warmonger. He told Buckley, another supporter of the turnover, that unless the canal was turned over, there would be guerrilla warfare in
the country.[58]

Explaining to fellow conservatives why he had called a press conference to
criticize Reagan was one thing; explaining to Reagan himself about this news
conference was a different matter altogether. From Reagan's perspective, it
looked like a stab in the back. Whatever else Barry Goldwater was, he was a
direct man. He wrote Ronald and Nancy Reagan, a week after his news conference, to say that he had become increasing "apprehensive about Ron's attacks
on the President relative to the Panama Canal." He said that he had tried to
phone them and that only after not being able to get hold of them had he called a
press conference. This was not at the president's encouragement; he had called
the press conference because "I have to put the interests of my country ahead of
that because, in my opinion, you were treading on very dangerous water,
although I will admit very popular water, and I wanted to remove the whole
thing from this campaign."[59]

Reagan replied to Goldwater's letter about a month later, questioning his
attempt to call him. "I don't know where your phone call went astray," he said.
"No one in my shop has any record of a call ever being received." Reagan then
got to the point, "Barry, I did not create the canal issue – the people did. In
question and answer sessions in New Hampshire, Florida, and Illinois the

[55] Charleton Heston to Senator Barry Goldwater, February 5, 1974, Alpha File, Barry Goldwater
Papers, Arizona State University.

[56] Barry Goldwater to Ronald Reagan, June 2, 1966, Alpha Files, Barry Goldwater Papers.

[57] Barry Goldwater, Memo, May 5, 1975, Alpha Files, Barry Goldwater Papers.

[58] Barry Goldwater to John Wayne, May 12, 1976; Barry Goldwater to William F. Buckley, May 13,
1976, Alpha Files, Barry Goldwater Papers.

[59] Barry Goldwater to Ronald Reagan, June 3, 1976, Alpha File, Barry Goldwater Papers.

audience brought it up." Goldwater responded that he hoped that, after the election, the two of them could renew their friendship. "I treasure the friendship," he wrote, "that we have always had. I hope that after the steam of the election calms down that we can resume that friendship for it is very dear to me."[60] Reagan did not respond, thus ending their correspondence for over a year. The Panama Canal issue did not go away, coming up again during the Jimmy Carter administration and again dividing conservatives in general and Hollywood conservatives in particular.

By the time the Republican National Convention met, it was clear that Ford had won the nomination. He won on the first ballot, although by a narrow margin. On the final night of the convention, Reagan delivered an eloquent speech on behalf of Ford that left many wondering if they had nominated the wrong man. Perhaps they had: the Democratic nominee, Jimmy Carter won a narrow victory over Ford for the White House.

The next four years under Carter proved a godsend to Republicans and to Ronald Reagan, setting the stage for him to win the presidency in 1980 with a united Republican Party. This unity obscured divisions that erupted over the Panama Canal treaty when it was brought up to a Senate vote in August 1977.

The buildup of the Soviet military and its adventurous foreign policy in Africa and Central America set the context for the rancorous national debate over the Panama Canal. Grassroots conservatives framed the issue as a battle between Wall Street and the American people. Conservatives claimed that the treaty was a way to obtain repayment of loans totaling $135 million that had been given by powerful eastern banks to the military government of Panama. They launched a massive mailing campaign, including a letter by Reagan that brought in more than $700,000 in contributions. The Torrijos government hired Clifton White, Reagan's campaign manager for his failed presidential bid in 1968, and Lawrence E. O'Brien, a former Democratic chairman, to lobby for the treaties.

John Wayne came out in support of the turnover as well. Wayne's third wife was Peruvian, and he was well connected with leading Central American businessmen and politicians.[61] Wayne believed that the American possession of the canal smacked of colonialism. He threw his support behind Carter and the treaty, writing hundreds of letters to influential Republicans, often using Republican National Committee stationery. He circulated a seven-page position paper he had written on the treaty to every U.S. senator.[62] Wayne's activities on behalf of the turnover were well received by Barry Goldwater. In a letter thanking Wayne for his support, he noted that he had taken "umbrage" with Reagan

[60] Ronald Reagan to Barry Goldwater, June 1, 1976; Barry Goldwater to Ronald Reagan, June 29, 1976, Alpha File, Barry Goldwater Papers.
[61] Wayne was entertained by close friends of General Torrijos, as well as Panama's former president Dick Aria and the minister of economics Nicolas Ardito Barletta, who assured him that they did not support revolution or terrorism. John Wayne to Barry Goldwater, February 13, 1978, Alpha File, Barry Goldwater Papers.
[62] Roberts and Olson, *John Wayne: American*, pp. 603–611.

during the 1976 campaign for his attacks on the turnover. At the time, he continued, he recalled that Wayne had written "a long, very interesting, and well-thought out letter" to Goldwater explaining his support for Reagan and his position. Goldwater was pleased that Wayne had changed his position, and he wanted his support because there were amendments he sought to introduce to the treaty. Wayne responded immediately, assuring Goldwater that he supported the treaty and hoped it was not going to become a political football. This was hopelessly naïve.[63] Wayne soon came under attack from the right for his pro-turnover stance. Wayne responded to these attacks by publicly answering conservative critics.[64] Wayne lamented to Goldwater that he was receiving hate mail from the "extreme right," but when he answered them, "they write back two more letters. I think they are as bad as the extreme left." Goldwater responded, "I know just what you are faced with by the far right. They now refer to me as a socialist, so move over."[65]

In the midst of the Panama turnover, Reagan reached out to Goldwater. He wanted his vote against the Panama turnover. More important, he needed to unify the party if he was going to win the Republican nomination in 1980. Goldwater was appreciative, telling Reagan, "Again, it was a pleasure hearing from you and I hope someday the hatchet, if there be a hatchet, can be buried." Reagan answered, "Maybe both of us thought there was a hatchet, thinking the other one was swinging it. I will admit I was hurt and as a result, I suppose, felt the same hesitancy you did about writing."[66] By 1977, Goldwater believed that banking and financial interests represented by the Trilateral Commission were playing a large role in supporting the treaty. The Trilateral Commission was a Rockefeller-supported private group bringing together international financial interests. Goldwater told Reagan, with whom he was now corresponding once again, that the more "I prowl around these treaties, the more I smell the Trilateral Commission. I think we are going to see more and more efforts being made around the world to pay back the very stupid and foolish loans that some of the big banks of our country have made." Reagan tried to reinforce Goldwater's opposition to the treaty by warning him not to be taken in by Torrijos. "He seems to have charmed," Reagan observed, "our mutual friend, Duke Wayne, who has been his houseguest, but I, like you, feel the Trilateral Commission and the dictators' own funding is very deep in this."[67] In the end, Goldwater, upset by what he viewed as the unfair tactics of opponents, came out

---

[63] Barry Goldwater to John Wayne, September 22, 1977; John Wayne to Barry Goldwater, October 4, 1977, Alpha File, Barry Goldwater Papers.

[64] John Wayne, "Response to Lofton 'Battleline,'" January 16, 1978, Alpha File, Barry Goldwater Papers.

[65] John Wayne to Barry Goldwater, March 7, 1978; Barry Goldwater to John Wayne, March 13, 1979, Alpha File, Barry Goldwater Papers.

[66] Barry Goldwater to Ronald Reagan, December 15, 1977; Ronald Reagan to Barry Goldwater, December 30, 1977, Alpha File, Barry Goldwater Papers.

[67] Ibid.

for the treaty.[68] Wayne had given conservatives cover for voting for a treaty despised by much of the right.

In March 1978, treaties turning the canal zone back to Panama were ratified in an extremely close vote in the Senate, passing with a single vote to spare. Goldwater was one of those who voted for ratification, even though he was extremely critical of the soft wording in the treaty. In their support for the treaty, neither Wayne or Goldwater had turned to the left. Wayne remained extremely anti-Soviet in his political views, and he was especially upset by what he perceived as Soviet involvement in Somalia, Ethiopia, and Nicaragua, where the revolutionary Sandinistas were about to take over. He feared the Soviet arms buildup.

He was joined in this concern by fellow actor Charleton Heston, who actively campaigned against the ratification of SALT II when it came before the Senate in 1979. Heston coordinated his lobbying effort with Goldwater, who instructed his office to send Heston the names of undecided votes in the Senate. Goldwater told his staff that "he's a very influential person in Hollywood." Goldwater also sent Heston a copy of the minority report on SALT II from the Armed Services Committee, assuring him that, for the first time in this Committee, "a minority position has become the majority position." Heston replied that he was following closely the debate on SALT II, and he realized the "enormity of the task facing the nation if we are to restore anything like parity with the Soviets. Though I'm not one of your constituents, I want to thank you for the stand you have consistently taken on what was until recently the unpopular side of this question."[69] Heston's stance against SALT II represented the transformation of Hollywood anticommunism into anti-Soviet, pro-defense nationalism. When SALT II reached the Senate in the summer of 1979, the Carter presidency was in deep trouble. When the Soviet Union invaded Afghanistan shortly after the Senate Foreign Relations Committee had barely approved the treaty, Carter decided to withdraw the treaty. It was a major victory for the GOP and defense hawks.

As the 1980 election approached, Reagan and Goldwater renewed their political ties. Reagan reported that, in his speaking tours across the country to Republican groups, "I have never known Republicans to be more unified in purpose, philosophy, strength, and determination to win – and never more enthusiastic than they are today." Goldwater feared another split within the Republican Party. He told Reagan in June 1979 that he still feared the "tendency of Republicans to choose up sides, and I hope to God we can prevent a fight." He suggested that Reagan select a running mate early to "overcome some of the

---

[68] For insight into Goldwater's vote on Panama, see Cal Thomas and Bob Beckel, *Common Ground: How to Stop the Partisan War That Is Destroying America* (New York, 2007), pp. 175–176.

[69] Charleton Heston to Goldwater, November 15, 1979; Barry Goldwater, Memo, November 26, 1979; Barry Goldwater to Charleton Heston, January 23, 1980; Charleton Heston to Goldwater, January 31, 1980, Alpha File, Barry Goldwater Papers.

problems that I pray will not exist." Reagan thanked Goldwater for his advice.[70]
Although he did not make an early choice, Reagan selected George H.W. Bush as
his running mate at the GOP convention as a signal to the party that Reagan was
a unifier.

During the campaign, Reagan drew upon his Hollywood connections, but, by
1980, the right in Hollywood was nearly gone. Indicative of this was the fact that
when the Reagan-Bush campaign set up the usual presidential Entertainment
Committee, the decision was made not to attract celebrities but "individuals who
represent commercial and creative agencies in the film and television industry."
This meant targeting, "network executives, agents, personal managers, direc-
tors/writers, and so forth."[71] The Entertainment Committee was headed by
Beverly Hills Republican activists Sue Tarog and Goldie Arthur, who had served
in this capacity in Reagan's 1966 governor's race. Reagan did find support
among Hollywood actors, but many were long in the tooth. Singer Dean
Martin, who had attracted a national following first with comedian Jerry
Lewis and later with a popular television program, joined Reagan at campaign
rallies. Also joining Reagan at rallies were actors Jimmy Stewart and Cesar
Romero, Efrem Zimbalist, Jr., and singer Tony Martin. Reagan attracted the
support of actor Leon Ames, comedian Morey Amsterdam, and country and
western singer Hoot Gibson. Television producer Fred DeCordova played an
important role in tapping Hollywood sources for fundraising. Character actor
Donald DeFore, born in 1913 in Cedar Rapids, Iowa, contributed to the campaign by writing a letter to his hometown newspaper endorsing Reagan. Heston,
who had emerged as a major defense hawk, publicly supported Reagan.[72] A few
of the younger crowd, such as actor Clint Eastwood and director John Milius,
who later gained attention with his cult classic anti-Soviet movie *Red Dawn*
(1984), supported Reagan, but they were not visible during the campaign.

On election day, Reagan won one of the largest victories in presidential
voting. He won by more than 7 points, carrying 489 electoral votes to Carter's
49, taking 44 states. Reagan, an avowed conservative, stepped into the White
House and it appeared that American voters had rejected the liberal vision for
America. After wandering in the desert for nearly thirty-five years, conservatives

[70] Ronald Reagan to Barry Goldwater, June 1, 1979; Barry Goldwater to Ronald Reagan, June 11,
     1979; Ronald Reagan to Barry Goldwater, July 9, 1979, Alpha Files, Barry Goldwater Papers.
[71] Peter Dailey to Bill Timons, August 8, 1980, Campaign Papers, Series X, Citizen Operations,
     Ronald Reagan Papers, Box 306.
[72] For Hollywood support of Reagan in 1980, see Goldie Arthur to Elaine Cripen, October 12,
     1980, 1980 Campaign, Series I, Ronald Reagan Papers, Box 7; Ronald Reagan to Leon Ames,
     June 16, 1980, Series I, Box 5; Ronald Reagan to Fred DeCordova, June 5, 1980, Series I, Box 3;
     Ronald Reagan to Don DeFore, June 4, 1980, Series I, Box 3; Ronald Reagan to Hoot Gibson,
     July 24, 1980, Series I, Box 3; Ronald Reagan to Dean Martin, February 19, 1980, Series I, Box 3;
     Ronald Reagan to Cesar Romero, February 19, 1980, Series I, Box 6; Ronald Reagan to Jimmy
     Stewart, February 16, 1980, Series I, Box 6; Ronald Reagan to Donald DeFore, June 4, 1980,
     Series I, Box 3; Ronald Reagan to Rudy Vallee, July 14, 1980, Series I, Box 6; Ronald Reagan to
     Efrem Zimbalist, Jr., February 19, 1980, Series I, Box 6, Ronald Reagan Papers.

had marched to the Promised Land led by a former actor who had gotten his start fighting communism in Hollywood a generation before. Through Reagan, the Hollywood Right's anticommunist, patriotic, small-government vision became the prevailing philosophy of the national Republican Party. Reagan's election marked the final triumph of the Hollywood Right.

Few who fought the battles of the 1950s lived to see Reagan's victory. One of those who did not was one of the great symbols of the Hollywood Right for more than thirty years – John Wayne, who died on June 11, 1979. Before he died, Wayne appeared to have found personal peace. He converted to Roman Catholicism with the encouragement of his son. His death from cancer was one of intense pain, and he found sleep nearly impossible without heavy medication. As he slipped in and out of consciousness before his death, he told his daughter Alissa that he dreamed he had just returned from a wonderful parade. Speaking with a blank, glazed stare, Wayne said he had marched in "the middle of many majestic horses, the drummers drummed and the streets were lined with children."[73] There were no elephants in Wayne's parade.

Perhaps the dream represents a metaphor for the Hollywood Right's struggle for a better America. They had fought the good fight, defeating the communist faction in Hollywood and helping to transform the Republican Party in California. The cultural war in Hollywood was lost, but they had won the political battle that culminated in Reagan's election to the White House in 1980. For Republicans across the country, in 1980, the gates of heaven had opened.

---

[73] Alissa Wayne, *John Wayne, My Father* (New York, 1991), p. 208; and Roberts and Olsen, *John Wayne: American*, p. 208.

Manuscripts

Cecil B. DeMille Papers, Brigham Young University
John Ford Papers, Indiana University
Barry Goldwater Papers, Arizona State University Library, Tempe, Arizona
Charleton Heston Papers, Academy of Motion Picture Arts and Sciences
Herbert Hoover Papers, Herbert Hoover Presidential Library, Iowa City, Iowa
Hedda Hopper Papers, Academy of Motion Picture Arts and Sciences
Goodwin J. Knight Papers, University of California, Berkeley
Ring Lardner, Jr., Papers, Academy of Motion Picture Arts and Sciences
Clare Booth Luce Papers, Library of Congress
Richard M. Nixon Papers, Richard M. Nixon Presidential Library, Yorba Linda,
   California
Westbrook Pegler Papers, Herbert Hoover Presidential Library, Iowa City, Iowa
Joseph L. Rauh, Jr., Papers, Library of Congress Archives
Ronald Reagan, Gubernatorial Papers, 1966–75, Ronald Reagan Presidential Library
Ronald Reagan Papers, 1976 election files, Eagle Forum Educational Archives, St. Louis
Records of the United States House of Representatives, House Un-American Activities
   Committee, Executive Sessions (1947), Exhibits, RG 233, Boxes 2, 3, 4, 5, 6, 8, 9, 11,
   and 120.
Nelson A. Rockefeller Papers, Rockefeller Archives
Upton Sinclair Papers, Indiana University

Index